Democracy's Empire:
Sovereignty, Law, and Violence

Edited by

Stewart Motha

BLACKWELL PUBLISHING
9600 Garsington Road, Oxford OX4 2DQ, UK
350 Main Street, Malden, MA 02148-5018, USA
550 Swanston Street, Carlton, Victoria 3053, Australia

First published 2007 by Blackwell Publishing Ltd as a special issue of *Journal of
Law and Society*

Library of Congress Cataloging-in-Publication Data
A catalogue record for this title has been applied for.

A catalogue record for this title is available from the British Library.

ISBN 13: 9781405163132

The publisher's policy is to use permanent paper from mills that operate a
sustainable forestry policy, and which has been manufactured from pulp processed
using acid-free and elementary chlorine-free practices. Furthermore, the publisher
ensures that the text paper and cover board used have met acceptable
environmental accreditation standards.

For further information on
Blackwell Publishing visit our website:
www.blackwellpublishing.com

Contents

JOURNAL OF LAW AND SOCIETY
VOLUME 34, NUMBER 1, MARCH 2007
ISSN: 0263-323X, pp. 1–2

Democracy's Empire: Sovereignty, Law, and Violence

Stewart Motha*

Since the end of the Cold War, juridical and political thought has featured triumphal assertions about the end of ideology and history. Much of this literature has proclaimed the universality of human rights, affirmed market-oriented democratic states, and urged risk management and privatization over state-controlled delivery of social goods. The increased integration of economies and markets was supposed to collapse national borders and lead to the extinction of national sovereignty. The challenges to this linear account came from multiple fronts – but some of these were attended, more often than not, by ethno-national violence and war. The problem of sovereignty also persists in various struggles for self-determination. But resistance to cultural and social homogenization such as the French eschewal of 'Americanization' and *mondialisation* fall prey to what is rotten in the republic, the production of a 'people', the enforcement of a civil religion, and a notion of democracy that must identify its 'friends and enemies'.

The essays in this volume take up the challenge of explaining the current formation of the relation between democracy, sovereignty, law, and violence in what is termed 'Democracy's Empire'. *Democracy's Empire* attempts to capture the *co-appearance* of democracy as an unavowable mode of politics that institutes and sustains freedom and equality – and modes of violence and subjection. The proliferation of 'anti-terror' measures and wars for democracy suggest that the exception, as Walter Benjamin predicted, is becoming the norm. This volume contains a situated discussion of the institution of democracy and related juridico-political concepts of sovereignty, law, and violence.

The formation of the *demos* and its rule has long been attended by forms of sovereign violence, and these are examined through essays which reflect on the historical and philosophical legacies which inform Democracy's Empire – such as the Roman Republic, the separation between Church and State, formations of revolutionary violence in the enlightenment, and the relation between norm and exception. The volume contains essays which offer a mixture of historical and philosophical treatment of democracy as a

* *Kent Law School, University of Kent, Canterbury, Kent CT2 7NS, England*
s.motha@kent.ac.uk

1

juridical problem of constitutional violence. For instance, South Africa was supposed to be the exemplary instance of democratization – an example of the constitutionalization of politics for all the 'failed states' and post-conflict, 'post-racist' societies to follow. From the death of politics in South Africa to the institution of a certain normalization of death in the 'constitutional' process in Iraq, the essays in this volume consider the problem of violence and death at the heart of the institution of democracy. The minutia of economic and embodied practices of power and politics are not neglected. By interrogating the 'interior' of global capital and the transnational corporation, regular narratives of an overarching globalization are disturbed. Modes of politics and embodiment are also examined through the tension between religion and democracy, heteronomy and autonomy.

2

JOURNAL OF LAW AND SOCIETY
VOLUME 34, NUMBER 1, MARCH 2007
ISSN: 0263-323X, pp. 3–13

Church, State, Resistance[1]

JEAN-LUC NANCY

This article problematizes a separation of Church and State that is nevertheless identified as constitutive of politics. Democracy has come to manifest a tension between the 'autonomy' of the political and a 'heteronomy' that, exceeding rationalist or social contractarian accounts of our co-existence, is here presented as an irreducible affect of our being together. Autonomy, it is argued, resists heteronomy through all representations of democracy; yet, by contrast, heteronomy resists autonomy, and does so with the force of this affect. So if civil religion is impossible – and if we know only too well where its realizations lead: by default, to republican celebration, or by excess, to fascism – then we must take up again, and from scratch, the question of the affect according to which we co-exist.

I

The separation of Church and State is the expression, linked in France to the dominant Catholic Church, for the complete distinction of competences, laws [*droits*] and powers between the religious order (be it ecclesiatical or otherwise constituted) and the political order. It is understood that in any civil or public matter the political order prevails; while in any religious matter – henceforth considered as private or as having to do with the intimacy of conscience – the authority exercised is defined by a religious body [*instance*] to which everyone is free to adhere.

Today this separation is recognized as a given of democracy, whatever the precise form of its enunciation in public law (and even where, as in England, there exists a very particular situation which may seem, but which is not really, one of non-separation). The constitutional and/or institutional affirma-

* *Université de Strasbourg, 22 rue René Descartes, 67084 Strasbourg, France*
nancy@umb.u-strasbg.fr

1 Translated by Véronique Voruz, Lecturer in Law at Leicester University, and Colin Perrin, Commissioning Editor with Routledge.

3

tion and imposition of the consubstantiality of religion and State contravenes the general rules of democracy and the rule of law [*Etat de droit*] – since, precisely, law must establish among other things the independence of religions and the appropriate conditions to be placed upon this independence, in the same way that it must establish the conditions for freedom of thought and of expression.

We are used to considering this separation between Church and State as an achievement of modern democracy. This is not wrong in so far as the juridical inscription of this separation is indeed recent in history (notwithstanding certain details that we will encounter later). But it is still necessary to recall that this separation, or at least its principle and its condition of possibility, appear at the very beginning of politics: in Greece. It is necessary to recall this because, to go straight to the point, it means that the separation of Church and State is not one political possibility among others, but a constitutive element of politics as such – if we agree to give this term the sense derived from its Greek origin, rather than a vague and distended sense which would encompass any possible kind of organization of the collectivity.

II

For sure, the *polis*, the city, has its own religion, celebrates its own rites and also makes room for other less public or less 'civic [*citoyens*]' forms of worship [*cultes*]. Yet in its principle, in its very being as *polis*, the city supposes a fundamental rupture with any kind of theocracy, whether direct or indirect. From Aristotle, and even Plato, to Machiavelli and Bodin, without awaiting the more official and more modern forms of separation [between Church and State], this principle is verified: politics encompasses any kind of '-cracy' except theocracy. Reciprocally, theocracy encompasses any kind of societal organization that rests on a religious principle, except politics – even where the latter seems to include a religious dimension. The stakes are high: in principle, what is the case for religion is not the case for freedom of thought. Religion is not first of all a *private* preference; it is a mode of representing and organizing both personal and collective existence. Therefore, religion is nothing but the other collective or communitarian possibility, besides that constituted by politics. The separation of Church and State should be considered as the only true act that gives birth [*acte de naissance*] to politics.

The *polis* rests firstly on the fact that it gives itself its own law [*loi*]. It can invoke a prescription or a divine guarantee for this law; but it is to the *polis* itself that the determined establishment, formulation, observation, and improvement of law belongs. In this respect, nothing is more instructive than, on the one hand, the displacement and progressive abandonment of various forms of trial by ordeal and, on the other hand, the development, which predates the *polis* itself (in Babylon in particular), of codes of property

4

and exchange (trade, inheritance, and so on) which themselves anticipate part of the general *auto-nomy* upon which the city will come to rely.

The political [*le politique*] – if we can use this [*masculin*] term to designate an essence or principle – is autonomy by definition and by structure. Theocracy, in the sense we have just given it as the other of politics – represents, on the contrary, heteronomy by definition and by structure. Manifestly, autonomy cannot but resist heteronomy, and reciprocally. In general, we can even say that any form of political or moral resistance implies a relation between an autonomy and a heteronomy; its most authentic form for us (perhaps even its only authentic form) being the resistance of autonomy – individual as well as collective – to any kind of heteronomy.

III

Under these conditions, the religion – where there is one – that is proper to the city has a double aspect. On the one hand, it appears as a survival of and as a substitute for theocratic religion. Everything takes place here as if the *polis* did not yet know how to organize [*ordonner*] its relationship to the very principle of its institution – let us say to the founding authority – without the customary form, which in reality is not political, of a recourse to the divine. From this perspective, and whatever its precise form, the separation of Church and State is the logical outcome – however remote in time it is or may seem to be – of the political invention. As such, civil autonomy is separated without ambiguity from religious heteronomy.

On the other hand, the religion of the *polis* tends, on the contrary, to constitute itself as a specific religion, distinct from the 'religion of the priests', to use the expression through which Kant seeks to distinguish religion in the ordinary sense from that which he puts to work 'within the limits of simple reason'. This religion purports to be political *and* religious, but religious in so far as political, and not the other way around.

In some respects at least, this is already the case with the religion of Athens, a city that does not bear the name of its tutelary goddess by chance. And this is even more visibly the case with the religion of Rome, which probably provides the most accomplished example in western history of a religion that is somehow consubstantial with the city and State – to the point that the Latin word *religio*, which we inherit to name a phenomenon that only Rome named as such, offers a sense which is consubstantially juridico-political and religious, whether we understand this according to the etymology of scrupulous observance or according to the more uncertain etymology of the establishment of a bond.

What does the Roman religion signify as a political, civic or civil religion? It signifies the inclusion of autonomy in a heteronomy which, without subverting this autonomy, gives it the double dimension of a transcendence and a fervour. 'Rome' transcends its own autonomous immanence; the

5

Roman body politic (*Senatus Populus Que Romanus*) is more and something other than the effective existence of the assembled Romans, of their laws and their institutions. Thus, for example, the Roman Republic is able to take up the legendary inheritance of the kings who preceded it: it is by virtue of the same truth – of 'Rome', precisely – that the Republic prides itself on having supplanted royalty, and that the kings are venerated as ancestors and precursors of the republican law.

Rome has at its disposal a heteronomy *of* its own autonomy, or a transcendence of its own immanent principle. Whether this Roman model does or does not strictly conform to the reality of history matters less here than the fact that Rome was able to create this image of itself and to leave its effigy to posterity, such that the exemplarity of the Roman model was regularly invoked by the French Revolution as much as by Italian fascism, to mention the most famous and the most representative cases. This model was characterized by the exemplarity of Roman civic virtue, of a tight combination of juridical observance and a patriotic cult, and of the representation of the Senate as an 'assembly of Kings' (Friedrich Schlegel), mixed with the exemplarity of an urban management that was as social as it was economic, of an army more national than ever before in antiquity, and finally with the *exemplum* par excellence, the magistrate-priest whose name – *pontifex* – carries a double meaning, a dual sacral and civil genius.

IV

The importance of the Roman example reveals how much we have wanted to associate with the image of Greek democracy – essentially represented by the agora and the free discussion on justice which, for Aristotle, constitutes the *politikon* character of the human *zôon* – the image of a religious reality of the public thing [*res publica*], anterior to any space and any articulation of relation. What does it mean that we have 'wanted' this ? Have we desired it, and why? Have we felt it as a need inherent to the public thing itself from the moment that it autonomizes itself – and where does this need come from? It is probably not possible – at least not now – to answer all these questions. But to broach the political question in all its breadth – as it is revealed to us today – it is necessary to underline the extent to which the image, idea or scheme of a 'civil religion' underpins more or less consciously our principal representations of the political.

This in fact is how one should understand the Schmittian motif of 'political theology'. Even if Carl Schmitt does not himself ask the question of civil religion – irrespective of the fact that he felt entitled to find some suitable equivalent of his 'theological' model in Nazism – or perhaps exactly because he does not ask this question as such, his rigorous thought of sovereignty shows that recourse to the religious remains or obscurely returns at the horizon of the politics of the Moderns. Failing such recourse, which

6

the idea of a 'Republic', in its French form in particular, will have kept alive until yesterday (to say nothing here of the model of the United States of America, of Habermas's constitutional patriotism, of everything that could be analysed in the Japanese and Chinese realities, in the constitutional monarchies of Europe, and so on), it seems that the political is destined to withdraw [*retirer*] the essence we assumed it to have, leaving it to dissolve itself in 'management' and in the 'police', which henceforth appear to us as the miserable remnants of what politics could or should have done.

Marx was right to link the critique of religion to that of politics. The point for him, at least according to his first and founding inspiration, was to undo political specificity and suppress its separate existence ('the State'), much as the critique of religion should suppress the separation of heaven and earth: but it was in order to arrive at a world that would no longer be a world 'devoid of spirit and heart'. In other words, the true spirit and heart, the spirit and heart of the true human community at work in the production of man himself, were to substitute their immanent authenticity for the false transcendences of the political spirit and the religious heart.

As we see, politics and religion were to be sublated *(aufgehoben)* together, in the same and unique movement, itself arche-political and – by way of consequence – arche-religious; the movement of the real social being beneath and beyond its politico-religious representations.

So everything happens as if the great alternative of modernity had been: either definitively emancipate politics so that it is entirely separate from religion, or expel them both, outside the effectivity and seriousness of the autoproduction of humanity. So either politics is conceived as the effectivity of autonomy (personal as well as collective), or politics and religion together are represented as heteronomous, and autonomy consists in freeing oneself from them. Resistance of the political to the religious or resistance to the politico-religious (and in this case, resistance of what, of whom? Let us leave this question in suspense).

V

This alternative had its condition of possibility in the second Roman event, the one which succeeded the Republic and the Empire in so far as it retained something of the *republican*. This event is none other than Christianity and, from the point of view that interests us here, Christianity brings nothing other than an essential separation between Church and State. In fact, this separation is so fundamental that it is even foundational: for it is in Christianity that this conceptual couple 'Church/State' is properly for-mulated. It is formulated with the constitution of the *ekklésia*, a term taken from the institutions of the Greek city and which now designates an 'assembly' and a specific mode of being together, as distinct from the social and political mode.

7

Already before the creation of the Church, or even the local churches, Christianity presented two major features: the distinction between two kingdoms and the correlative distinction between two laws. The Kingdom of God and the kingdom of Caesar, the law of Moses ('the law of sin' according to Paul) and the law of Jesus or the law of love ('the law of freedom' according to James). Heir to a dehiscence which appeared within Judaism, Christianity constitutes a major political event – or an event in relation to the political: in the same operation, it rigorously, ontologically separates the political from the religious (since there are two 'worlds', and for its part this division entails great religious consequences). And further, in a paradoxical gesture, it constitutes the religious itself on the political model of the kingdom or of the city ('kingdom' in the Gospels, 'city' for Augustine).

The origin of this entirely novel formation in the religious order is to be found in the meaning [*signification*] of Messianism: where the Messiah was expected to restore the kingdom of Israel, he becomes the instaurator of an entirely different Kingdom, which totally escapes nature and the laws of the human kingdom. Or rather: it is only in this way that the political is unveiled as a human order, only human and 'all too human'. . .

From then on civil religion is impossible. All manner of alliances will become possible between Church and State. And as we know, it is even by way of the conversion of the Empire to the new religion that a new age begins, an age that will know the double destiny of the Empire between the Orient and the Occident, according to a double articulation of the relation between the two kingdoms. Still, the fundamental principle of the heterogeneity of the two orders will never be fundamentally called into question.

(In passing here, this is also why an important aspect of the tradition or the diverse traditions of Islam has to do with the relation between temporal and spiritual authorities – a formulation which is only possible *stricto sensu* in a Christian terminology.)

The separation of Church and State that democracy came to produce is in a way the direct consequence of the double regime instituted by Christianity, a double regime that at the same time displaced the order of the city and the order of religion. This displacement itself intervened as the consequence – here again, in a way direct – of the precarious and always repeatedly destabilized situation in the ancient world of the city endowed with civil religion.

VI

It is not surprising under these conditions that the modern thought of the political should have passed through two decisive stages with regard to the relationship between the State and religion.

8

The first stage is the invention of sovereignty. From Machiavelli to Bodin – and without wanting to over-valorize the motif of a certain continuity from one to the other – it is clear that the centre of gravity of the political problem has not ceased to move towards a profane, temporal and even atheist, to use Bayle's word about Bodin – condition of the State. The very notion of 'State', with its value of establishment and stability, testifies to the necessity of discovering a principle of grounding [*principe d'assise*] and of solidity where an absolute foundation [*fondement*] is definitively lacking. The expression 'absolute monarchy', although it is applied to regimes surrounded by ecclesiastical and theological guarantees, speaks for itself: the sovereignty of the monarch, that is, of the State, cannot by definition depend upon any authority other than itself, and its religious consecration does not, despite appearances, constitute its political legitimacy.

The sovereign State is the State that must derive its legitimation from itself. Without even emphasizing how essential the right to decide the state of exception (according to which Schmitt defines sovereignty) is in this context, we have to acknowledge that *autonomy*, as the principle of the political, here makes its major demand: it must or it should in one way or another found, authorize, and guarantee its own law by its own means. Is this possible in any other way than by invoking the necessities of security born of the weakness and the hostility of men? But can such necessities found more than an expedient – or even in some cases, more than a usurped authority for the sole good of some? Thus we see delineated the general scheme of the political problematic from the classical age onwards.

The second stage is none other than the demand for a civil religion as formulated by Rousseau. What is this about? To render 'perceptible to the hearts of citizens' all of the rules and conditions deduced from the transcendental deduction of the social contract. Why this need for a specific affectivity? Why, if not because the affect was excluded from the contract – the very notion of which implies rationality, but not fervour, nor desire, nor sentiment.

Despite appearances, Rousseau's civil religion is not something added in the manner of a more or less gratuitous ornament to the edifice constructed by the contract. On the contrary, it comes to try and repair the intrinsic flaw of the contract, which does not know how to bring about a regime of assembly [*régime d'assemblement*] other than on the basis of interest – even as this contract forms man himself at the same time as it forms the citizen. (As to the protestant source or provenance of this civil religion, it obviously deserves a development which will have to take place elsewhere.)

VII

As we know, Rousseau's civil religion remained a dead letter. At least, give or take a few things, it remained a dead letter as to the execution of Rousseau's programme. It nevertheless left two traces that are both durable

9

and problematic, under the dual guises of 'fraternity' and 'secularism' [*laicité*].

Like the 'separation of Church and State', the political senses of 'fraternity' and 'secularism' [*laicité*] constitute a French specificity. Yet, as with 'separation', one must interpret them broadly and as designating notions of general value for the current representation of democracy. (I leave the task of justifying this affirmation in a more detailed way for another time.)

With 'fraternity', added as we know as an afterthought to the motto of the French Republic, we are faced with the residual minimum of the political affect. This is also to say with the minimal form of a latent question, more or less clearly resurgent, about the force of affect supposed by the simplest being-with. It is not that the idea of 'fraternity' necessarily accounts for it well – this is another debate, which Derrida reopened several times in opposition to Blanchot and myself. Even if we debate the term, what matters to me here is that it is in order to substitute other terms with an affective denotation or connotation: 'friendship', in Derrida's case, or elsewhere 'solidarity' or even 'responsibility', terms which – as well as in the last analysis that of 'justice' if we think about it – cannot be entirely divested of an affective tone. To say it as briefly as possible, what resists with 'fraternity' is affect, and so something of affect resists, under one term or another, at the heart of the political order considered as an order of integral autonomy – supposing the latter to be thinkable without affect (or thinkable at all, which perhaps amounts to the same thing).

With 'secularism' [*laicité*], another aspect of the same resistance manifests itself: namely, not the sole possibility of holding the politico-social order exempt from any religious interference, nor that of charging this order with organizing the free practice of worship [*cultes*] according to necessary conditions, but beyond that – and somewhat contradicting the two preceding propositions – the necessity of conceiving and practising something like the observance and celebration of the values, symbols, and signs of recognition which attest to everyone's adhesion to the community as such.

For sure, the previous sentence cannot fail to produce the suspicion that what is being defined here is a kind of vague fascism ... but I would like precisely to point out that fascisms, and with them 'real' communisms as well as some types of dictatorship, have well and truly seized upon an unemployed desire for the celebration of community, and that if this desire remained unemployed – as it does today – it is because politics was not able to take it up. That is to say, because politics did not know how to or could not fulfil the intentions or expectations which the words 'fraternity' and 'secularism' [*laicité*] designate as best they can. Or, to put this in an inverted form, because the general idea of tolerance, and of the State as a space of tolerance remains inferior or even foreign to what is rightfully expected of the political: namely, the taking up of a force of affect inherent in being-with.

10

If autonomy resists heteronomy through all representations of democracy, by contrast, heteronomy resists autonomy with the force of affect. The affect is essentially heteronomous, and perhaps we should even say that affect *is* heteronomy.

Christianity put into effect a sharing that the Greek foundation of the political implied: the sharing of two orders and two cities; on the one side the order and the city of the useful and the rational (in the restricted sense that we more often than not give to this word), and on the other side the order and the city of a law which does not call itself the law of love by accident.

For the whole duration of the civilization known as Christian, love has not failed to return, at least as a question, exigency or concern – which is to say also and fundamentally as resistance – on the side of the political. Thus the subjects of kings were supposed to love their sovereigns; Hegel thinks love as the very principle of the State; fraternity, patriotism (up to and including Habermas's 'constitutional patriotism'), and national liberations; democracy itself or the Republic (European style) or the Nation (American style); and a number of generous representations of Europe: all these will have amounted to so many efforts to take up and reactivate something of this love. For the inventors of democracy, like Rousseau and in accordance with him, always knew that democracy could not abandon love to the other kingdom, and that it should perhaps even take it up for itself without leftover, since failing that it would be merely ... a democracy, that is to say, a simple order of the useful and rational management of a world in itself devoid of affect, which is also to say of transcendence.

Democracy is thus by birth (we could even say its double birth, Greek and Modern) too Christian, and not Christian enough. Too Christian because it fully assumes the separation between the two kingdoms, not Christian enough because it fails to re-find in its kingdom the force of affect that the other has reserved for itself. But at the same time, Christianity, deprived of the public positions through which it recovered with one hand the material power that it had abandoned with the other – and through which it also continued to instil a little bit of love or the pretence of love in the political order – this Christianity has dissolved itself as a social religion and because of this it has tended to dissolve itself as a religion *per se*, thus tending to take all religions with it.

Neither of the two kingdoms resists the other any more – except under the brutal form of fanaticisms, whether they be of Church or State. But in reality, this is not a relation of resistance, it is a relation of wills of domination and of the absorption of one kingdom by another, of a pure and simple conquering and destructive hostility.

11

We no longer live in [a time of] resistance, but in [one of] confrontation. We no longer live in [a time of] the different nature of two kingdoms, but in [a time of] the different force between empires. If it is certain that we will return neither to a Christian civilization [*chrétienté*], nor to the Roman republic, nor to the Athenian city, and if it is certain that it is not desirable in any way that we return to any of these forms, it is just as certain that we must now invent a new way to refigure [*rejouer*] the political institution itself, from now on by clearly formulating its exigency as that of the *impossibility of civil religion*. For if civil religion is impossible – and if we know only too well where its realizations lead, by default (republican celebration ...) or by excess (fascist celebration), and that its 'just measure' is precisely the impossible itself – so we must take up again, and from scratch, the question of the affect according to which we co-exist. After this we will have to ask ourselves how we should truly separate Church and State – or rather how we should from now on renounce, just as much as the political hold of a given religion, the desire for a politics that would be able to take up this affect and its heteronomy. It seems that it is too much to ask for the two things together. Yet this is what we must give ourselves at least as an exploratory and heuristic rule.

We could start (again) as follows.

Being in common, or being together, and more simply still, or in a starker [*dénudée*] form, being several, is being in affect: being affected and affecting. It is being touched and touching. 'Contact' – contiguity, brushing together, encountering, and clashing – is the fundamental modality of the affect. For what the touch touches is the limit: the limit of the other – of the other body, because the other is the other body, that is to say the impenetrable (penetrable only through the wound, and not penetrable in the sexual relation where 'penetration' is only a touch that pushes the limit to its farthest point). What is at stake above all in being-with is the relation to the limit: how to touch, and to be touched, at the limit, without its violation? For we desire to violate the limit in so far as it exposes finitude. The desire for fusion or the desire for murder constitute the double modality of an essential trouble that agitates us in our finitude. To swallow or to annihilate others – and yet at the same time wanting to maintain them as others, because we also sense the horror of solitude (which is properly the exit from sense, if sense is essentially exchanged or shared). This said, the relation to the limit is dealt with or has been dealt with in two ways in [the history of] humanity: either by a given modality of the sacrifice, which consists in crossing the limit by establishing a link with the totality (more generally still, I would say: a modality of consecration, for the bloody sacrifice is not the only one at stake), or outside of consecration, as in the Occident, in politics and law, that is to say, essentially in the recourse to an autonomy of finitude. The city may want to be regulated according to some cosmic, physical or organic model, but the very fact of this will and this representation indicates that it is the totality, the 'consecration through wholeness [*consécration au tout*]' which is experienced as lacking.

Thus the city establishes itself, if I can say so, in a problematic situation with respect to affect: the relation to the limits, the relation of limits between themselves, is no longer taken up by a virtually total 'consecration'. The political emerges from the outset as a regulation of affects. It is not by chance that Christianity appears in a context where the city that will soon be named a 'human city' experiences itself as failing with regard to personal relations and where the empire testifies to a failure or a halting of the *polis* and of *autonomia* to the benefit of a model of domination (of the *imperium*) which, despite its efforts, does not succeed in capturing the affect (because it is no longer truly sacred: it itself emanates from civil law, from 'dictatorship' in the Roman sense). It is not by chance that Christianity – that is to say prophetic Judaism and the Judaism of the diaspora (I mean to say: the two figures of a certain separation between the kingdom of Israel and Israel as the people of God), having reached a decisive point of transformation precisely in the midst of and in the face of empire (in the same way as, in a converging mode, Stoic and Epicurean philosophy seeks a regulation of affect) – should respond with both the 'law of love' and the 'kingdom of God'. At the same time, Christianity proposes the distinction between two kingdoms or two cities, and the distinction between the legal law and the law of love, that is also to say of the other of law or of its reverse. Christian love signifies above all the reverse of law: its inversion or its subversion, its hidden side also; that is to say, where the law comes from without being able to recognize it – namely, the very sense of being-with.

What resists in these conditions is no more the Church to the State than the State to the Church – but it is being-with itself which resists *itself* and which refuses to accomplish itself under any form of hypostasis, configuration, institution or legislation. What resists is being-with in its resistance to its own gathering [*rassemblement*]. This resistance touches the truth of being's 'with', of this proximity of the *with* forever impossible to effectuate as a being and always resistant. Neither autonomous, nor heteronomous: but rather anomic in the mutual resistance of the autonomous and the heteronomous.

13

JOURNAL OF LAW AND SOCIETY
VOLUME 34, NUMBER 1, MARCH 2007
ISSN: 0263-323X, pp. 14–30

Constitutional Violence

DAVID BATES*

The eighteenth-century is usually looked to as the theoretical source for modern concepts of constitutionality, those political and legal forms that limit conflict. And yet the eighteenth century was also a period of almost constant war, within Europe and in the new global spaces of colonial rule. Though it is well known that new concepts of international law emerged in this period, surprisingly few commentators have established what connections there are between the violence of war and the elaboration of new ideas about constitutional limit. I will show that war played a crucial role in the Enlightenment invention of a modern existential concept of the political, where the violence of constitution was understood to be foundational.

ENLIGHTENMENT AND VIOLENCE

In its theorization both of war and of government, the Enlightenment has been defined by its emphasis on the idea of 'limit.' In the discipline of international law, for example, new normative concepts were developed that aimed to humanize the violence of war – or even eliminate that violence altogether.[1] This theorization of war seems consistent with the actual practices of warfare in eighteenth-century Europe. The post-Westphalian 'cabinet wars' were essentially positional, often indecisive, embedded in a complex diplomatic network, and nothing like the destructive, even annihilatory conflicts of an earlier age. Enmity, we might say, was 'domesticated' in the largely dynastic and territorial confrontations of the Absolutist era, at least within the European sphere.[2]

* *Department of Rhetoric, 7408 Dwinelle Hall, University of California, Berkeley, CA 94720-2670, United States of America*
dwbates@berkeley.edu

1 G. Best, *Humanity in Warfare* (1980) especially ch. 1, 'The later Enlightenment consensus'.
2 See, for example, J. Black, *European Warfare 1660–1815* (1994) especially ch. 1, 'European warfare and its global context', and J.A. Lynn, 'International rivalry and

14

At the same time, the sovereign 'absolutist' state that was the actor in these wars was itself domesticated over the course of the Enlightenment. The state was newly imagined as a political entity defined by foundational legal limitations that flowed from the constitution of political society by individuals with certain natural rights. The idea of the 'people' gradually usurped – theoretically – the unconditioned sovereignty of the traditional historical ruler.[3] Key modern concepts can be traced to this period: the division of powers, popular sovereignty, the rule of law, individual rights. All were different ways of construing state institutions as rational construc-tions 'constituted' in order to preserve peacefully the interests and well-being of individual citizens in society. Both international concepts of limit and constitutional political ideas were linked by an Enlightenment redefini-tion of sovereignty as a rational power in the service of pacification – within the state and between states in the international sphere.

But as we know, the end of the eighteenth century saw the total break-down of social, political, and inter-state order. The civil forms of violence paralleled in intensity the great religious and political upheavals of the sixteenth and seventeenth century. In the larger spaces of conflict, the European practice of limited war broke down entirely, as states sought to annihilate their enemies or violently transform them into an image of themselves. And civil war, particularly in revolutionary France, mirrored and perhaps even exceeded the unrestrained violence of this inter-state warfare. In the revolutionary wars and in the French counter-revolutionary conflicts we can see the first instances of modern 'total war,' with its blurring of the border between combatants and non-combatants on the battlefield and on the domestic front. The revolutionary era marks the beginning of a new form of warfare, characterized by a deadly intensity that would only be exacerbated by new technologies of destruction in the industrial age.

So how do we explain this paradoxical situation, that a century invested in the concept of limit would produce the most stunningly violent breaching of all limits in the revolutions and revolutionary wars that followed in the wake of 1789? For those with a stake in the Enlightenment legacy of limit (both its political and international variants), the French Revolution must be a kind of pathology. Discourses that countered the liberal constitutional tradition can be blamed for the radical political ideas that animated the revolutionaries; for example, republican concepts of unity that emphasized the total power of the people and relegated law and institutional forms to mere instruments.[4] Similarly, one could point to dangerous ideas of 'nationalism' at odds with the largely cosmopolitan

warfare' in *The Eighteenth Century: Europe 1688–1815*, ed. T.C.W. Blanning (2000). Less sanguine is A. Starkey, *War in the Age of Enlightenment, 1700–1789* (2003).

3 K. Baker, *Inventing the French Revolution: Essays on French Political Culture in the Eighteenth Century* (1991).

4 H. Arendt, *On Revolution* (1963).

Enlightenment ideal as a source that helped fuel the totalizing violence of the revolutionary period.[5]

At the very least, it seems clear that we cannot isolate thinking about the theory and practice of war from the conceptualization of the constitutional state in eighteenth-century Europe. It is this connection that I want to pursue. If theories of international law and war in this period have received a great deal of attention, they are not often integrated into accounts of classic political theory, which in turn often ignore the broader inter-state context of those arguments. What I want to show here is that a reading of some classic Enlightenment theorizations of constitutional 'limit' reveals the critical importance of violence and war in those accounts.

My goal is to show how this conceptualization of the state in relation to violence and war in fact made possible a new concept of sovereignty in this period, one that drew on older notions of state autonomy as well as newer discourses of individual freedom in the context of new forms of political administration and organization. I will suggest that the Enlightenment concept of the political was a radically existential concept; in other words, political sovereignty was newly defined in terms of the existence (and not the content or even the institution) of the state. This redefinition of political sovereignty (which itself reflected critical transformations of the state in the eighteenth century) in turn transformed the ways in which warfare could be understood (and practiced) in this period. In other words, political theory in the Enlightenment was not about the establishment of normative limitations to the exercise of power within the state and between military powers. Rather, theoretical concepts of the state made visible emergent relations between state authority and its exercise of violence in this period. My focus here will be on these theoretical formulations of state 'constitutions,' though understood as instantiations of a broader historical development.

WAR, STATES, AND INDIVIDUALS

As Quentin Skinner has demonstrated, by the start of the seventeenth century, 'the concept of the State – its nature, its powers, its rights to command obedience – had come to be regarded as the most important object of analysis in European political thought.' The state would be positioned, theoretically and practically, as the institution that would bring order and maintain it in a Europe fraught with religious, civil, and political division. To fulfill that role, the state was reconceived as a modern institution, freed, Skinner says, from its submissive status in medieval thought and culture. The modern concept of the state relied on the idea that politics was its own

5 D. Bell, 'Les origines de la guerre absolue, 1750–1815' in *La Révolution à l'oeuvre: Perspectives actuelles dans l'histoire de la Révolution française*, ed. J.-C. Martin (2005).

16

distinct branch of moral philosophy. But, more important, this concept underwrote the total independence of each political unity 'from any external or superior power'. Thus the principle of sovereignty was embedded in the new concept of the state: 'the supreme authority within each independent *regnum* should be recognized as having no rivals within its own territories as a law-making power and an object of allegiance.' As Skinner notes, this 'unitary image of political sovereignty' was a dramatic innovation because in medieval Europe the Church's power as a law-making entity in its own right, alongside legal assumptions grounding feudal social organization, precluded this radical political autonomy. However, a crucial limit built into this modern state concept was the idea that the state exists *solely* for political purposes. That is, the legitimation of state supremacy derived from its ability to produce and preserve political unity. The existence of other objectives would, in fact, undermine the independence and sovereignty of the state *as a political institution.*[6]

Historically, the emergence of the modern state in the seventeenth century brought some measure of order and security to Europeans after decades of brutally violent war and civil war. As Carl Schmitt has noted, any account of the sovereign state must be integrated within the larger context of inter-state relations, as Europe was reconstituted in the aftermath of religious upheaval and the destruction of an old spatial order.[7] ' "Statehood" is not a universal concept, valid for all times and all peoples. Both in time and space, the term described a concrete historical fact.'[8] For Schmitt, the modern state could assert its 'sovereignty' and independence only when other emergent states acquired the same status. This modern sovereign entity, with its distinct conceptual and territorial borders, was always part of a comprehensive European order. The annihilatory violence of a European 'civil war' was overcome by the institution of an inter-state legal order grounded in political units which had the ability to restore order and security within their own borders, maintaining order within Europe as a whole because they recognized each other as legitimate counterparts. 'The equality of sovereigns made them equally legal partners in war and prevented military methods of annihilation.'[9]

As Schmitt relates, a new international law, and with it a new concept of war and peace, developed in this period, one that turned away from older Christian moral paradigms to focus on the 'sovereign territorial state'[10] as the sole axis of jurisprudence. The natural law theorists of the early modern

---

6 Q. Skinner, *The Foundations of Modern Political Thought*, Vol. 2: *The Age of Reformation* (1978) 349–53.
7 C. Schmitt, *The 'Nomos' of the Earth: The International Law of the 'Jus Publicum Europeaum'* (2003 [1950]) tr. G.L. Ulmen.
8 id., p. 126.
9 id., p. 142.
10 id., p. 126.

era reconceived law based on how natural individuals endowed with 'natural reason' would and should behave to one another in what was called by Hobbes a 'state of nature.' The state, freed from any legitimating discourse, was the agent of a new order, and the only foundations for this juridical order were the rights and obligations derived from this radical autonomy. Jurists would rediscover Roman legal structures to think about how states could be understood as 'public persons' in the international arena: 'the analogy between states and human persons in international law ... became prominent in all international law considerations', with Hobbes's *Leviathan* the best exemplar of this way of thinking.[11] International law and the problem of war were thus deeply implicated in the formation of sovereign states and the elaboration of a legal justification for their autonomy.

Richard Tuck has recently argued that the natural law tradition that developed this 'reason of state' justification of sovereign political autonomy *within* the state, and of restricted forms of warfare *between* European states, paradoxically marks a crucial stage in the emergence of a modern liberal tradition of thinking about individuals and the state.[12] Tuck claims, in effect, that the predominance of a social contract theory of the liberal, constitutional state in the eighteenth century can only be understood as the unintended effect of thinking about *states* as independent actors on the world stage. If the state was a kind of autonomous 'agent' analogous to an individual, it was possible to redescribe the individual as 'a miniature sovereign state to which the vocabulary of liberty and sovereignty could be applied'.[13] As we see in Hobbes, who first used the term, the 'state of nature' was from the start ambivalent, modeled on the anarchic condition that obtained between powerful states lacking any real restraint, but used simultaneously to describe individuals confronting one another prior to the foundation of any civil or political society. It was the natural law jurisprudence of war and peace in the sixteenth and seventeenth century that forged a strong *juridical* argument for radical individual autonomy based on the key concept of a natural right of 'self-preservation', paving the way for a powerful liberal discourse of individual rights beginning in the later seventeenth century.

At the dawn of Enlightenment, then, we can see how the European inter-state order was intertwined with the concept of the independent sovereign state, while new legal conceptions of the individual subject drawn from 'reason of state' jurisprudence were poised to threaten the very idea of this sovereign state – and with it, potentially, the greater spatial order constituted in Europe after 1648.

---

11 id., p. 146.
12 R. Tuck, *The Rights of War and Peace: Political Thought and the International Order from Grotius to Kant* (1999). Compare Tuck's earlier work, for example, *Philosophy and Government 1572–1651* (1993).
13 id. (1999), p. 84.

18

Hobbes's *Leviathan* was the greatest attempt to control these various analogies in a tight, logically coherent system – autonomous individuals, in a state of nature akin to the international condition, recognized the dangers of their situation and came together to form a sovereign state authority with total independence, a state that in turn could participate in the post-Westphalian inter-state order that preserved security within Europe as a whole. But as critics such as Pufendorf realized early on, the problem with this argument was that the success of the constitution of the sovereign state was not in fact paralleled by the construction of some 'higher' sovereignty at the inter-state level.[14] For Enlightenment thinkers in the liberal tradition, this difficulty undermined the argument for absolute sovereignty, opening the way for alternate conceptions of state formation in the originary condition, and providing a new language for speaking about international order as well. So while writers (from Locke on) would appropriate the legal discourse of war to underwrite their own conception of the acquisitive individual, they also assumed that a 'natural sociability' would bring human beings together, and (potentially at least) bring states closer together as well. Tuck thinks that this was a doomed project, for once the strict analogy between sovereign state and liberal individual was loosened, both the state and the individual were bound to lose their radical autonomy. Only with Rousseau and, following him, Kant, was Hobbes 'rediscovered' and a pure liberal theory made possible again on the analogy between reason of state and the social contract.

Countering this interpretation, I will argue that beginning with Locke, the complex interplay between concepts of inter-state violence and the originary condition of individuals in nature spurred the development of a wholly new idea of the state, one that was inherently political, self-legitimating, and not dependent on other concepts, while at the same time deeply bound up with a radical democratic understanding of individuals in society. This was not, as it might seem, an entirely paradoxical conception, as I will try to show. Tracing three exemplary formulations (Locke, Montesquieu, Rousseau), we can see how ideas about foundational violence and the demands of war prepared the invention of a modern concept of the political, reflecting a whole new way of thinking about the autonomy of sovereign entities in a 'democratic' age. Individuals were tied to a *collective* identity whose function was to defend individuals in moments of extreme crisis. The organs of that collective identity emerged as a new site of power, legitimated not by transcendental concepts but, instead, the very ideal of preservation, enacted in two registers: the community of individuals, and the concrete vehicles of that existential unity.

14 id., p. 140.

19

Locke's *Second Treatise* is a crucial first step in the reconceptualization of the individual in relation to the state after Hobbes. This rethinking of the individual on the model of the war-making sovereign leads to a crucial theoretical transformation of that original sovereign state. In Locke's analysis, this newly framed state structure retains much of the authority and power of the original political entity, however, with important new limitations. Political action is, for Locke, never wholly autonomous, driven as it was by the logic of individuality linked to the principle of property.

Locke begins his origin narrative by distinguishing the state of nature from what he calls the state of war. In the state of nature, human beings can live together, 'according to reason,' though there is no common superior to judge their controversies. The state of war is that condition where force (or its 'declared design') disrupts this natural state. In this new position, individuals cannot appeal to a common superior for relief and are thus threatened. Therefore, as Locke relates, one must kill to protect oneself. In this state of war, one is justified in killing even a lowly thief, for example, because *any* intervention of force is a threat to one's security, and only when force disappears (when the opponent is *destroyed*) does the state of war end. This subtle rewriting of Hobbes clears the way for a foundational moment that arises from this originary violence but is, in an important sense, not at all legitimated by that violence. For it is the natural state *before* the state of war that will be 'refounded' in the new political society created to neutralize the threat of war. While Locke assumes here the existence of some kind of society prior to this decisive moment, the point is that we have no *political* entity until a common force is created to prevent the state of war from ever developing.[15]

The created political power has two main functions according to Locke. First, it has the ability to create 'law' inside the community and protect individuals from each other. This is the legislative form of authority. Second, it makes 'war and peace' to defend the rights and existence of the political society of property-owning individuals. This is what Locke calls the 'executive' authority, and it is worth paying closer attention to this power, since it rather strangely seems to exceed any liberal constitutional limitation.

Locke derives executive authority from an analogy between the individual and the political body as a whole. The executive decides who the enemy is and whether to kill or not, based on the original condition of war first encountered by individuals. Since Locke cleanly divides the 'internal' management of the society from the duty to protect the society as a whole, he is led to conclude that the legislative order has no role to play in executive action. That is, because the executive power by definition operates in the

---

15 J. Locke, *Second Treatise of Government*, in *Two Treatises of Government*, ed. P. Laslett (1988) ch. 3, ss. 16–18.

state of war that characterizes the relations between independent states, the executive should not at all be limited by any legal regulation – for this state of war is a realm of unpredictability and pure force, not law and controlled behaviour.[16] One must rely on prudence here (not 'precedent') in order to succeed. Here then is the logic behind the Lockean division of powers. The realm of contingency and violence must never enter the internal world of law, otherwise disorder and ruin can be the only possible result. Locke was of course hardly unaware of the dangers of executive power in this context. Yet his reflections on the limitations of that power are revealing. This is not a 'constitutional' problem for him but an existential one. When the legislative power (the vehicle of law and order within the state) is threatened, it must decide whether the executive has exceeded its authority or misused its power. And if the executive tries to hinder the legislative power from functioning, then the people have the right to counter force with force and resist the sovereign power.[17]

At the same time, Locke admits that the prerogative of the executive logically *exceeds* the law in exceptional circumstances – namely, those where the *law itself* might well endanger the state. Here, the executive cannot but help transgress the boundary between inside and outside; or rather, the problem of 'war' invades the body politic itself:

> ... in such cases, which depending upon unforeseen and uncertain occurrences, certain and unalterable laws could not safely direct; whatsoever shall be done manifestly for the good of the people, and the establishing the government upon its true foundations, is, and always will be, just *prerogative*.[18]

However, there is a fundamental limit to these interventions – defined not in terms of law but as a logic of political organization itself. The foundational legitimacy of any government is the preservation of *all* its members who come together to constitute it. Thus, in extreme crisis, when 'a strict and rigid observation' of the 'laws themselves' may threaten the state, law must give way *not* so much to executive power per se, but rather to this fundamental consideration. Prerogative, though it is the acting without a rule, defends a state of affairs to which it is always subordinate.[19]

The prerogative of the sovereign state is the persistent reminder that the political body is founded in a condition of violence. If the legislative authority represents the desire to manage and thus eliminate 'force' from human existence, the executive power at times must repeat the foundational autonomy of the individual, who must, when necessary, counter force with force, and kill to produce security. The decisive intervention of sovereignty is not a violation of the spirit of the legal state. Just the opposite – the almost unlimited authority of sovereignty 'without rule' in Locke's text merely

16 id., ch. 7, s. 88.
17 id., ch. 13, ss. 155–6.
18 id., ch. 13, s. 158.
19 id., ch. 14, s. 159.

21

affirms (as Tuck would have it) the absolute autonomy of the liberal individual. In this mirroring of individual and executive, there exists no space for a political sphere with its own constitutional ground. The right of killing those who threaten us is not 'constituted' as a particular political responsibility. It is merely the re-enactment of a prior natural right in the service of an *original* intention to eliminate the very need for such violent interventions. The political condition only *reproduces* the state of nature, albeit on a new level, and does not thereby introduce any new political principle.

While Locke's political theory was on one level a direct engagement with the particularities of English political and constitutional history, it is obviously also the case that his thinking about war and violence was very much influenced by his thinking about, and practical involvement with, the colonies of the New World and their relationship to British political life. We might therefore read his views on interventional power 'beyond the law' as a response not so much to the relatively peaceful state of Britain (and Europe) at that particular time, but instead as a reflection of the anarchic and often bloody conditions that characterized the colonial spaces of conflict – spaces inhabited by European states but also pirates, Indians, and other organized entities that threatened commercial and agricultural activity.[20]

THE CULTURE OF POWER IN MONTESQUIEU

Unlike Locke, Montesquieu attempted to locate a domain that we might call *purely* political, outside the logic of association we find in early forms of contract theory. Indeed, embedded in Montesquieu's justly famous typological analysis of governmental regimes is an origin story, a narrative account of the formation of power that has important repercussions for his understanding of the political. And, as Tuck has noted, Montesquieu, in contrast to earlier natural law theorists such as Grotius or Hobbes, here weakened the analogy between sovereign state and individual in nature when he (like many other Enlightenment figures) assumed that the affections and natural sexual bonds would produce a social organization without any 'rational' calculation on the part of these individuals.[21] Though the state remained, in Montesquieu's formulation, a radically autonomous entity, the resources of 'reason of state' juridical argumentation could not be marshalled for a defence of individual liberal freedom.

While this may well be the case, Montesquieu's aim was somewhat different I believe. His description and analysis of regimes is founded on a

20 See J. Tully, 'Rediscovering America: the *Two Treatises* and Aboriginal Rights' in *An Approach to Political Philosophy: Locke in Contexts* (1993); D. Armitage, 'John Locke, Carolina, and the *Two Treatises of Government*' (2004) 32 *Political Theory* 602–27; and Tuck, op. cit. (1999), n. 8, pp. 177–8.
21 Tuck, op. cit., n. 12, pp. 186–7.

22

prior understanding of what I call their intrinsic politicality. In fact, his assumption of some kind of prior social order allowed him to look at the origins of politicality in a new way. Montesquieu showed how political power is not in fact derived from scenarios of free individuals who associate and form civil society. Montesquieu tries instead to pinpoint an autonomous concept of the political, one with its own logic, and this will take Enlightenment thinking in an altogether new direction.

Montesquieu begins with the assertion that we find men in society, as a result of natural human affections. Immediately, however, something critical happens: 'As soon as men are in society, they lose their feeling of weakness; the equality that was among them ceases, and the state of war begins.' These are rather ambiguous phrases – for as Montesquieu will tell us, this condition of war has two dimensions (the one internal and the other external) and it is their *intersection* that helps explain the origin of the political. That is, in contrast to Locke, the 'legislative' management of the social and the 'executive' management of foreign affairs cannot at all be separated. 'Each particular society comes to feel its strength, producing a state of war among nations.' And at the same moment: 'the individuals within each society begin to feel their strength; they seek to turn their favor the principal advantages of this society, which brings about a state of war among them.' Analytically, we see that each space of conflict grounds a constitution of law – the civil law (internal to the nation) and the law of nations.[22]

Yet Montesquieu's famous typology of power as it develops *within* the state can only be understood with respect to this initial condition of war *between* societies. For the foundational political moment in any civil society occurs, Montesquieu implies, when individuals or groups take up the challenge of defending the pre-existing society at war and in civil war. The social would disappear without this foundational act to preserve unity. Allusively, Montesquieu writes: 'the strength of the whole society may be put into the hands of *one alone* or in the hands of *many*.'[23] How unity is preserved, and by whom, depends on the contingent conditions of the social order. Montesquieu's key point is that this original constitution of power, if it is to preserve unity and not merely continue civil war, must reflect a real unity of *all* the wills of the society. That sounds simple enough, but what drives much of Montesquieu's immensely complicated text is the serious challenge faced by these primitive communities. How can one maintain the radical unity of wills, the total unanimity of the society, when power is not shared equally by all? The 'spirit' of law is what can produce stabilizing institutions and effective defensive capacities to meet future challenges. Each type of regime – republican, monarchical, despotic – represents a

---

22 Montesquieu, *The Spirit of the Laws*, tr. A.M. Cohler, B.C. Miller, and H.S. Stone (1989) 1.1. 3.
23 id.

23

particular structure of power *and* a kind of cultural form of compensation that maintains unity even in the presence of sometimes striking inequality.

In republics, a whole people or a large part defended the society and overcame any internal division with a collective effort of defence. In the absence of enmity, some form of order must preserve the power structure, if civil strife is not continually to reappear. Paradoxically, it is much more difficult, Montesquieu says, to achieve order in a democracy, despite its radical equality of power. For the unity of wills that constitutes a political body can be maintained in periods of relative peace only if the individual can renounce his or her interests and love the abstract unity of the state itself. This is the political function of virtue.[24]

The origin of monarchical authority is not hard to imagine, and indeed, the eighteenth century abounds with conjectural histories that legitimate the power of kings and the privileges of the nobility, by showing how these figures protected communities and founded unity and order in times of radical violence and insecurity.[25] But how can we explain the stability of a power structure where only one person claims sovereign rule? The answer lies in the function of the many corporate bodies and intermediary powers that constitute the monarchical regime. If the monarch retains the ultimate power, other segments of the social order have specific functions and rewards that compensate for this lack of political power. What keeps this system running is honour – the passionate desire, that is, to uphold the specific practices of one's particular social form. In a monarchy, a complex set of institutions maintains equilibrium by distributing activity in various subsystems, all of which serve the unity of the whole almost by accident.[26]

In the despotic state there is no genuine order. Whatever stability the despot brings to a society in times of war and crisis, it is ephemeral and does not found any compensatory system, thus requiring constant reactivation. Fear is the regime's motor force because the people will remain united only by the real and terrible presence of force. Republics and monarchies order themselves, so to speak, because power is *integrated* into a social system that works to provide stability by compensating individuals for their lack of political power. In the despotic state, there is no spirit of unity. The state exists only as it is maintained through the exercise of direct force on the population.[27]

In all three regimes we see that the political is located in the space of sovereignty; the political is the origin and foundation of a unity discovered only in the dangerous times of war and civil conflict. The political is not

---

24 id., 1.2.2–3, 1.3.3–4.
25 F. Furet and M. Ozouf, 'Deux légitimations historiques de la societé au XVIII siècle: Mably et Boulainvilliers' (1970) 34 *Annales: Economies, societés, civilizations* 438–50.
26 Montesquieu, op. cit., n. 20, 1.2.4, 1.3.5–7.
27 id., 1.25, 1.3.8–9.

directly linked to the natural form of the social but rather emerges only in crisis when unity is *produced* in the crucible of enmity. Montesquieu's analysis here raises a difficult question. If the political unity of any society is bound up with a specific, historically contingent organization that shapes the very identity of the individuals that populate it, what happens when changes in historical conditions threaten the stability of that organization? To be more particular, what happens when (as in eighteenth-century France), the emergence of a commercial society erodes the feudal order of society, an order that grounds the very structure of sovereignty in the realm?

I think that Montesquieu's famous invocation of England's constitution as a model of political liberty is one answer to this challenge. Montesquieu did not believe, as naive readers often assume, that societies should aspire to this idealized constitutional order. We must remember that Montesquieu portrays England as an *exception*, a peculiar society (and state) that does not really follow the proper development of normal regimes, however thereby accidentally revealing the nature of political liberty most clearly. The English constitutional regime (at least the idealized picture Montesquieu gives us) is a reverse image of the despotic state. Despotisms are unified, but only by force, and thus there is no liberty because there is no security, no predictable order of things. In contrast, England is not at all unified, but its citizens are free precisely because there is no supreme political authority. We have to imagine how England might have escaped the normal paths of history. Perhaps because it is an island, there was no original threat of existence to spur the emergence of sovereignty. And perhaps because the miserable climate made everyone so morose, a mutual distrust kept its inhabitants apart enough so that internal conflict was never that intense. Whatever the story, it is clear that there is no sovereign power in England (in the sense of a monopoly of force and legitimacy) and therefore no compensatory mechanisms. The division of powers is not really a form of governmental power but rather a circuit of competing powers – which do not, incidentally, even represent different sectors of the society. As Montesquieu notes, individuals switch allegiances all the time in this system. Nothing is stable in England, yet a divisive institutional organization gives this instability an amazing security.[28]

The pathology of England is crucial for Montesquieu because it reveals a constitutional structure of liberty divorced from the political. This allows him to imagine the reform and restabilization of *political* regimes using the technology, so to speak, of constitutional mechanisms as developed in England. England does not provide some model of 'liberty' that would spur radical political change in nations such as France. Rather, if the monarchical regime was threatened because the functions of the orders were not fully compatible with modern economic and social realities, the English division

28 id., 2.11.

25

of powers could, as an institutional structure, provide renewed security if adapted by the sovereign state – but not by substituting for the state, as in the example of England. The English constitution exemplified a pure principle of balance, in contrast to normal nations where stability was located in very *particular* cultural forms. Constitutional devices like England's would not replace these cultures of compensation, or the structure of sovereignty from which they derived. The political (as principle and expression of foundational unity) would never be effaced from government; it might, however, be constrained by external mechanisms of control grafted onto it from the outside. Once Montesquieu had outlined an autonomous concept of the political, he realized that political power could never guarantee its own stability. The political was inevitably tied up with discrete cultural forms of order whose transformations might expose the society again to the foundational crisis with which it began.

Montesquieu therefore upheld the principle of balance. He was not naive about this – he knew that balance was something that was *achieved* in a complex historical process that was at its origin linked to warfare and civil unrest. And he knew that when these cultures began to break down, balance was threatened. His ideal of the technology of balance in the English constitution was just that – a technology that would support, but not substitute, for systems of sovereignty that defined the essence of modern states. Montesquieu's legal state was the quintessential post-Westphalian entity. It could preserve itself within its domain because it 'neutralized', so to speak, the internal divisions that had threatened its existence. And it could participate in a balance of power in Europe because it sought only to maintain its position and defend its borders.[29]

ROUSSEAU'S 'SOCIAL CONTRACT' AND THE LOGIC OF THE POLITICAL

The narrative of foundation in the *Social Contract* opens with the threat of violence – indeed, the radical threat of the extermination of the human species itself.[30] Individuals in the state of nature are forced, Rousseau says, to band together in order to survive. So unlike Locke or Montesquieu, Rousseau does not assume the existence of some contingent historical community that produces or faces its own *particular* threat. Rather, Rousseau zeroes in on the abstract character of an existential threat. Individuals know they must unite to combine strength, but this moment of recognition leads to another – that by uniting with other human beings, the proximity with other individuals opens up new and significant dangers. The answer to the

---

29 id., 2.9.
30 J.-J. Rousseau, *Social Contract* in *The Social Contract and other later Political Writings* (1997) tr. V. Gourevitch, 1.6, 'Of the social pact'.

predicament is well known – the social contract as figured by Rousseau draws on Hobbes's logic of security but gives it a democratic twist. To avoid the dangers of the 'other' while defending the unity of this (somewhat reluctant) new political community, one must give up all of one's powers to the unity itself – and not to any one particular figure or group. This story also radically rewrites Montesquieu's narrative of the political, which was framed as essentially *contingent* in two ways: the political was contingent on *what* was being defended in the first place, and on *who* emerged to defend that particular community. Rousseau denies both of these contingent preconditions in order to isolate what we might call a *pure concept of the political*, and from this pure concept he derives a logic of political legitimacy that transcends the specificity of any one kind of regime.

If the threat of violence and death is what drives individuals together, it does not drive them to form a particular social system which itself resolves the threat, and which would then only subsequently be the object of the political. The political precedes the social, in Rousseau's formulation. The political emerges as the real power to protect *not* the specific bonds of any one human grouping, but instead, the fictional *political* unity whose only goal is to protect the well-being of this newly formed group. The political speaks in the name of the unity alone, and by definition, Rousseau implies, that unity can have no specific content since its function is only to preserve itself as a unity. The general will speaks for all, in the sense that it speaks for the unity that they constitute, and not the interests that define them as concrete individual people. The sovereign is in Rousseau a necessarily abstract configuration. Neither the Lockean figure tied to the concrete particularities of the property-owning citizens, defending their *particular* public good, nor the sovereign in Montesquieu who seizes political supremacy and who is then integrated into a culture that sustains that *particular* constellation of power, the sovereign in Rousseau is more or less a logical principle only. It 'owes its being solely to the sanctity of the contract.'[31] The general will voices the interest that binds these individuals together in political society, which is the interest to maintain a political unity that preserves the radical autonomy of the natural individual.

Of course, the general will cannot remain in this suspended realm of generality. First, at any one moment, the general will must decide what, in this moment, for *this* particular community, is in its best interests as a unitary being. This demand for a decision that moves us from the pure logic of defence opens up the risks and challenges of the contingent. It also prepares another crucial transition. Because for the general will to speak and do anything, it must have 'organs' to express itself. This is the place for what Rousseau will call 'government' – the mediate body that expresses the general will of the sovereign but which can never be completely identified

31 id., 1.7.

27

with that will. Of course it is in these two transitional moments where the logic of the political as the defence of a contractual unity risks contamination and thus 'deflection' from the pure desire of preservation. And clearly, the second transition (the concretization of will in specific human organs) is the riskiest, since by Rousseau's definition, individuals always have their own interests, their own desires.[32]

But for Rousseau, the actual mechanisms of government were not the most important considerations. Or, at least, he realized that many different regimes were possible, with differing forms of organization and power structures, as Montesquieu had already demonstrated. What Rousseau provided with his radical story of the social contract was not a historical justification for a particular kind of government but, rather, a logical principle that demonstrated that social formations (which were inevitably contingent and defined by inequalities of all kinds) were strictly outside of the logic of the political. The unity formed at the origin of the political was existential: the group must be defended, and the individual must be defended *within* that group. The political was derived only from that logic of defence – the *content* of the grouping and the actual interests of individuals were immaterial. The conclusions Rousseau draws in this text (we are familiar with his claims about equality, the nature of laws, and so on) are grounded in the constitution of unity *as* unity, and not any one form of unity. The *Social Contract* provided, then, a critical tool for the evaluation of any one particular form of government. The limits of sovereignty were defined not by constitutional structures of the traditional sort, but instead by the radical constitution of any political community formed as a response to absolute crisis. This is why Rousseau's argument tells us a lot about the nature of 'democratic' and liberal forms of government, but at the same time seems to justify radical expressions of sovereign will beyond the law. Rousseau was neither republican nor liberal in the traditional sense. His concept of the political identified a pure logic of preservation that had no predetermined limit. Sovereignty is indivisible and without any 'rule' – it is an 'absolute power':

> If the State or the City is only a moral person whose life consists in the union of its members, and if the most important of its cares is the care for its self-preservation, then it has to have some *universal and coercive* force to move and arrange each part in the manner most conformable to the whole.[33] (my emphasis)

32 id., 2.6.
33 id., 2.4.

28

CONCLUSION: ENLIGHTENMENT WAR

With Rousseau we see a whole new perspective on war opening up in late eighteenth-century Europe. The logic of the political entailed a sovereign power whose responsibility was not to any particular social goal or interest but simply the demands of maintaining political unity. The coming to consciousness of this autonomy helped to prepare the way for a trans-formation in the understanding of war and its inherent legitimacy. Rousseau articulates the growing awareness in the eighteenth century of the independence of states (and cultures) and their mutual enmity in a ruthless global competition for dominance. After the Seven Years War, then the War of American Independence, it was increasingly difficult to imagine European states linked via traditional dynastic and historical bonds, especially as the very principle of monarchical sovereignty was being contested and dramatically reformulated in the Enlightenment. This is to say that the idea whose development we have been tracing – the idea of the state as an independent political power capable of preserving a unity founded in violence and war – reached its culmination in the late eighteenth century: historically with the emergence of true global warfare, and theoretically in the notion of absolute popular sovereignty of the Rousseauist sort. The result is the appearance of what Rousseau himself called a new state of nature.

It was, I would suggest, this logic (and not the emergence of specific ideas of national identity) that can explain the escalation of war in the late eighteenth century and the emergence of totalized warfare in the revolu-tionary period. For the political had been freed; no longer was it embedded in the distinct cultural forms whose very specificity had often limited the excesses of sovereignty. Rousseau predicted a time when the state would become newly conscious of itself as the incarnation of political unity:

> once things have reached a point where a being endowed with reason is convinced that his preservation is inconsistent not only with another's well-being but with his very existence, he takes up arms against the other's life and tries to destroy him as eagerly as he tries to preserve himself, and for the same reason. . . . The manifest will to destroy one another and all the actions that result from it produce between the two enemies a relation that is called *war*.[34]

But this coming to consciousness took place gradually in a century of (relatively) limited war for the European powers – at least on the Continent itself. What was forgotten at just this moment was the fact that the state as a concrete autonomous political unity was itself born in the very midst of an inter-state order that had conditioned and delimited that unity from the very start. We can speculatively argue that it was this forgetting that paved the way for a new concept of the state, a state whose autonomy was not constrained by any legal boundaries, within the state or in the global sphere.

---

34 J.-J. Rousseau, *The State of War*, in id., p. 163.

Not surprisingly, then, the open confrontations that had been limited to the colonial spaces outside of Europe would return to the Continent with the collapse of the French monarchy and the revelation of this pure logic of the political in the French Revolution – with predictably disastrous results.

The post-revolutionary challenge was to rebuild this unitary state within a new global order of states. Contests over political unity within industrial societies would of course complicate that goal. So would the unintended consequences of the drive for unification, in Italy and especially Germany. But this was, I think, the true legacy of the Enlightenment. Not the choice between constitutional governments and their irrational 'others,' or between 'international law' and brutal military competition in a realist vein. Instead, the legacy of Enlightenment was the challenging, almost paradoxical task of constituting a political spirit of unity within complex and divided social bodies, while founding a pluralistic inter-state order that lacked any form to express its own inherent unity.

JOURNAL OF LAW AND SOCIETY
VOLUME 34, NUMBER 1, MARCH 2007
ISSN: 0263-323X, pp. 31–45

Sovereignty, Exception, and Norm

ANDREW NORRIS*

Carl Schmitt's Political Theology *is the* locus classicus *of contemporary discussions of sovereignty. I argue that Schmitt's conception of sovereignty is excessively metaphysical and that it posits an incoherent 'sovereign' ability to decide what shall count as normal. Schmitt follows and radicalizes the late Bodin's claims – themselves the product of a political theology, namely, Bodin's conversion to Judaism – regarding the necessity of an indivisible and absolute sovereignty. In each, the relation between the executive and the other parts of government is reduced to what Schmitt describes as an 'either/or.' This move is a disastrous mistake. The question is not whether exceptions and emergencies such as terrorist attacks are real, but to what extent the executive branch can rightly claim a monopoly on the ability to determine whether an exception exists, and whether its resulting actions will be permanently unchecked and unregulated. Recent work by Bruce Ackerman is a better guide in these matters than the metaphysics of either Schmitt or Bodin.*

All significant concepts of the modern theory of the state are secularized theological concepts not only because of their historical development – in which they were transferred from theology to the theory of the state, whereby, for example, the omnipotent God became the omnipotent lawgiver – but also because of their systematic structure, the recognition of which is necessary for a sociological consideration of these concepts. The exception [*Ausnahmezustand*] in jurisprudence is analogous to the miracle in theology.

Carl Schmitt, *Political Theology*[1]

The sovereign decision is the absolute beginning, and the beginning ... is nothing else than a sovereign decision.

Carl Schmitt, *Über die drei Arten des rechtswissenschaftlichen Denkens*[2]

* *Department of Political Science, University of Pennsylvania, 208 S. 37th Street, Philadelphia, PA 19104-6215, United States of America*
anorris@sas.upenn.edu

1 C. Schmitt, *Political Theology: Four Chapters on the Concept of Sovereignty* (1985) tr. G. Schwab, 36; I silently modify the translation throughout when accuracy demands. German references are from *Politische Theologie* (1996, 7th edn.).
2 C. Schmitt, *Über die drei Arten des rechtswissenschaftlichen Denkens*, 2. Auflage (1993) 23–4.

The *locus classicus* of contemporary discussions of sovereignty, the first volume of Carl Schmitt's *Political Theology*, opens with the infamous proclamation, 'Sovereign is he who decides on the exception.'[3] For Schmitt, one can understand sovereignty only if one first grasps the nature of the exception. But this is, as Schmitt emphasizes, not as easy as it sounds. For what is *the* exception? The etymology of the German *die Aus-nahme* and the English *exception* (*ex-capere*) give us some help here: the exception is what is *taken outside*. But out of what is the exception taken, by whom, and under what circumstances? It may seem quite impossible to answer such questions, as there are so many different exceptions, made by so many different sorts of agents in different sorts of circumstances. But it is clear enough that not all exceptions are instances of *the* exception, whatever that might be. If I write of someone, say in a letter of recommendation, 'She is an exceptional student,' *exceptional* here means, simply, outstanding, significantly better than average. Such rankings may raise questions of justice or accuracy, but they do not raise any significant philosophical questions, in part because they do not truly *take anything out* of a norm or standard or rule, but are simply a matter of gradation. That is to say, the exceptional is here *determined by* the rule of rank, as the student is said to be at a point that, though not on the current scale, lies on the trajectory of any extension of that scale. The exception upon which Schmitt's sovereign decides stands in a considerably more vexed relation to rules, norms, and ordinary life.

But what relation exactly? As a way into an answer, let us consider two images, one philosophical, and the other literary, one a picture within which the problem and indeed the category of the exception does not and cannot appear, and the second a depiction of the exception in perhaps its most radical form. The first is the picture John Dewey paints of the human life of adaptation, reaction, and inquiry. In Dewey's picture, human beings are adaptive organisms that constantly modify their environment and themselves in the course of their interaction with their surroundings. As Dewey puts it in his 1938 *Logic*:

> Modification of both organic and environmental energies is involved in life-activity. This organic fact foreshadows learning and discovery, with the consequent outgrowth of new needs and new problematic situations. Inquiry, in settling the disturbed relation of organism-environment (which defines doubt) does not merely remove doubt by recurrence to a prior adaptive integration. It institutes new environing conditions that occasion new problems. What the organism learns during the process produces new powers that make new demands upon the environment. In short, as special problems are resolved, new ones tend to emerge. There is no such thing as a final settlement.[4]

As these are 'the conditions of life itself,' they are never surpassed, even by philosophical inquiry: 'The moment philosophy supposes it can find a final

3 Schmitt, op. cit., n. 1, p. 5.
4 J. Dewey, *Logic: The Theory of Inquiry* (1938) 35.

and comprehensive solution, it ceases to be inquiry and becomes either apologetics or propaganda.'[5] Properly understood, logic is the theory of inquiry understood in the terms of biological adaptation. In this picture, there is no room for fixed rules or norms, nothing from which an exception might be taken. All settlement is provisional, and the fundamental fact is the experience of particular disruptions and adaptations. At best, we can develop 'principles' and try to apply and modify them in the emerging 'problematic situations' within which we find ourselves. As such situations are 'individual or unique,' it follows that the decisions made there will be neither applications of a rule nor exceptions to it, but 'irreplaceable' situational goods.[6] On this account, '*the* exception' is no more helpful a term than Dewey took '*the* state' or '*the* individual' to be. It, like them, would at best be a 'general [answer] supposed to have a universal meaning that covers and dominates all particulars.' Such general concepts, Dewey argues, 'do not assist inquiry. They close it.'[7] Given the exception's oft-stated connection to the particular as opposed to the general or the universal, this would be a rather ironic outcome, but not an incoherent one. If Dewey is right, there is little for any given sovereign to do.

Things are very different in our second image, from G.K. Chesterton's 1908 *The Man Who Was Thursday*. This somewhat hysterical novel depicts a philosophical/political struggle between its hero, the 'philosophical policeman' Syme, and a band of mysterious philosophical revolutionary anarchists that Chesterton goes out of his way to associate with German Idealism. The Dostoyevskyian premise of the novel is that 'the most dangerous criminal now is the entirely lawless modern philosopher,' one who rejects 'the essential idea of man' and who hates life itself.[8] Syme is the perfect foil to such lawless nihilism, his very name announcing his commitment to unity and order (sym- coming from syn-, together, same, similar, union). He is not a simple figure of reason opposed to unreason, however, but a 'poet of law' who finds authentic poetry in the Underground Railway rather than 'the

---

5 id.
6 J. Dewey, *Reconstruction in Philosophy* (1920) 161, 163. As Alan Ryan emphasizes, Dewey's stance here makes it difficult to see how he could claim, as he did, that it was absolutely crucial to align science and aesthetics if humankind were to be more than 'a race of economic monsters, restlessly driving hard bargains with nature and one another.' As Ryan puts it:

   If there is no logical contradiction, there is some rhetorical tension between the largeness of the claims about what is at stake in the well-being of an entire civilization and the methodological injunction to look at each case in its own right. What one misses is what Dewey's hero Francis Bacon called *axiomata media*, middle-range principles that connect the large concern and the particular case.

   (A. Ryan, *John Dewey and the High Tide of American Liberalism* (1995) 232.)
7 Dewey, id., pp. 188–9. Compare Dewey's critique of the focus on 'the State' in his response to Walter Lippmann's at times almost Schmittian manifesto, *The Phantom Public* (1925), in J. Dewey, *The Public and its Problems* (1927) 8–9.
8 G.K. Chesterton, *The Man Who Was Thursday* (1986) 45.

33

lawlessness of art and the art of lawlessness'. 'The rare, strange thing,' he argues, 'is to hit the mark; the gross, obvious thing is to miss it.'[9] It is as such a poet that he is open to a 'sense of an unnatural symbolism' when confronted with the leaders of the anarchist conspiracy, each of whom is named for a day of the week and hence for a day in the Lord's creation of the world they are bound to destroy. In Chesterton's depiction of these men:

> Each figure seemed to be, somehow, on the borderland of things, just as their theory was on the borderland of thought. He [Syme] knew that each one of these men stood at the extreme end, so to speak, of some wild road of reasoning. He could only fancy, as in some old-world fable, that if a man went westward to the end of the world he would find something – say a tree – that was more or less than a tree, a tree possessed by a spirit; and that if he went east to the end of the world he would find something that was now wholly itself – a tower, perhaps – of which the very shape was wicked. So these figures seemed to stand up, violent, and unaccountable against an ultimate horizon, visions from the verge. The ends of the earth were closing in.[10]

We do not, I think, require Chesterton's repeated allusions to the Idealist tradition to be reminded here of Kant: the notions that the 'borderland of thought' reveals a 'borderland of things,' and that where the world thus ends one finds things that are either impossibly identical with themselves or else uncannily not themselves is almost too perfect an evocation of Kant's thing in itself, a 'thing' that, as the noumenal substrate of the phenomenal, is at once the true essence of the thing (the tower) and no-thing at all (the tree that is the spirit).[11] As for Kant, so for Syme there is in the end no difference between these two visions: the band of anarchists calls them both up, without distinguishing between them, and as the ends of the earth 'close in', Syme finds himself in a 'borderland' where east and west are one. And, as in Kant, it is impossible to dispel this paradox, one that Friedrich Jacobi for one took to lead directly to a form of pure subjective idealism he first named *nihilism*. Syme's nightmarish vision suggests that we don't know what we want and expect a thing to be: neither the absolute identity of form and content of the tower nor the uncanny, beside-itself quality of the tree make up a world in which one feels at home, a dismal realization that leaves one forever on the border, the verge, or tending towards it. What the anarchist conspirators represent is a rejection of the lawful, the orderly, the normal, and the ordinary. Syme's double vision of this rejection presents him and us with two ways a lawless, abnormal, extraordinary object might appear: as something either wholly itself, or as something ecstatically beside itself. In either case,

---

9 id., pp. 11, 10, 12.
10 id., p. 61.
11 I note that this is a reading of Kant that has recently been challenged; on the alternative account, though Kant might have been somewhat confused both in his exposition and his own understanding of the matter, in the end things in themselves are not objects of reference to which we intelligibly refer. For a helpful summary, see S. Gardner, *Kant and the Critique of Pure Reason* (1999) 284 ff.

34

the object defies inclusion in a general scheme, destroying the *arche* that Syme defends and the union he names.[12]

The very hysterical quality of Chesterton's vision is an important part of what I think recommends it to us. For it is matched in Schmitt's own reflections on the exception in *Political Theology*, a number of features of which it anticipates. This might sound quite counterintuitive, given Schmitt's distaste there and elsewhere for anarchists of any stripe. But then, such aversion is shared by Syme, the man who becomes Thursday, the fourth day in the doing and the undoing of the Lord's work. (It being on the fourth day that the Lord sets sun, moon, and stars in the sky, 'to rule over the day and over the night, and to divide the light from the darkness.'[13] To undo the fourth day is to mix light and darkness such that they cannot be distinguished, and thus render any Enlightenment impossible from the start.) Like Syme, Schmitt the theorist of the exception is a poet of order who cannot decisively break with disorder. When Syme meets the band of anarchists, he is pretending to be one of them, and like Syme, Schmitt's struggles for order require that he appear at times as a champion of chaos.

As in Chesterton's novel, the exception for the Schmitt of *Political Theology* is a 'borderline concept', 'not a confused concept, but one pertaining to the outermost sphere'.[14] As such it is something much more radical and difficult to grasp than a mere 'construct applied to any emergency decree or every state of siege'.[15] The exception is a borderline concept in the sense that it is neither within the legal order not outside it. When the sovereign decides on the exception, he:

> decides whether there is an extreme emergency as well as what must be done to eliminate it. Although he stands outside the normally valid legal system, he nevertheless belongs to it, for it is he who must decide whether the constitution needs to be suspended in its entirety.

Since 'it is precisely the exception that makes relevant the subject of sovereignty, that is, the whole question of sovereignty', it follows that the

---

12 Chesterton brings out the political implications this vision has for him elsewhere, where he emphasizes that if society is to function in any but a destructive way, people must be allowed to live 'normal' lives, where normality is the precondition of law, not its product. Though lines need to be drawn in order to give our lives the order they need, such lines cannot be drawn just anywhere. G.K. Chesterton, *The Outline of Sanity* (2001) 182, 52, and 156–7.

13 Genesis 1:18. The fourth day thus repeats and continues the work of the first (or last).

14 Schmitt, op. cit., n. 1, p. 5. Schmitt describes sovereignty, not the exception, as a borderline concept. But he does so because of its essential association with the 'borderline case'. And since the exception is not a particular case or *Fall*, it should itself be understood as a concept that covers various cases – as Schmitt here indicates ('the exception is to be understood to refer to a general concept [*Begriff*] in the theory of the state').

15 id.: 'hier unter Ausnahmezustand ein allgemeiner Begriff der Staatslehre zu verstehen ist, nicht irgendeine Notverordnung oder jeder Belagerungszustand.'

exception likewise lies within and without the legal order, on the border of law.[16]

> What characterizes an exception is principally unlimited authority, which means the suspension of the entire existing order. In such a situation it is clear that the state remains, whereas law recedes. Because the exception is different from anarchy and chaos, order in the juristic sense still prevails even if it is not a legal kind [*Rechtsordnung*].[17]

The exception might be confused with 'anarchy and chaos' because of its status as *Grenzbegriff*: the active withdrawal of the legal order looks like the withdrawal of order as such to eyes that confuse state and law and hence are blind to *the political*.

Schmitt is not, however, simply asserting the priority of the state over the legal order. The US Supreme Court did something like that in its 1936 decision, *United States* v. *Curtiss-Wright Export Corp.*, when it held that the sovereignty of the United States was acquired prior to the writing of the US Constitution when the nation won its independence from Great Britain. Here the fact of the nation precedes and make possible the Constitution – as Schmitt himself suggests in his *Verfassungslehre* when he attributes the fundamental 'concrete political existence' of 'the American states' to the Declaration of Independence, and not the Constitution as we know it.[18] But Schmitt's claims in *Political Theology* go considerably beyond this. It is not simply that the unified political entity – *die politische Einheit* – must precede and make possible the norms and laws that will govern it. It is, rather, that the sovereign's decision on the exception determines what shall count as *normal*. The exception occupies the border between not just law and state, but between order and disorder in its most radical or primordial sense. 'The exception', Schmitt writes:

> is that which cannot be subsumed; it defies general codification, but it simultaneously reveals a specifically juristic element – the decision in its absolute purity [*Reinheit*]. The exception appears in its absolute form when a situation in which legal prescriptions can be valid must first be brought about. Every general norm demands a normal, everyday frame of life to which it can be factually applied and which is subjected to its regulations. The norm requires a homogenous medium [*homogenes Medium*]. This effective normal situation is not a mere 'superficial presupposition' that a jurist can ignore; that situation belongs precisely to its immanent validity. There exists no norm that is applicable to chaos. For a legal order to make sense, a normal situation [*normale Situation*] must exist, and he is sovereign who definitively decides whether this normal situation actually exists.[19]

As Giorgio Agamben puts it:

---

16 id., p. 6.
17 id., p. 12.
18 C. Schmitt, *Verfassungslehre* (1989) 23.
19 Schmitt, op. cit., n. 1, p. 13.

36

The exception does not subtract itself from the rule; rather, the rule, suspending itself, gives rise to the exception and, maintaining itself in relation to the exception, first constitutes itself as a rule ... The sovereign decision of the exception is the originary juridico-political structure on the basis of which what is included in the juridical order and what is excluded from it acquire their meaning.[20]

As the fluctuating boundary between order and disorder, the exception and the sovereign decision upon it (which are but two sides of the same thing) are themselves instances of neither order nor disorder, but – as in Chesterton – a more primordial, *ecstatic* mix of these opposites.

Schmitt was fond of styling himself the Hobbes of the twentieth century, but he here goes well beyond anything found in Hobbes. On Hobbes's account, the legitimacy of the state rests upon its ability, in general and for the most part, to guarantee the security of the embodied life of its citizens. The citizen ought to think of himself as having been brought into a situation of order only by virtue of the coming into being of the state. What *kind* of order that order might be is not for the citizen to determine, but for the sovereign who rescues him from the state of war. And Hobbes indicates that the specific characteristics of that order will be in some flux. To recognize an order as a *good* order, even for the sovereign, is to make decisions that reflect the changing state of the body of the one (or ones) deciding that as much as they do the actual structure of that order.[21] But if we cannot agree on the characteristics of a good order, we can all agree on the characteristics of order and disorder *as such*. Our ability to do is indeed required if Hobbes's mythic presentation of the social contract is to be persuasive at all. If, for instance, a Catholic order were the only true (or orderly) order, it would be impossible to acknowledge the need for a sovereign who will guarantee order by making its own independent decision whether that order will be Catholic or Protestant, Muslim or secular. In a condition of disorder, life is nasty, brutish, and short. In a condition of order, it is not. All can perceive this, and hence all can receive Hobbes's teaching as well as the benefits of an authoritarian sovereign, who guarantees an order that we recognize to be orderly whether we like it or not.

When Schmitt argues that only the sovereign 'definitively decides whether [the] normal situation actually exists', he thus goes far beyond Hobbes. The 'decision in its absolute purity' is not a decision as to what goods the social order shall embrace and encourage, but *what shall count as order as such*. This is a necessary feature of the 'purity' of the absolute decision, the fact that *he* who is sovereign must *make* it, rather than *all* or *most* of us *acknowledging* it. Schmitt's claim in *Political Theology* is thus a far more *metaphysical* claim than anything found in Hobbes. It is thus little

20 G. Agamben, *Homo Sacer: Sovereign Power and Bare Life* (1998) tr. D. Heller-Roazen, 18, 19.
21 See T. Hobbes, *Leviathan*, ed. C.B. Macpherson (1968) 120.

surprise that Schmitt emphasizes there the conceptual and metaphysical nature of his understanding of the exception. In the second chapter of *Political Theology* he argues that only 'the sociology of concepts ... has the possibility of achieving a scientific result for a concept such as sovereignty', and, by extension, that of the exception.

> This sociology of concepts transcends juridical conceptualization oriented to immediate practical interest. It aims to discover the basic, radically systematic structure and to compare this conceptual structure with the conceptually represented social structure of a certain epoch. There is no question here of whether the idealities of radical conceptualization are the reflex of sociological reality, or whether social reality is the result of a particular way of thinking and therefore also of acting. Rather this sociology of concepts is concerned with establishing proof of two spiritual but substantial identities.[22]

The radicality of Schmitt's conceptualization is crucial here:

> The presupposition of this kind of sociology of juristic concepts is thus radical conceptualization, a consistent thinking that is pushed into metaphysics and theology. The metaphysical image that a definite epoch forges of the world has the same structure as what the world immediately understands to be appropriate as a form of political organization. The determination of such an identity is the sociology of the concept of sovereignty.[23]

The references here to metaphysics and theology seem calculated to make one think of Comte's very different sociology, with its theological, metaphysical, and positive stages. It is certainly clear enough that Schmitt's emphasis upon radical conceptualization precludes any form of positivism. He marks a similar break from Weber in insisting that:

> To trace a conceptual result back to a sociological carrier is psychology; it involves the determination of a certain sort of human motivation. This is a sociological problem, but not yet a problem of the sociology of a concept.[24]

For Schmitt, only a *radical conceptualization* beyond psychologism will allow us to understand the concepts that structure our world, including that of the exception.

For the Schmitt of *Political Theology*, if there is such a thing as *the* exception, it is a *metaphysical* matter. It is not a practical problem of deciding when the relative balance of order and disorder tips towards the former rather than the latter. This is something that all of us do, non-sovereigns included. Was our fight so bad that it signalled the end of our marriage? Has our casual disregard of the rules of the game become so regular and obnoxious that we are no longer playing but rather fighting? Has the band's smashing of their instruments at the close of the show gone on so

---

22 Schmitt, op. cit., n. 1, p. 45.
23 id., p. 46.
24 id., p. 44. Contrast Weber's definition of sociology as 'a science concerning itself with the interpretive understanding of social action' in M. Weber, *Economy and Society, Vol. I*, eds. G. Roth and C. Wittich (1978) 4 f.

long as to cease being a part of the performance and become a cry for help? Schmitt is adamant that 'rationalism' has denied the necessity of the exception.[25] But who denies that in every situation of order there is disorder mixed in, or that the question of when one predominates is always easily settled? These may be matters where the answer is 'confused' and not clearly outlined, but they are not for all that 'borderline cases.'

But can anyone be said to *decide* what is normal? What would this entail? To decide what is normal is, among other things, to *say* what is normal. But is what is normal for us whatever we say it is? There is a sense in which the answer is, yes, and a sense in which the answer is, no. The sense in which the answer is yes is tied to the fact, which has been at the forefront of philosophical reflection for almost a hundred years now, if not since Nietzsche, that our concepts are bound up with our language. What is normal, and what is not, are bound up with the way we think and talk. However, we cannot think and talk however we might like. Take the famous example of J.L. Austin's, that of when we can and cannot say that we did something *voluntarily*. It might seem that this adverb can be tacked on to any old sentence. But Austin observes that, whatever we might think in philosophy class, in our actual practice we say of an act that it was *voluntary* only if there is something unusual or fishy or out of the ordinary about it – as when I say (rightly or wrongly), the heiress Patty Hearst voluntarily joined the Symbionese Liberation Army in the bank robbery. But of an unremarkable visit to the bank by an unremarkable person in unremarkable circumstances, we would not say, 'She voluntarily went to the bank to deposit the check.' But neither would we say the contrary. The act is neither voluntary nor involuntary but, as Austin puts it, normal:

> The natural economy of language dictates that for the *standard* case covered by any normal verb – not, perhaps, a verb of omen such as 'murder,' but a verb like 'eat' or 'kick' or 'croquet' – no modifying expression is required or even permissible. Only if we do the action named in some *special* way or circumstances, different from those in which such an action is naturally done (and of course both the normal and the abnormal differ according to what verb in particular is in question) is a modifying expression called for, or even in order.[26]

25 Schmitt, op. cit., n. 1, p. 14.
26 J.L. Austin, 'A Plea for Excuses' in *Philosophical Papers*, eds. J.O. Urmson and G.J. Warnock (1961) 138. Austin presents no argument for this. I recently had a student insist that Austin is wrong in his claims here, and that it would be perfectly in order for him (the student) to say, for example, to his roommate after arriving home from school on his bicycle, 'I rode home normally'. But when pressed to say how his roommate might respond to such an utterance, he admitted that this would hardly be accepted at face value, and the roommate would probably respond, 'What do you mean? Do you mean you rode home in the normal way, that is, up Walnut and then down 44th Street?' And he likewise acknowledged that his only option here would be just to say, 'No, I just rode my bike in the normal way, in that I didn't stand on my head when I rode, or anything crazy like that.' How the roommate might respond to such 'information' was not thought important.

Stanley Cavell argues that such uses of 'voluntary' are not just impermissible, as Austin says, but *meaningless*.[27] This is a difficult claim to get one's head around, as the words are so plainly meaningful: she voluntarily went to the bank! But things look this way, Cavell argues, because we can imagine a possible setting in which the sentence might be meaningfully used, and we silently assume that the words alone have the meaning that they would in such a situation. 'We had been fighting about how to split up errands, and before today I felt I had to constantly threaten or cajole her into doing her share.' But in the absence of such a context – in a normal context – the word *voluntary* loses its meaning. We can, as Cavell puts it, understand how the word *could* meaningfully be used, but we don't yet understand what *you* mean by it here and now. One can't, that is, simply announce a claim at any time, in any place, and be (oneself, in one's claim) intelligible. One will not yet have quite *said* or *claimed* anything.[28]

The same, I want to suggest, would go for an attempt on the part of the sovereign to decide and hence say what counts as normal and what does not. Legal rules and norms can be given, and imposed. But *the normal* cannot; and because it cannot, the exception in the strong sense is an illusion. No decision being possible, there is nothing to decide.[29] To some extent, Schmitt himself reached a very similar conclusion, intermittently at least.[30] As is well known, by the time of 1934's *Über die drei Arten des rechtswissenschaftlichen*

---

27 See S. Cavell, 'Must We Mean What We Say?' in *Must We Mean What We Say?* (1969) and S. Cavell, *The Claim of Reason: Wittgenstein, Skepticism, Morality, and Tragedy* (1979).

28 For further discussion of this argument, see the introduction to A. Norris (ed.), *The Claim to Community: Essays on Stanley Cavell and Political Philosophy* (2006). Some will object that Austin and Cavell are not the best places to look for an instance of ordinary language philosophy engaging with the question of the exception, but that we would do better to look to Wittgenstein, whose account of language use as an ongoing engagement with the aporias of rule following appears to place the exception at the heart of the ordinary. I argue against Chantal Mouffe and Simon Critchley that this reading of Wittgenstein is deeply mistaken in A. Norris, 'Cynicism, Skepticism, and the Politics of Truth' (2006) 9(4) *Theory & Event*.

29 I was thus quite wrong to argue that the decision as Schmitt characterizes it is *unavoidable*, as I did in A. Norris, 'Carl Schmitt's Political Metaphysics: On the Secularization of the Outermost Sphere' (2000) 4(1) *Theory & Event*. What I took to be an investigation of metaphysics was itself an instance of metaphysics.

30 Indeed, as Gopal Balakrishnan emphasizes, Schmitt in *Political Theology* treats questions of political theology in such different ways than he does in the almost exactly cotemporaneous *Roman Catholicism and Political Form* that 'it is hard to believe that the author had written one book immediately after the other.' G. Balakrishnan, *The Enemy: An Intellectual Portrait of Carl Schmitt* (2000) 51. Where the first draws upon the theological roots of sovereignty so as to emphasize the 'unlimited' character of the decision that defines it, the second presents the Church as a potentially universal institution capable of genuinely political mediation and representation. For a helpful discussion of the reappearance of earlier themes in Schmitt's 1933 *Staat, Bewegung, Volk*, see the first chapter of B. Scheuerman, *Carl Schmitt: The End of Law* (1999).

Denkens, Schmitt had explicitly moved from decisionism to 'concrete order thinking.' As he there notes, decisionism of the sort he had embraced in his discussion of the exception in *Political Theology* assumed that order was being produced from disorder by means of a 'decision' that at the same time made the one making it sovereign.[31] In concrete order thinking, in stark contrast, order is not produced by law or the command that Bodin and Hobbes saw behind the law; rather, the norm or rule rests upon the *Ordnung* that gives it function and a relatively determinate meaning.[32] A similar conclusion is actually hinted at in the more significant texts of the twenties. In *The Concept of the Political* Schmitt repeats almost word for word *Political Theology*'s claim regarding norms and the normal situation – but with a significant twist. Schmitt writes:

> The endeavor of a normal state consists above all in assuring total peace within the state and its territory. To create 'tranquility, security, and order' and thereby establish the normal situation is the prerequisite for legal norms to be valid. Every norm presupposes a normal situation, and no norm can be valid in an entirely abnormal situation.[33]

In *Political Theology*, Schmitt makes plain that only the sovereign can say what the normal situation is, and he provides no criteria by which it might be recognized, other than the vague and openly metaphoric reference to a 'homogeneous medium' that he says norms and laws require if they are to function. Here he refers to '*Ruhe, Sicherheit und Ordnung*' (tranquility, security, and order). If *The Concept of the Political* were to follow *Political Theology* – as I once thought it did – then these words would be a red herring, unable alone to provide enough determinate content to do much of anything, and in need of an interpretive sovereign decision to give them enough precision to distinguish between what is allowed and what is not, what is order and what is not, and hence what is normal and what is not. Schmitt indicates, however, that this is not his understanding of the matter in his *Verfassungslehre*, which was written as he was working on *The Concept of the Political*. In chapter 17 of the *Verfassungslehre*, Schmitt explicitly discusses the sections of the *preußischen Allgemeinen Landsrechts* that discuss the police's duty to produce and maintain '*Ruhe, Sicherheit und Ordnung*', and notes that 'every single word' there led to a series of 'precedent cases' that gave the terms 'calculability' and a 'controllable, *normal* content'.[34] He goes on to note that in a state of exception, the controlling statutes would be suspended rather than reinterpreted. It is true that in the history of precedents whereby *Ruhe, Sicherheit und Ordnung* are given

---

31 Schmitt, op. cit., n. 2, p. 24.
32 id., p. 11.
33 C. Schmitt, *The Concept of the Political* (1996) tr. G. Schwab, 46. Schmitt's quotation marks – which I initially took to be scare quotes – are silently omitted in the translation. Compare C. Schmitt, *Der Begriff des Politischen* (1932) 34.
34 Schmitt, op. cit., n. 18, p. 176, emphasis mine.

41

determinate content, the way of life of the people is the single most important factor. As Schmitt emphasizes in the opening pages of the *Verfassungslehre*, 'the authentic political question' is, who is sovereign?[35] The 'same state of affairs that in a Monarchy appears as "a threat to public tranquility, security, and order" is', Schmitt writes, 'judged quite differently in a democratic republic.'[36] On his account, this reflects a 'concrete political decision' made by the bearer of constitution-giving power in the society.[37] The decision here does not prowl the borders of the polity, but determines its heart; in *Political Theology*, however, it appears whenever the normal is thought to verge into the abnormal, a decision only the sovereign can make. 'All law,' as Schmitt there puts it, 'is "situational law".'[38] And it is the exception in this sense that I am arguing is illusory and, ultimately, incoherent. Dewey, in the end, was almost right. He was only wrong to think that the mere assertion of his naturalism would be enough to dispel metaphysics – and, with it, the exception and the exceptional sovereign.

Political Theology echoes Bodin's 1576 *Six Books of the Commonwealth* in beginning with a *definition* of sovereignty; and it resembles its predecessor in approaching political philosophy through the analysis of the concepts it thus defines. As Quentin Skinner observes, in the *Six Books* (as opposed to the 1566 *Method for the Easy Comprehension of History*) Bodin 'not only treats the doctrine of non-resistance as an analytical implication of sovereignty, but goes on to treat the idea of absolute sovereignty as an analytical implication of the concept of the state'.[39] For Bodin, 'Sovereignty is the absolute and perpetual power of a commonwealth ... that is, the highest power of command.'[40] Since, as Bodin puts it, 'the very word "law"

---

35 id., p. 8; compare Schmitt's discussion of the sovereign decision on p. 49.

36 id., p. 37.

37 id., pp. 24, 25. Andreas Kalyvas argues incorrectly that Schmitt is concerned with only this sort of decision, and not the 'dictatorial' ability 'to violate and transgress an established legal order' – though Kalyvas grants that this 'is not always clear,' and describes *Political Theology* as Schmitt's 'most obscure and ambivalent text'. A. Kalyvas, 'Carl Schmitt and the Three Moments of Democracy' (2000) 21 *Cardozo Law Rev.* 1534. I would argue that the language of an absolute *decision* is misleading here as well, as it is almost incoherent to say, as Schmitt does, that a constituent power in founding a new state makes a decision 'born out nothingness'. Neither the revolutionaries who founded the United States nor those who founded the French Republic nor those who created any of the more contemporary states that might be cited as being instances of the emergence of this constituent power occupied a vacuum. What they wanted was not simply to produce a future, but to protect established accomplishments: families, property, relationships, and conceptions of themselves as individuals who would in the future have to negotiate with the state they set out to found.

38 Schmitt, op. cit., n. 1, p. 13. History is thus set aside, by the sovereign, and by Schmitt.

39 Q. Skinner, *The Foundations of Modern Political Thought*, II (1978) 287.

40 J. Bodin, *On Sovereignty: Four Chapters from The Six Books of the Commonwealth*, tr. and ed. J. Franklin (1992) 1.

42

in Latin implies the command of him who has the sovereignty', this means that the sovereign is the source of all law.[41] As Skinner notes, in casting the sovereign as a legislator, Bodin thus downplays the sovereign's role as judge, a role that had been emphasized by medieval constitutionalists such as Legists and Bodin himself in his *Method*.[42] This makes the sovereign less *receptive* and more *active*, and hence considerably less responsible to the existing norms and laws. D. Engster argues that this reflects not just Bodin's oft-noted anxiety in the face of the St. Bartholomew's Day massacre of 1572, but the influence of distinctly *theological* concerns, namely, Bodin's late conversion to Judaism and his resulting turn away from history towards the Old Testament.[43] As we have seen, such theological, metaphysical commitments are poor guides for political theory. Schmitt's own political theology completes the movement of Bodin's thought when it casts the sovereign not as legislator but rather, in George W. Bush's words, as a 'decider'.[44] In doing so, Schmitt tosses aside the remaining limits that the Bodin of the *Six Books* had been willing to place upon the sovereign's power.[45] He maintains, however, what is possibly the most problematic feature of Bodin's account: its emphasis upon the idea that the sovereign is indivisible as well as absolute. As has been widely noted, this is hardly a necessary feature of a successful legislative or political system, many of which are 'mixed' in a manner that Bodin had to deny was possible.[46] (Indeed, Bodin's casting of the sovereign as the sole legislator reverses what in England at least became a movement in the opposite direction, whereby formerly juridical bodies increasingly took on active roles in legislation, and by extension, the exercise of the emergency powers of the Royal *ius majestatis*.[47]) Schmitt endorses just this aspect of Bodin when he comments that Bodin stands at the beginning of the modern theory of the state:

41 id., p. 11; compare p. 51.
42 Skinner, op. cit., n. 39, p. 289.
43 D. Engster, 'Jean Bodin, Scepticism and Absolute Sovereignty' (1996) XVII *History of Political Thought* 489 ff.
44 As Bush put it in a defence of his embattled Secretary of Defense, 'I'm the decider, and I decide what's best'. J. VandeHei, 'Bush Names New Budget Chief; More Changes Coming But Rumsfeld Will Stay In Job, President Says' *Washington Post*, 19 April 2006.
45 On these limits, see Skinner's discussion at op. cit., n. 39, pp. 293 ff. and J.H.M. Salmon, 'The Legacy of Jean Bodin: Absolutism, Populism or Constitutionalism?' (1996) XVII *History of Political Thought* 503 ff.
46 See Julian Franklin's helpful discussion of this 'incoherent' claim in the Introduction to Bodin, *On Sovereignty*.
47 See Jeremy Elkins's helpful review of these developments in Tudor England in J. Elkins, 'Declarations of Rights' (1996) 3 *University of Chicago Roundtable* 261–81. As Elkins there notes, the analogy between sovereign and God that lies at the heart of Schmitt's political theology is found in fourteenth-century discussions of the Pope's ability to perform the legal equivalent of 'miracles,' but explicitly repudiated in James I's 1610 'Speech to the Lords and Commons of the Parliament at White-Hall.'

because of his teaching [*seiner Lehre*] ... rather than because of his oft-cited definition [of sovereignty]... The decisive point about Bodin's concept is that by referring to the emergency he reduced his analysis of the relationships between prince and estates to a simple either/or.[48]

This either/or is a false dilemma, and a dangerous one. Today, as in Tudor England, the question is not whether the state must at times go beyond the law to confront unanticipated emergencies, but to what extent the executive branch can rightly claim a monopoly on the ability to determine or decide whether such is necessary, and whether its resulting actions will be permanently unchecked and unregulated. In the Ship Money crisis of the 1630s, Charles I had claimed both that he as sovereign must have the power to raise military forces to defend the nation *and* that the Crown must be the sole judge of whether such a threat existed. It was the latter claim that was opposed in 'Hamden's Case' in 1637. Such threats were not, it was argued, matters of decision, but of *recognition*; and other parties, such as public opinion as registered in Parliament, could perform such acts of recognition as well as the Crown.[49] Similar debates are being replayed today in the wake of the terrorist attacks of the 11th September 2001, particularly in the United States. Though the Bush-Cheney administration does not claim to be making Schmittian decisions, but rather regularly traces its supposed *legal* authority to the September 2001 congressional Authorization for Use of Military Force (Public Law 107–40 [S. J. RES. 23]), it does repeat claims such as Charles's.[50] The claims of Charles's opponents are in turn made by political and legal theorists such as Bruce Ackerman, who argues that states of emergency need to be addressed by an executive branch that is much more responsive to and limited by the other branches of government than the executive branch in the United States currently is. Ackerman proposes that

---

48 Schmitt, op. cit., n. 1, p. 8.
49 Richard Tuck nicely relates this dispute to the role of scepticism in modern political thought in general and Hobbes in particular in his short *Hobbes*, reprinted in R. Tuck, *Great Political Thinkers* (1992) 137 ff.
50 The extreme and disturbing writings of John Yoo complicate this judgment somewhat. In a less irresponsible if still Schmittian vein, Richard Posner argues that presidential acts undertaken in response to what Posner *very* loosely describes as a state of national emergency should be understood as belonging to 'a class of criminal acts that are not excused but nevertheless permitted.' Posner would defend such exceptions as being analogous to civil disobedience, which he thus severs from its connection with public debate on the proper meaning of shared political values. Posner argues that his view provides a 'partial defense' of such acts and he in effect argues that the courts should honour this defence, though he acknowledges that they need not. R. Posner, *Not a Suicide Pact: The Constitution in a Time of National Emergency* (2006) 153, 155. As Posner's own analysis indicates, if his reading is correct and the Administration's wrong, we are confronted with a series of criminal acts, ones that we or the judiciary might choose to forgive, but that are not, for all that, themselves exceptions to the law unless we choose to make them so. Posner does not so much demonstrate the inevitability of the exception as advise us to make it real, and a real part of the legal system.

the Executive be given the ability to declare a state of emergency, but that this declaration must be ratified by the Congress at regular intervals, and each time by a supermajority with an increasing percentage of the vote.[51] The issues in such debates are only obscured by metaphysical analysis such as Schmitt's. Consider in this regard the ambiguities of the work of Giorgio Agamben, the most prominent contemporary philosopher to have adopted a version of Schmitt's political theology in his consideration of contemporary politics and jurisprudence. In his most widely read contribution to this discussion, *Homo Sacer: Sovereign Power and Bare Life*, Agamben writes as if the exception were a logically and metaphysically necessary moment in any system of rules or laws, one that is fated to come ever more into the light.[52] But this metaphysical destiny, for whom no-one can be blamed and which cannot be directly addressed or warded off, is less prominent in Agamben's more recent *State of Exception*. Here, as in his numerous public statements, Agamben suggests that the Bush-Cheney administration is culpable for the production of such 'states of exception' as Guantánamo Bay. But one cannot have it both ways. If the Bush-Cheney administration is simply providing the sovereign decisions that are metaphysically necessary to maintain public order in the United States, one cannot fault it for acting tyrannically. Conversely, if it is indeed acting tyrannically, this is something that requires not metaphysical analysis and political theology, but practical, political resistance and institutional change. The choice between these two is hardly a decision in the sense of Schmitt's 'absolute decision.' But it is, I would argue, the choice that we face.[53]

---

51 Ackerman attacks Schmitt's *Political Theology* as 'melodramatic' and takes care to give criteria of what is and is not an 'existential threat' to the nation. B. Ackerman, *Before the Next Attack: Preserving Civil Liberties in an Age of Terrorism* (2006) 56, 21, 171, and throughout.

52 Agamben goes so far as to argue that all *examples* are exceptional (instances of *the* exception) in that they are, as examples, taken outside of the class they allegedly exemplify. I discuss the disastrous implications of this position in 'The Exemplary Exception: Philosophical and Political Decisions in Giorgio Agamben's *Homo Sacer*' in *Politics, Metaphysics, and Death: Essays on Giorgio Agamben's Homo Sacer*, ed. A. Norris (2005).

53 I am extremely grateful to Jeremy Elkins for his comments on an early draft of this essay.

45

JOURNAL OF LAW AND SOCIETY
VOLUME 34, NUMBER 1, MARCH 2007
ISSN: 0263-323X, pp. 46–64

Undoing Legal Violence: Walter Benjamin's and Giorgio Agamben's Aesthetics of Pure Means

Benjamin Morgan*

Giorgio Agamben calls for a 'playful' relation to law as a way to counteract its inherent violence. Such a relation would prevent law from functioning as a means to an end, instead treating it as a 'pure means.' This article evaluates the significance of Agamben's proposal and of the concept of pure means, arguing that both implicitly draw on a Kantian model of aesthetic experience.

Giorgio Agamben's *State of Exception* paints an ominous picture. Agamben asks whether law can regulate its own suspension not because this is an interesting, if abstract, legal problem, but because the state of exception has become a worldwide 'paradigm of government'.[1] According to Agamben, a global state of exception is the only way to explain our current state of affairs, in which:

> law can ... be obliterated and contradicted with impunity by a governmental violence that – while ignoring international law externally and producing a permanent state of exception internally – nevertheless still claims to be applying the law.[2]

The state of exception enables this contradiction since it is neither inside nor outside law. On the one hand, it is not a 'special kind of law' since it is 'a suspension of the juridical order itself';[3] on the other, it is not merely the absence of law, since law contains provisions for its suspension. This topographical paradox means that law functions unusually within the state of exception. The state of exception doesn't create chaos or anarchy; it separates the law's force from its application. Law's purely formal applicability comes loose from its direct impact on life. As a result, acts that are not

* *University of California, Berkeley, 7408 Dwinelle Hall, Berkeley, CA 94720, United States of America*
bjmorgan@berkeley.edu

1 G. Agamben, *State of Exception* (2005) 1.
2 id., p. 87.
3 id., p. 4.

authorized by any law can employ the force of legal action:

> in extreme situations 'force of law' floats as an indeterminate element that can
> be claimed by both the state authority ... and by a revolutionary organization.[4]

Agamben argues that this ultimately makes law and life indistinguishable:
every action is potentially a legal action. Unfortunately, however, we can't
simply return to a situation prior to the state of exception:

> from the real state of exception in which we live, it is not possible to return to
> the state of law, for at issue now are the very concepts of 'state' and 'law'.[5]

If we take Agamben's claims about the reach of the state of exception
seriously, we are left to grapple with the odd solution that Agamben
suggests. This solution is what I would like to interrogate here. Agamben
argues that to get beyond the state of exception we must do something more
radical than modify the law, since the exception has revealed that the normal
functioning of law depends on violent force. As a consequence, we must
pursue 'the only truly political action ... which severs the nexus between
violence and law'.[6] But it is difficult to imagine how we might actually take
this 'truly political' action, which Agamben calls 'play':

> One day, humanity will play with law just as children play with disused
> objects, not in order to restore them to their canonical use but to free them
> from it for good.... [T]his studious play is the passage that allows us to arrive
> at ... justice.[7]

'Play' is a surprising answer to the problems that Agamben has dramatically
sketched: it seems simultaneously too abstract and not serious enough. But can
we take play seriously? Play might be able to counteract the law's violent
application to life *because* of its lack of seriousness: play suspends both
instrumentality and normativity. In this sense, play deinstrumentalizes what
Agamben frequently calls the 'machine' or 'apparatus' of the state of exception.

This attempt to think beyond the instrumentality of law is as a
continuation of Walter Benjamin's project in 'Critique of Violence', which
Beatrice Hanssen describes as the creation of a 'politics of pure means':

> Benjamin hoped once and for all to break the vicious circle of violence by
> radically rethinking a long-standing philosophico-political tradition according
> to which violence was to be conceived as *instrumental* in nature, that is, as a
> means or implement to be put to the service of (political) ends.[8]

What makes this rethinking radical is its fundamental challenge to the way we
think not only about violence, but about means themselves. Against our normal

---

4 id., pp. 38–9.
5 id., p. 87.
6 id., p. 88.
7 id., p. 64.
8 B. Hanssen, 'On the Politics of Pure Means: Benjamin, Arendt, Foucault' in *Violence,*
   Identity, and Self-Determination, eds. H. de Vries and S. Weber (1997) 239.

47

understanding of means as always being 'for' something – a hammer as a means for nailing; an automobile as a means for travelling – Benjamin tries to imagine a sphere of pure means, where means would not be related to their ends in any conventional way, and could even appear to be means *without* ends. I will argue that Benjamin's and Agamben's attempts to undo the link between law and violence by deinstrumentalizing politics are informed by Kant's theory of aesthetic judgement. To the politics of pure means corresponds a less manifest but no less significant aesthetics of pure means.

This argument depends on a passage in Kant's third critique where he claims that an aesthetic judgement does not take into account how well an object functions as a means to an end – whether that end be some sort of subjective gratification (as in the case of good food or a warm bath) or some sort of conceptual good (political harmony, our definition of what a rose ought to look like). The former is a judgement about what is agreeable and the latter about what is useful or correct; neither is a disinterested aesthetic judgement. But objects we judge to be beautiful *do* produce pleasure, even though this is not what they are for. As such, they have no end in the context of our aesthetic judgement and yet still function as a means:

> nothing other than the subjective purposiveness in the representation of an object without any end ... consequently the mere form of purposiveness ... can constitute the satisfaction that we judge [as] the determining ground of the judgment of taste.[9]

In so far as the object functions as a means, it does so only subjectively (in that it causes the 'play of the cognitive powers of the subject'[10]), and not as the fulfilment of an objective end (since the real purpose of the object is not to cause this play). The aesthetic object is neither instrumental nor normative: it cannot be judged in its capacity as a means to an end or in its agreement with a preconceived concept of what it ought to be. A careful reading of Benjamin and Agamben reveals that they work with and around Kant's definition in their constructions of theories of pure means.

The possibility that the theory of the state of exception is related to enlightenment aesthetic philosophy has been explored by those writing on Carl Schmitt – mostly (as Victoria Kahn points out) to expose contradictions within Schmitt's thought.[11] Peter Bürger writes that Schmitt's theory of the state of exception describes a non-normative realm that invokes Kantian aesthetic judgement:

> That which Kant concedes to art, with manifold restrictions, Carl Schmitt will transfer to the realm of the political. The decision that constitutes the sovereign is the irreducible originary act. The decision is a sphere free of norms.[12]

9 I. Kant, *Critique of the Power of Judgment* (2000) ed. P. Guyer, 106.
10 id., p. 107.
11 V. Kahn, 'Hamlet or Hecuba: Carl Schmitt's Decision' (2003) 83 *Representations* 42.
12 P. Bürger, 'Carl Schmitt oder die Fundierung der Politik auf Ästhetik' in *Zerstörung, Rettung des Mythos durch Licht*, ed. C. Bürger (1986) 173 (my translation).

48

This suspension of normativity is also the grounds on which Habermas, in an almost offhand remark, alludes to an aesthetics in Benjamin's 'Critique of Violence':

> above all it is the aesthetics of violence that fascinates [Schmitt]. Interpreted on the model of the *creatio ex nihilo*, sovereignty acquires a halo of surrealistic meanings through its relationship to the violent destruction of the normative as such. That ... explains why at this time Carl Schmitt felt impelled to congratulate the young Walter Benjamin on his essay on Sorel [that is, 'Critique of Violence'].[13]

Habermas intends to expose a possible political affinity with Schmitt, but we might read his comment more charitably. Benjamin and the Frankfurt School, after all, found productive political possibilities in the idea of an autonomous aesthetic realm that could critique a dominating instrumental logic by refusing to be instrumental. Such a reading, however, would require that we ask whether the non-instrumentality that Agamben proposes as the way out of the state of exception refers back to the same notion of aesthetic autonomy.

BENJAMIN'S THEORY OF PURE MEANS IN 'CRITIQUE OF VIOLENCE'

Benjamin's 'Critique of Violence' produces its theory of a 'sphere of pure means' through an attempt to respond to a familiar question: what criteria can we use to decide whether or not violence is justifiable? Benjamin immediately closes down the easiest way of answering that question, which would be to examine the purposes for which violence is used. Benjamin is unsatisfied with any solution that relies on a consideration of the justness of the purpose of violence to evaluate the justness of violence itself. Such an approach doesn't offer a 'criterion for violence itself as a principle, but, rather, the criterion for cases of its use'.[14] In other words, critiquing violence retroactively, in light of our ethical judgements regarding its effects, bases an evaluation of violence on something other than violence. What we judge is not really violence, but rather what it achieves. Benjamin, however, wants to examine violence 'as a principle'. This raises the question of how we are to determine whether violence in and of itself, independent of its relation to just or unjust ends, could be a 'moral means'. Might it be possible for violence itself to be unethical, even if it were used so judiciously as to never produce effects in conflict with an ethical framework? Or, conversely, might it be possible for violence itself to be ethical, even if it is generally at odds with

13 J. Habermas, 'The Horrors of Autonomy' in *The New Conservatism: Cultural Criticism and the Historians' Debate*, ed. S.W. Nicholsen (1989) 137.
14 W. Benjamin, 'Critique of Violence' in *Selected Writings, Vol. 1*, eds. M. Bullock and M.W. Jennings (1996) 236.

ethical ends? Both questions demand a language for describing the very principle of violence as a means without considering, in particular cases, the purposes for which it is used or the effects that it has.

Legal and philosophical questions are inextricable here. By structuring his inquiry into the ethics of violence in terms that distinguish the event of violence from its effects, Benjamin indicates that it is possible to consider a means independent from its ends. If the legal question is 'what criterion is capable of judging the justness of violence itself?' the philosophical question is 'how do we think about a sphere of means separate from a sphere of ends?' Benjamin makes this distinction explicit when he determines to find a 'more exact criterion' for violence that would be located within 'the sphere of means themselves, without regard for the ends they serve'.[15] In looking for this criterion, Benjamin's critique will challenge the 'most elementary relationship within any legal system', that between means and ends. This challenge is necessary since means-ends-based analyses of violence arrive at an impasse. Namely, 'natural law attempts, by the justness of the ends, to "justify" the means, positive law to "guarantee" the justness of the ends through the justification of the means'.[16] Neither natural nor positive law is capable of considering means alone since both are engaged in a project of justifying means with respect to their results. Natural law justifies violence 'as a natural datum'[17] by assuming that it is the 'only original means'; this original status within nature renders it 'appropriate' and 'legal'. Positive law takes what looks like a 'diametrically opposed' stance but employs the same logic of means and ends: adequately ensuring that only just means are used necessarily entails the arrival at just ends. Both schools of thought assume a direct progression from means to ends. This is what Benjamin calls their 'common basic dogma: just ends can be attained by justified means, justified means used for just ends'.[18] It is this assumption about the nature of means and ends, and the circularity that it entails, that Benjamin wants to think beyond – and only by doing so will it be possible to establish a space from which we can inquire into violence as a principle, separate from its ends.

Benjamin complicates the problem by arguing that any time we consider law as a means to an end we are taking for granted the violence that law is capable of inflicting. Law cannot serve as a framework for determining whether or not violence is inherently just or unjust, since law itself depends upon violence both in its origin and in its continued existence. Revolutions and wars highlight the 'lawmaking' character of violence: in their wake, conflicting parties sanction new conditions as 'new "law"'.[19] In this sense, law is a product of violence and violence is the origin of law. But violence

15 id.
16 id., p. 237.
17 id.
18 id.
19 id., p. 240.

50

remains crucial for maintaining law – Benjamin here identifies the 'law-preserving' character of violence. We experience law-preserving violence not only when we break the law and are threatened with punishment, but any time that we make a contract. For Benjamin, even the apparently most peaceful contractual agreements are underwritten by this violence: he argues that a legal contract, 'however peacefully it may have been entered into by the parties, leads to a possible violence. It confers on each party the right to resort to violence in some form against the other, should he break the agreement.'[20] Benjamin suggests that the error of liberal parliamentarianism is that it forgets that its peaceful discussion, deliberation, and agreement are not nonviolent, and that the institution of the parliament is the product of historical violence. In fact, violence undergirds parliamentary actions even at those moments when it least appears to: 'what a parliament achieves in vital affairs can be only those legal decrees that in their origin and outcome are attended by violence'.[21] These two types of violence – law-making and law-preserving – aren't, however, compatible with each other. Law-preserving violence maintains itself only by continually suppressing counter-violence and revolution – the precise form of violence that created the present legal situation. Benjamin writes that 'this lasts until either new forces or those earlier suppressed triumph over the hitherto lawmaking violence and thus found a new law, destined in its turn to decay'.[22] The movement from law-making to law-preserving violence is temporal, but its temporality is circular and dialectical rather than linear and teleological.

Benjamin's essay thus proposes two related problems: first, in evaluating the ethics of violence, is there a measure we can use that doesn't rely upon the means-end rationality of natural and positive law?; second, how can we overcome the cycle of law-preserving and law-creating violence that so far has determined historical progress? Benjamin responds to both of these questions through his inquiry into a 'sphere of pure means' where law and violence would shed their instrumental quality. Rather than describing a law without violence, however, Benjamin describes a form of violence that would be absolutely unrelated to any familiar notion of law and, that would ultimately destroy law's normative character. This would be among 'other kinds of violence than all those envisaged by legal theory'.[23] Such violence would no longer be a means to an end; Benjamin inquires whether there might be a 'different kind of violence ... that certainly could be either the justified or the unjustified means to [an] ends, but was not related to them as means at all but in some different way?'[24]

---

20 id., p. 243.
21 id., p. 244.
22 id., p. 251.
23 id., p. 247.
24 id.

51

Benjamin describes two 'different ways', which correspond to what he describes as 'mythic' and 'divine' violence. The former posits an identity between the means and ends of violence; the later disconnects violent means from ends by placing the latter in an unknowable, divine sphere. An outburst of anger is an example of mythic violence, which is not directed toward any specific end. It is a 'nonmediate violence':

> as regards man, he is impelled by anger, for example, to the most visible outbursts of a violence that is not related as a means to a preconceived end. It is not a means but a manifestation.[25]

Distinct from violence that punishes or destroys, an outburst of anger isn't a strategy for achieving something. Its only aim is to manifest itself. This example moves violence from a realm of calculation to a realm of appearance, where what distinguishes 'nonmediate violence' from mediate violence is that the former is a performance (rather than a performative).

But these mythic manifestations of violence appear to operate independently of their ends only momentarily, reducing, upon analysis, to a special kind of law-making violence. The manifestations of the gods, it turns out, ultimately produce new law. Arriving at this conclusion, Benjamin asks 'the question of a pure immediate violence that might be able to call a halt to mythic violence'.[26] Benjamin names this pure immediate violence 'divine', defining it as violence whose expiatory ends are impossible for humans to see: 'only mythic violence, not divine, will be recognizable as such with certainty, unless it be in incomparable effects, because the expiatory power of violence is invisible to men'.[27] Where the recursive visibility of mythic violence offers a criterion for understanding it as its own end, the *in*visibility of the ends of divine violence allows it to appear as pure means. Hence the different ways in which mythic and divine violence might appear to us as nonmediate: the former for having an end in itself, the latter for having an end in the realm of the unknowable. Because its ends are invisible, it is impossible to analyse divine violence within our frameworks of law or morality, frameworks which are based on systems of just ends.

Divine violence thus answers the question with which Benjamin begins in a surprising manner. Benjamin's critique doesn't arrive at a criterion for judging which violence is just and which is not; it arrives at an aporia where the very possibility of human judgement is no longer secure. The very attempt to consider violence as a means apart from its ends produces a second-order violence that not only eliminates the possibility of elaborating its relation to law and justice, but which destroys the very boundaries which it is law's project to create:

25 id., p. 248.
26 id., p. 249.
27 id., p. 252.

52

if mythic violence is lawmaking, divine violence is law-destroying; if the former sets boundaries, the latter boundlessly destroys them; if mythic violence brings at once guilt and retribution, divine power only expiates.[28]

Destructive of the categories useful to law, divine violence refuses to become a useful yardstick for action:

This commandment ['thou shalt not kill'] precedes the deed, just as God was 'preventing' the deed. But just as it may not be fear of punishment that enforces obedience, the injunction becomes inapplicable, incommensurable, once the deed is accomplished. No judgment of the deed can be derived from the commandment. And so neither the divine judgment nor the grounds for this judgment can be known in advance.[29]

As 'pure immediate violence', divine violence can never be used as an instrument for legally controlling action; its commandments precede the deeds they proscribe but refuse to be generally applied.

POETIC LANGUAGE AND DIVINE VIOLENCE

This concept of a sphere of pure means integrates Benjamin's early linguistic and political concerns. Werner Hamacher and Agamben both identify 'pure language' in Benjamin's earlier essay 'On Language as Such and on the Language of Man' as the origin of the concept of 'pure violence'.[30] Hamacher argues that both essays are 'based on the same fundamental conception' of the relation between means and ends; in 'On Language as Such':

in opposition to what he terms 'the bourgeois conception of language',[31] Benjamin insists on the immediacy of a mediality, which constitutes all isolated instances of the linguistic process and which is therefore not reducible to them.[32]

Hamacher uses this similarity between the essays to argue that Benjamin's category of divine violence can be the starting point for a theory of a linguistic performative without an end, an 'afformative'. I would like to suggest that there is another way to connect Benjamin's linguistic and political concerns. If we look to 'The Task of the Translator' (which Benjamin worked on at the same time as the violence essay) rather than 'On Language as Such', we find Benjamin addressing a similar set of concerns about the relation between means and ends, but in a way that pays particular attention to the poetic rather than the epistemological quality of language.

28 id., p. 249.
29 id., p. 250.
30 Agamben, op. cit., n. 1, p. 62.
31 W. Benjamin, 'On Language and Such and on the Language of Man' in Bullock and Jennings, op. cit., n. 14, p. 63.
32 W. Hamacher, 'Afformative, Strike' in *Walter Benjamin's Philosophy: Destruction and Experience*, eds. A. Benjamin and P. Osborne (1994) 129.

53

An analysis of the two essays together will allow us to give depth to Habermas's suggestion that 'Critique of Violence' contains within it an aesthetics of violence.

Like 'Critique of Violence', 'The Task of the Translator' is an extended reflection on the relation between means and ends. In the essay, Benjamin challenges the view that translation is simply a way to convey the same meaning in a different language. According to Benjamin, this assumption produces an inferior translation that conflates 'the sense of a linguistic creation' with 'that of the information it conveys'.[33] Translation then treats language homogeneously as a communicative tool. Against this understanding of language, Benjamin argues first, that there is something incommunicable in poetic language, and second, that successful translation does not translate the incommunicable aspect of language but instead allows us to recognize its existence. The incommunicable is what makes language poetic; Benjamin begins the essay by directing our attention to the fact that in literary works we recognize that something is 'beyond communication . . . the unfathomable, the mysterious, the "poetic".'[34]

Benjamin's concept of 'pure language' plays a crucial role in challenging the theory that language is always a means of communication. Pure language resists transmission: translation can testify to its existence, but cannot reconstruct it. Benjamin writes that 'pure language . . . no longer means or expresses anything but is, as expressionless and creative Word, that which is meant in all languages'.[35] 'Pure language' thus names the non-instrumentality of language: it is language that continues to be language but ceases to communicate. Its 'purity' is a product of this suspension of meaning. Meaning is not seamlessly transmitted from language to reader, because pure language does not aim at expression. It thus interrupts the mediality of language itself. For Benjamin, the literary work has a privileged relation to pure language because it manifests the difference between literal and uncommunicated meaning: in a poem, a calculation of the former does not yield the latter. Benjamin asks, 'what does a literary work "say"? What does it communicate? It tells very little to those who understand it. Its essential quality is not communication'.[36] Literature unhinges the communication of information from an arrival at understanding. The work's resistance to immediate apprehension characterizes what Benjamin calls 'the realm of art' itself:

> in the appreciation of a work of art or an art form, consideration of the receiver never proves fruitful. . . . No poem is intended for the reader, no picture for the beholder, no symphony for the audience.[37]

33 W. Benjamin, 'The Task of the Translator' in Bullock and Jennings, op. cit., n. 14, pp. 260–1.
34 id., p. 253.
35 id., p. 261.
36 id., p. 253.
37 id.

54

We can read the translation essay as Benjamin's articulation of the idea of pure means within his aesthetic (rather than legal) philosophy. This makes it clear why pure language does to meaning what pure violence does to normativity: both are manifestations of the resistance to a means-ends logic that a theory of pure means is capable of mounting. Where divine violence destroys law's forceful application to life, pure language 'extinguishes' the capacity of language to signify, to apply to the world. Benjamin writes that 'in this pure language ... all information, all sense, and all intention finally encounter a stratum in which they are destined to be extinguished'.[38] As in the violence essay, this destruction creates the possibility for a higher justice; Benjamin writes that 'this very stratum furnishes a new and higher justification for free translation'.[39] It is at this level that Benjamin's aesthetic interest in pure language connects definitively with his political interest in pure violence. In both essays Benjamin makes the same move, relocating the ends of a means (violence, language) to a 'higher' sphere, thus showing how the means can appear pure, unrelated to an end. But where the violence essay depends on a messianic realm of justice to effect this dislocation, the translation essay depends upon 'the realm of art,' where we can find meaning in a poem beyond the content that it communicates.

The translation essay is significant not merely because it illustrates yet another way in which Benjamin reworks the philosophical relationship between means and ends, but because it uses the figure of pure means as the grounds for identifying the difference between the quotidian and literary uses of language, between the everyday and the aesthetic. In other words, it is through pure means that language becomes susceptible to aesthetic appreciation – becomes something that, in Kant's terms, we approach not for what it does or how well it does it, but in the absence of its functional or normative aspects. Indeed, it is at Kant's terms that Benjamin himself arrives. Benjamin writes that the process of translation:

> is governed by a special high purposiveness [*Zweckmässigkeit*]. The relationship between life and purposiveness ... reveals itself only if the ultimate purpose [*Zweck*] toward which all the individual purposiveness of life tends is sought not in its own sphere but in a higher one. All purposeful manifestations of life ... have their end not in life but in the expression of its nature, in the representation of its significance.[40]

'Representation' and 'expression' thus serve the same structural function in the translation essay that divinity serves in 'Critique of Violence', naming a realm capable of separating an end from its means. As such, the translation essay makes it clear that pure means need not be formulated in messianic terms: it is equally possible to describe means without ends as a Kantian purposiveness without purpose. Doing so calls upon aesthetic rather than

38 id.
39 id., p. 261.
40 id., p. 255.

55

religious experience as a model for understanding a means without ends. In 'Critique of Violence,' the experience of pure means depends on a divinity to whom alone the ends of violence are known; in 'The Task of the Translator', however, this same experience depends on the work of art, which manifests itself as an purposive object without purpose.

GESTURE AS AN UNENDED MODE OF ACTION

This figure of means without end, of 'pure means', is central to Agamben's theorization of sovereignty and the political because it enables a kind of thinking about political action that doesn't evaluate it only in terms of what it achieves. Agamben highlights the ethical possibilities of a sphere of pure means in *Means Without End*, a collection of essays written during his work on *Homo Sacer*. Throughout the collection, Agamben argues that domains which have traditionally been understood as political have lost their political significance; it is thus necessary to find politics in 'experiences and phenomena that usually are not considered political (or are so only marginally)'.[41] Agamben proposes a constellation of concepts that stakes out a new territory for the political: natural life, the state of exception, the concentration camp, the refugee, language itself, and 'the sphere of pure means or of gestures (that is, of means that even while remaining such, emancipate themselves from their relation to an end)'.[42] The last is particularly important as it is 'the proper sphere of the political'.[43] Where Benjamin uses a theory of pure means in 'Critique of Violence' to define a kind of violence that would destroy the normative as such, Agamben uses it in an attempt to reclaim authentic political experience.

The concept of pure means is dealt with most explicitly in the essay 'Notes on Gesture', which imports the major concepts of 'Critique of Violence' without directly referencing Benjamin. Agamben asks what kinds of phenomena allow us to experience 'pure mediality', and is interested, as Benjamin is, in the possibility of 'breaking the false alternative between ends and means that paralyzes morality'.[44] Gesture – of the kind we see in miming, the cinema, even pornography – is capable of breaking this alternative because it allows us to see 'the sphere ... of a mediality that is pure and without end'.[45] The essay thus follows the same logic as 'Critique of Violence', dissolving an impasse of means-ends logic by positing a kind of action that is unrelated – or related unusually – to its end. Although gesture sounds as though it would be the same thing as Benjamin's expressionless

---

41 G. Agamben, *Mezzi senza fine* (1996) 9 (all translations are my own).
42 id., p. 10.
43 id.
44 id., p. 51.
45 id., p. 52.

56

language, Agamben's version of gesture doubles its mediality rather than suspends it: 'Gesture is the exhibition of a mediality, the rendering visible of a means as such.'[46] Much like mythic violence, gesture's recursivity allows means to appear for their own sake and not in order to achieve something else. In contrast to actions that are directed toward an end – Agamben gives the example of marching 'as a means for moving the body from point A to point B'[47] – gesture calls attention to action itself. Agamben asks us to think of a mime whose movements don't accomplish the tasks they perform, but rather exhibit the performance. For the mime, 'gestures directed towards the most familiar ends are exhibited as such'.[48] When we watch a mime, we don't interpret his or her action by observing what it achieves, but rather see only the action. Such unendedness is the hallmark of what Agamben wants to call authentic political action, which (unlike economic calculation) is started without a predetermined end: 'The political is the sphere of pure means, that is of the absolute and complete gesturality of humanity.'[49]

If this reminds us of Benjamin's politics of pure means, then 'Notes on Gesture' is particularly interesting for what it leaves out. It does not, for example, connect the sphere of pure means to violence or law, the phenomena that motivate Benjamin's development of the concept originally. Nor does Agamben describe the breaking of the continuity between means and ends as a violent event. But perhaps most significant is Agamben's conscious exclusion of aesthetic experience from the sphere of pure means: unlike Benjamin's expressionless word, the expressionlessness of gesture carries no relation to a theory of the work of art. Agamben knows that his description of pure means comes close to Kant's definition of the aesthetic object as something that has a subjective purposiveness without an objective purpose – in fact, he writes that only through the figure of pure mediality does 'the obscure Kantian expression "purposiveness without purpose" [*finalità senza scopo*] acquire a concrete significance'.[50] But Agamben's examples of pure mediality reveal his attempt to avoid equating 'pure means' and 'purposiveness without purpose'. Using dance as the model of a situation in which action appears to have no end, Agamben brackets an understanding of dance as aestheticized movement and treats it instead as a series of gestures. This perhaps unusual way of thinking about dance is necessary for the larger claim that aesthetic experience does not have the structure of pure mediality. Only as long as we experience dance as movement that, like miming, renders means visible in themselves, can dance function as an example of pure means. This is not because otherwise dance is a means for producing aesthetic pleasure in an audience but, rather, because

---

46 id.
47 id., p. 51.
48 id., p. 52.
49 id., p. 53.
50 id., p. 52.

dance as an artistic performance, for Agamben, is its own end. It is what it is for. This reasoning clarifies Agamben's definition of the aesthetic within the essay: aesthetics is the realm of pure ends, not pure means. Dance shows 'an endedness without means [*finalità senza mezzi*]', a sphere where gesture 'is a movement that has in itself its own end [*fine*]'.[51] Agamben makes explicit the connection between Kantian purposiveness and pure means which Benjamin only implies, but does so in order to cordon it off.

If dance only works as a qualified example of pure means, because it seems to display at once pure mediality and pure endedness, then it would seem that miming itself might work better. But here, too, Agamben must cover over the possibility that watching a mime could be an aesthetic experience. Miming, Agamben writes, holds gestures:

> in suspense, '*entre le désir et l'accomplissement, la perpetration et son souvenir*' [between desire and fulfilment, perpetration and remembrance], in that which Mallarmé calls a *milieu pur* [pure medium].[52]

Agamben's quotation of Mallarmé's 'Mimique' provides an elegant instance of the relation between miming and pure means. In his empty action, Mallarmé's mime allows an audience to witness means alone; Mallarmé writes that the mime's 'act is confined to a perpetual allusion without breaking the ice or the mirror'.[53] But this appeal to Mallarmé is problematic for Agamben's argument in ways that remain unaddressed. As a whole, Mallarmé's text is paratactic and polyvalent, and, as Barbara Johnson points out, plays with syntax in a way that obscures meaning.[54] In so far as this signifies that 'its essential quality is not communication or the imparting of information',[55] 'Mimique' may tell us more about the kind of poetic language that characterizes Benjamin's work of art than about miming itself. Agamben's essay thus formally reintroduces the Benjaminian continuity between the literary work and pure means in the very moment that it tries to subtract the aesthetic from the gestural, speaking more to 'that which lies beyond communication'[56] than to 'the communication of a communicability'.[57] Mallarmé's mime doesn't offer the corrective to the example of dance that we might expect, but raises the question once again of whether it is possible to think of a sphere of pure means separate from the aesthetic object. This question is exacerbated by what Agamben leaves out of his quotation of Mallarmé: that the viewer of the mime is trying to articulate 'the aesthetics of the genre' of miming.[58] For this viewer, it is fictionality as

51 id., p. 51.
52 id., p. 52.
53 S. Mallarmé, 'Mimique'. Quoted in B. Johnson's introduction to the English translation of J. Derrida, *Dissemination* (1981) xxii.
54 id., p. xviii.
55 Benjamin, op. cit., n. 14, p. 253.
56 id.
57 Agamben, op. cit., n. 41, p. 52.
58 Mallarmé, op. cit., n. 53.

58

much as purity that defines the means of miming: 'he thus sets up a medium, a pure medium, *of fiction* [*il installe, ainsi, un milieu, pur, de fiction*]'.[59] Agamben's use of Mallarmé's prose poem is not only strange, as he has just asserted that the aesthetic dimension can be 'just as alienating'[60] as pure instrumentality; it is also selective in a way that attempts to prevent the infiltration of Mallarmé's aesthetics of miming into Agamben's politics of pure means.

Why might Agamben, unlike Benjamin, resist using literary language as a manifestation of pure means? The answer has to do with the difference between what Benjamin and Agamben mean by the term 'aesthetic'. Though both draw upon Kant's formulation that 'beauty is the form of the pur-posiveness [*Zweckmässigkeit*] of an object, insofar as it is perceived in it without representation of an end',[61] the two interpret 'purposiveness' differently. For Agamben, unlike Benjamin, Kantian purposiveness repre-sents pure endedness, not pure mediality. This is clear from the way in which Agamben plays on the relation between the words *fine* ('end') and *finalità* (the standard Italian translation of Kant's *Zweckmässigkeit*).[62] Agamben writes that if we experience dance aesthetically, we see it as movement that 'has in itself its own end'.[63] This endedness closes the aesthetic off from the realm of pure means: 'a purposiveness without means [*una finalità senza mezzi*] is just as alienating as a mediality that makes sense only with respect to a purpose.'[64] As '*finalità senza mezzi*', the aesthetic aspect of dance is perfectly opposed to means without ends, '*mezzi senza fine*'. (Hence, as we have seen, Agamben's distinction between the aesthetic and the gestural.) For Benjamin, this is not the case; in 'The Task of the Translator', *Zweckmässigkeit* alludes to a sphere of means rather than a sphere of ends. Benjamin views translation as related to 'purposeful manifestations of life' whose ends are located in the higher realm of expression or representation, manifestations which thus appear to us as means without end. Thus, where Agamben's essay excludes aesthetic endedness from an authentic politics of pure means, Benjamin connects pure means to the incommunicable in the work of art.

59 id., pp. xxii and xx (my emphasis).
60 Agamben, op. cit., n. 41, p. 51.
61 Kant, op. cit., n. 9, p. 120.
62 It is worth noting that in Vincenzo Binetti and Cesare Casarino's translation of *Means Without End*, '*finalitá*' is translated as 'finality', which loses, for English speakers, the allusion to Kantian purposiveness.
63 Agamben, op. cit., n. 41, p. 51.
64 id.

This philosophical effort to describe noninstrumental means is the basis for Agamben's political response to our 'global state of exception'. A theory of pure means can counteract a central problem of the state of exception: its exacerbation of the 'nexus between violence and law'.[65] Benjamin, as we have seen, views law as inherently violent in both its creation and preservation in so far as it is conceived as instrumental. Agamben argues that the state of exception extends this legal violence beyond its own boundaries by making it possible for extra-legal actions to acquire legal status. Tracing the legal history of the term 'force of law' (the title Derrida gave to an essay in which he analyses 'Critique of Violence'), Agamben describes those actions that, though not legally authorized, nonetheless draw upon the violence that guarantees law's dictates: 'decrees, provisions, and measures that are not formally laws nevertheless acquire their "force".'[66] What is peculiar – and dangerous – about the state of exception is that its suspension of legal norms allows *any* action to potentially acquire legal force.[67] As such, in suspending the law, the state of exception does not also suspend the violence that creates and maintains law, but rather makes it available for appropriation by revolutionary groups, dictators, the police, and so forth: 'It is as if the suspension of law freed a force ... that both the ruling power and its adversaries, the constituted power as well as the constituent power, seek to appropriate.'[68] Agamben terms this potential coincidence of every human action and legal force the inseparability of law and life.

Given that suspending law only increases its violent activity, Agamben proposes that 'deactivating' law, rather erasing it, is the only way to undermine its unleashed force.[69] It is in this context that Agamben offers the apparently strange solution of 'play' with which I began:

> One day humanity will play with law just as children play with disused objects, not in order to restore them to their canonical use but to free them from it for good. What is found after the law is not a more proper and original

---

65 Agamben, op. cit., n. 1, p. 88.

66 id., p. 38.

67 In both *State of Exception* and *Homo Sacer*, Kafka is the theorist par excellence of such a situation: his characters live in a state where 'a distracted knock on the door can mark the start of uncontrollable trials'. G. Agamben, *Homo Sacer* (1998) 52.

68 id., p. 51.

69 This 'deactivation' of law tempers Benjamin's 'destruction' of law. Through his reading of Paul, Agamben is able to, in effect, use the figure of weak messianic force from Benjamin's 'Theses on the Philosophy of History' to soften the conclusions of 'Critique of Violence':

> Just as messianic power is realized and acts in the form of weakness, so too in this way does it have an effect on the sphere of law and its works, not simply by negating or annihilating them, but by de-activating them, rendering them inoperative, no-longer-at-work.

G. Agamben, *The Time That Remains* (2005) 97.

60

use value that precedes the law, but a new use that is born only after it. And use, which has been contaminated by law, must also be freed from its own value. This liberation is the task of study, or of play.[70]

In proposing this playful relation Agamben makes the move that Benjamin avoids: explicitly describing what would remain after the violent destruction of normativity itself. 'Play' names the unknowable end of 'divine violence'. Agamben himself may not be entirely comfortable with this moment; in the final paragraph of *State of Exception*, he replaces this prediction with a question and a possibility:

> only beginning from the space thus opened [that is, by law's deposition] will it be possible to pose the question of a possible use of law after the deactivation of the device that, in the state of exception, tied it to life.[71]

Playfulness disappears completely in *The Time That Remains*, where Christian love instead designates our relation to the fulfilled law: 'once he divides the law into a law of works and a law of faith ... and thus renders it inoperative and unobservable ... Paul can then fulfil and recapitulate the law in the figure of love.'[72] Despite Agamben's apparent hesitation, this idea of play is instructive because of its resonance with Agamben's own articulations of aesthetic experience.

In an essay arguing that play derives from ritual, Agamben claims that 'everything pertaining to play once pertained to the realm of the sacred'.[73] Play is the participation in a ritual whose meaning has been forgotten: it converts sacred objects into mere toys. This is what gives it its (literally) revolutionary force: Agamben notes that play 'overturns' the sacred 'to the point where it can plausibly be defined as "topsy-turvy sacred".'[74] This mediation between the sacred and the secular is the function that Agamben would like play to perform on the law: overturning it without destroying it. Play would do this by retaining law's form while forgetting its meaning; Agamben writes that 'Playland is a country whose inhabitants are busy celebrating rituals, and manipulating objects and sacred words, whose sense and purpose they have, however forgotten.'[75] This ritual with a forgotten purpose articulates a means without end in so far as the end has become unknowable through its forgetting. This account also amounts to a

---

70 Agamben, op. cit., n. 1, p. 64.
71 id., p. 88.
72 Agamben, op. cit., n. 69, p. 108. The book on Paul offers a more developed account of a deactivated law, but it notably does not make the polemical claims for political relevance that *State of Exception* does. Although it may be possible to discover a connection between Paul's fulfilling of the law as Christian love and the proposed deactivation of the law through play, the former is not immediately applicable to the problems articulated in Agamben's more political work.
73 G. Agamben, 'In Playland: Reflections on History and Play' in *Infancy and History: The Destruction of Experience* (1993) 71.
74 id., p. 69.
75 id., p. 70.

61

transposition of Benjamin's often-cited account of the relation between the sacred and the profane in 'The Work of Art in the Age of its Technological Reproductibility':

> *the unique value of the 'authentic' work of art always has its basis in ritual.* This ritualistic basis, however mediated it may be, is still recognizable as secularized ritual in even the most profane forms of the cult of beauty.[76]

Agamben's toy is thus not opposed to, but the counterpart of Benjamin's 'authentic' work of art.

Furthermore, Agamben's claim that law that has opened itself to play 'no longer has force or application'[77] depends upon the logic that, for Agamben, characterizes Kantian aesthetics. This negative definition of the figure of law – as law minus force and application – removes law's functionality and normativity while maintaining that something called law still exists. Defining 'pure law' as what it is not repeats a rhetorical move for which Agamben criticizes Kant, namely that in the third critique, 'judgment identifies the determinations of beauty only in a purely negative fashion'[78] and consequently 'our appreciation of art begins necessarily with the forgetting of art'.[79] Agamben thus glosses Kant's fourth definition of the beautiful (that 'which is cognized without a concept as the object of a necessary satisfaction'[80]) to emphasize its constitutive negativity: the beautiful, he says, is 'normality without a norm'.[81] In *State of Exception*, it may not be problematic that our appreciation of law would begin with the forgetting of law; indeed this forgetting may be the difficult work that the book proposes. But it is not only the negative structure of the argument but also the *kind* of negativity that is continuous between Agamben's analyses of aesthetic and legal judgement. In other words, 'normality without a norm', which paradoxically articulates the subtraction of normativity from the normal, is simply another way of saying 'law without force or application'.[82] To the degree that this is true, Kantian aesthetic judgement hasn't disappeared in our experience of pure mediality; in fact, its name has barely changed.

But perhaps most interesting is the similarity between Agamben's description of the disused law and a much less famous passage in Kant's

---

76 W. Benjamin, 'The Work of Art in the Age of Its Technological Reproductibility' (Second Version), *Selected Writings, Vol. 3*, eds. H. Eiland and M.W. Jennings (2002) 105.
77 Agamben, op. cit., n. 1, p. 63.
78 G. Agamben, *The Man Without Content* (1999) 41.
79 id., p. 43.
80 Kant, op. cit., n. 9, p. 124.
81 Agamben, op. cit., n. 78, p. 42.
82 This sort of negative formulation characterizes the fulfilled or extra-legal law almost every time Agamben describes it; in *The Time That Remains*, Agamben writes that the 'paradoxical figure of the law in the state of messianic exception' is 'a manifestation of "justice without law" … This amounts, more or less, to "observing the law without law".' Agamben, op. cit., n. 69, p. 107.

third critique. In a footnote to his definition of the beautiful as 'an object's form of purposiveness insofar as it is perceived in the object *without the presentation of a purpose*',[83] Kant describes an object much like Agamben's disused law. Anticipating a possible quarrel with his explication, Kant imagines someone who would point out that there are all sorts of objects whose use we don't know, but which still aren't considered beautiful:

> It might be adduced as a counterexample to this definition that there are things in which one can see a purposive form without cognizing an end in them, e.g., the stone utensils often excavated from ancient burial mounds, which are equipped with a hole, as if for a handle, which, although they clearly betray by their shape a purposiveness the end of which one does not know, are nevertheless not declared to be beautiful on that account.[84]

These stone utensils whose ends are unknown and unknowable give us an idea of what the law would look like to the humanity that Agamben hopes will play with it. Where Agamben imagines a future in which the law will still exist but will have lost its purpose, Kant describes a present in which we discover instrumental objects whose purpose is unknown. These objects offer us yet another figure of 'means without end': things which 'betray by their shape a purposiveness', but whose end has been erased by historical time. Kant argues that these objects are not actually susceptible to aesthetic reflection on the grounds that the counter-argument assumes. But they are significant because their obscured ends allow them to raise a question about their status as aesthetic objects. This is the precise question raised by Agamben's figure of a law to be played with after its use value has been superseded.

To say, however, that Agamben's theory of a deactivated law returns to a theory of aesthetic judgement is not to say that Agamben aestheticizes law – at least in the sense of this term that makes it an accusation. In *The Time That Remains*, Agamben argues that a certain way of thinking about messianism runs the risk of aestheticization: reducing 'ethics and religion to acting *as if* God, the kingdom, truth, and so on existed' amounts to 'an aestheticization of the messianic in the form of the *as if*'.[85] But I am not suggesting that the infiltration of aesthetic experience into Agamben's messianic law amounts to a substitution of fictional for real redemption. It is not some fictionality in our relation to the deposed law that renders our experience of it aesthetic but, rather, its suspension of the relation between means and ends. As such, Agamben's argument against the aestheticization of the messianic – that 'the messianic is the simultaneous abolition and realization of the *as if*' – does not address the aesthetic trace that remains in the messianic law as formulated in *State of Exception*. This trace, I think, may testify more to the productive political possibilities of Kantian aesthetic judgement itself than to some falsity of Agamben's solution.

83 Kant, op. cit., n. 9, p. 120.
84 id.
85 Agamben, op. cit., n. 69, p. 35.

Even so, this still amounts to a reading of Agamben against Agamben's own intention. Agamben ends *State of Exception* by suggesting that our experience of the law as a pure means is capable of reclaiming the political space that he believes has been eclipsed:

> a space between [life and law] for human action, which once claimed for itself the name of 'politics'.... To a word that does not bind, that neither commands nor prohibits anything, but says only itself would correspond an action as pure means, which shows only itself without any relation to an end.[86]

If it is as difficult to separate the figure of pure means from aesthetic purposiveness as Benjamin's and Agamben's own writings suggest, then one can easily see the beauty inherent in 'action as pure means, which shows only itself'.[87] This leaves us with a different answer to the question with which Agamben opens his book – 'What does it mean to act politically?'[88] – than Agamben gives. We might say that what it means to act politically is to act aesthetically. To enlist the figure of pure means in a call for the return of an authentic politics is to partially ground the political on that moment in aesthetic judgement when we appreciate something not because it is useful or because it fits with our conceptual understanding of the world, but simply because we have a relation to it, independent of its purpose.

86 Agamben, op. cit., n. 1, p. 88.
87 id.
88 id., p. 2.

64

JOURNAL OF LAW AND SOCIETY
VOLUME 34, NUMBER 1, MARCH 2007
ISSN: 0263-323X, pp. 65–76

The Normality of the Exception in Democracy's Empire

PETER FITZPATRICK* AND RICHARD JOYCE*

The motif is one of inversion. In its received mode, the exception – the exceptional decision suspending the normal legal order – generates both the sovereign and the law. Here, on the contrary, the exception is found to be of the 'normal' law and, thus endowed, law goes to constitute the sovereign. This normality of the exception is then matched with the sovereign claim of democracy's empire. That empire is thence shown to have an oxymoronic quality, democracy and its constituent law being conducive to empire yet ultimately opposed to it. The empire of the United States of America provides a 'case'.

INTRODUCTION

Guantánamo is influentially taken to be the paradigm for our time of the state of exception and its attendant sovereign rule.[1] In this rendition, so to speak, Guantánamo is a place of pervasive sovereign control where people are comprehensively contained beyond the law. Yet it has been cogently shown that law flourishes in this very scene supposedly devoid of it.[2] This revisionist account of Guantánamo indicates at least that there is a question about the adequacy of the received version of the exception and its attendant sovereign rule. The abrupt answer offered here is that the exception to the law is itself of the law and that the exception's attendant sovereign rule is constituted by law. Such an answer is then related to the sovereign claim of democracy's empire. In the result, democracy and its law are found to be

* School of Law, Birkbeck, University of London, Malet Street, London WC1E 7HX, England
peter.fitzpatrick@clickvision.co.uk   r.joyce@law.bbk.ac.uk

1 J. Butler, *Precarious Life: The Powers of Mourning and Violence* (2004) 51, 57; G. Agamben, *State of Exception* (2005) tr. K. Attell, 4.
2 F. Johns, 'Guantánamo Bay and the Annihilation of the Exception' (2005) 16 *European J. of International Law* 613; N. Hussain, 'Beyond Norm and Exception: Guantánamo' (2007) *Critical Inquiry* (forthcoming).

conducive to empire yet also and ultimately opposed to it. The empire of the United States of America provides a telling 'case'.

THE RECEIVED EXCEPTION

The inevitable starting point is Schmitt's pronunciamento: 'Sovereign is he who decides on the exception.'[3] There is a dual constitution involved here. The immediate one is the constitution of the sovereign. The consequential constitution is that of a distinct legal order. It is the sovereign who, in deciding when a state of exception exists and the normal legal order has to be suspended, also decides what is the normal legal order.[4] The normal order is one of a 'boring', repetitive application of pre-existent rules.[5] 'In the exception the power of real life breaks through the crust of a mechanism that has become torpid by repetition.'[6] The exception is, then and of necessity, illimitable. It 'cannot be circumscribed factually or made to conform to a preformed law'.[7] Rather, it 'frees itself from all normative ties'; it 'departs ... from the legal norm'.[8]

That is one side of the story. The other has to do with the primacy of law and the sovereign's dependence on it. That side will be recounted shortly. Its intimations are, however, already present in Schmitt's account. The sovereign decision on the exception needs the norm to which it is excep-tional. Hence for Schmitt the exception only suspends the legal order. This legal order remains in the wings ever awaiting its return. And return it must if there is to be a sustaining of the norm to which the exceptional can continue to be exceptional. But that is not all. Law invades the realm of the exception, and does so despite the surpassing determinative force which Schmitt would accord the decision on the exception. Law constitutes the terms in which the exception can be decided on: it 'suspend[s] itself', and although the sovereign 'stands outside the normally valid legal system, he nevertheless belongs to it', and sovereignty remains 'a juristic concept' or remains 'within the framework of the juristic'.[9] Nor is it simply the case that the sealed completeness of the decision on the exception is contaminated by legal matter – rather, the contamination is mutual. The exceptional inhabits the norm. With the operation of the norm, and for Schmitt, the 'autonomous moment of the decision recedes to a minimum',[10] but it exists. There is

3 C. Schmitt, *Political Theology: Four Chapters on the Concept of Sovereignty* (2005) tr. G. Schwab, 5.
4 id., p. 13.
5 id., p. 15.
6 id.
7 id., p. 6.
8 id., pp. 12, 13.
9 id., pp. 6–7, 12, 13–14, 16.
10 id., p. 12.

always 'space' for the norm in itself to be other than what it may be at any one time, 'space' for the entry from within the domain of the legal order itself of what is exceptional to the norm. In like vein, Schmitt recognizes that 'every juristic decision' involves a generative creativity, that it cannot simply be read off from what is already there but that it entails 'an independently determining moment'.[11] The mutual contamination of the exception and the legal order will soon prove crucial for an argument placing the exception in and as law, but what must be considered first is another hugely influential elevation of the surpassing exception and of its attendant sovereignty, an elevation that now becomes pointedly challenging for it incorporates within itself a contamination that for Schmitt seemed merely to derogate from the purity of the separation between the sovereign exception and the legal order.

Agamben's exception has the same components as Schmitt's but the composition of each is different. For Schmitt the decision on the exception 'frees itself from all normative ties'.[12] Agamben's exception likewise frees itself but not as an occasional suspending of an otherwise distinctly enduring legal order. Rather, the exception now continuously enters into and comprehensively subordinates the legal order:

> Indeed, the state of exception has today reached its maximum worldwide deployment. The normative aspect of law can thus be obliterated and contradicted with impunity by a governmental violence that – while ignoring international law externally and producing a permanent state of exception internally – nevertheless still claims to be applying the law.[13]

The exception 'everywhere becomes the rule' says Agamben,[14] and whereas for Schmitt, the exception brings with it 'the power of real life [which] breaks through the crust' of the legal order, for Agamben, the exception itself becomes a power ruling pervasively over life.[15]

The disparity between these lines of thought carries over into the relation between sovereignty and the exception. For Schmitt, as we saw, the sovereign is constituted as 'he who decides on the exception', and that power of decision somehow 'becomes in the true sense absolute' – something it would have to become if it is to match the illimitable exception.[16] With Agamben it is 'life that constitutes the first content of sovereign power', and the 'production' of that life is 'the originary activity of sovereignty', an originating sovereignty within which 'law refers to life and includes it in itself by suspending it'.[17] In so doing, sovereignty assumes complete control

---

11 id., p. 30.
12 id., p. 12.
13 Agamben, op. cit., n. 1, p. 87.
14 G. Agamben, *Homo Sacer: Sovereign Power and Bare Life* (1998) tr. D. Heller-Roazen, 9.
15 Schmitt, op. cit., n. 3, p. 15; Agamben, id., generally.
16 Schmitt, id., pp. 5, 12.
17 Agamben, op. cit., n. 14, p. 28.

67

over that life – a life that is thence decidedly 'bare'.[18] It is not only that this bare life is produced by sovereignty; it is the very power over bare life that constitutes sovereignty.

That aside, in its encompassing of life, of life that remains infinitely protean if now bare before sovereignty and its law, sovereign power would have to be at least co-extensive with life. How that could be or how it could be known to be is left aptly mysterious. Indeed, where the sovereign of Schmitt and of Agamben comes from is a mystery. Most immediately, it floats on tautology. The decision of Schmitt's sovereign creates the exception which creates the sovereign. Agamben's sovereign is constituted by the bare life it produces. More intriguingly, in both cases there is the evocation of a sacred foundation to sovereignty. Schmitt's sovereign is announced into existence in the opening sentence of a work on 'political theology', the gist of which Schmitt explains in this way:

> All significant concepts of the modern theory of the state are secularized theological concepts not only because of their historical development – in which they were transferred from theology to the theory of the state, whereby, for example, the omnipotent God became the omnipotent lawgiver – but also because of their systematic structure, the recognition of which is necessary for a sociological consideration of these concepts.[19]

Part of this systematic structure not exactly recognized by Schmitt is that his sovereign would have to be deiform in order to fuse its determinate presence with the illimitability of the exception. That same fusion endows Agamben's sovereign, only in his case it derives from an ersatz sacred tradition.[20]

Even if a quixotic credence were allowed these grounds of sovereignty, an intriguing irresolution would remain. Schmitt's overweening sovereign, as we saw, remained 'a juristic concept' and 'belongs to ... the normally valid legal system', a system able to decide autonomously even if Schmitt would arbitrarily confine this ability 'to a minimum'.[21] The inability of Agamben's sovereign to contain the law can be discerned more obliquely. The pervasion of this sovereign, its commensuration with life, is qualified by Agamben's finding that this is a catastrophe which is coming rather than already realized, and a catastrophe that could somehow in life be reversed.[22] So, this sovereign is less than comprehensive in its effective coverage of life, but the law it supposedly encompasses and subordinates is not so restricted but

18 id., pp. 11, 83.
19 Schmitt, op. cit., n. 3, p. 36. Even more strongly: 'The juridic formulas of the omnipotence of the state are ... only superficial secularizations of the theological formulas of the omnipotence of God': C. Schmitt, *The Concept of the Political* (1996) tr. G. Schwab, 42.
20 For an account and criticism of which, see P. Fitzpatrick, 'Bare Sovereignty: *Homo Sacer* and the Insistence of Law' in *Politics, Metaphysics and Death: Essays on Giorgio Agamben's* Homo Sacer, ed. A. Norris (2005) 49–73.
21 Schmitt, op. cit., n. 3, pp. 12, 16.
22 Agamben, op. cit., n. 14, pp. 12, 153, 188.

remains co-extensive with suspended life. This law becomes attenuated or is eventually eliminated only in Agamben's expectation of a new form of life alternative to the coming catastrophe.[23]

THE LAW OF THE EXCEPTION

Not without a touch of the tendentious, then, we find Schmitt and Agamben instancing persistent irresolutions in jurisprudence and in the field of law and society. Law is autonomous, or has some significant degree of autonomy. Yet law is receptively subordinated to some other power, usually conceived in terms of society or sovereign. There are various mediations of this divide. In jurisprudence, for example, law has been notably endowed with a 'core' of stilled meaning and with a 'penumbra' of receptive adaptability.[24] Nothing remotely resembling a general line of division between these categories has been identified. Taking another example, now from the domain of law and society, a 'constitutive theory' would have it that whilst indeed society constitutes or 'shapes' law, law also constitutes or 'shapes' society.[25] Again, no dividing line has been identified, and no barrier to stop either pervading the other. The corresponding alternation with Schmitt would have the sovereign generating the legal order *and* law not only retaining an autonomy but also constituently inhabiting the sovereign realm. With Agamben, the contrast, as we saw, was one in which a sovereign power encompassing life subordinated a law of equal extent, yet this same sovereign power also found itself to be less extensive than life leaving the extent of law's own relation to life undiminished.

That these contraries are not simply stark oppositions can be discerned in a more practical perspective on law. The notion of autonomous law usually imports law's providing some determinate reference, some available concentration of enforceable relations between us, some present normative hold on the futurity of our being together. To do all this, however, law has to be continually receptive to the ever-changing quality of those relations and of that futurity. Once, so the moderns say, these two dimensions of law, the determinate and the receptive, could be joined in a transcendent determination. Resort could be had to a deific or sacral resolution much like those evoked by Schmitt and by Agamben. Modernity is bereft of such resort. As the iterative tomes of jurisprudence attest, no resolution is to be found in one

---

23 id., p. 29; Agamben, op. cit., n. 1, p. 64. Compare the law seemingly amenable to the new form of life which Agamben evokes in G. Agamben, *Potentialities: Collected Essays in Philosophy* (1999) tr. D. Heller-Roazen, 165; and G. Agamben, *The Time that Remains: A Commentary on the Letter to the Romans* (2005) tr. P. Dailey, 122.
24 H.L.A. Hart, *The Concept of Law* (1961) 125, 149.
25 A. Hunt, *Explorations in Law and Society: Toward a Constitutive Theory of Law* (1993) 174–5.

69

side of the division or the other. Law cannot subsist as fixedly determinate. For law to accommodate the ever-pending infinity of possible relation in our being together, it must be utterly receptive. Yet if it were only receptive, it would be purely evanescent and, in the result, a vacuity.

More constructively, and more to our overall point, law is continuously constituted in a connecting receptivity to what is ever beyond its determinate self. The call for law always comes from beyond its determinate realization for the time being. If law could not actively and receptively respond to that call, it would wither in cumulating irrelevance. But for law to bring what is beyond into its determinant existence, it must be in a position apart from that existence, a position that opens to, and that can be held open to, what is beyond its determinate existence. Yet that same position apart must also be one that resists what is beyond, selecting and gathering it in terms which maintain a connection generatively affirming law's continuing and determinate existence. This position is that of the exception, the exception now as normal.[26] This position is, then, like Schmitt's exception in that it combines being beyond and yet of the existing 'legal order'.

That self-transcendent position of law also positions the exaltation of the sovereign in both Schmitt's and Agamben's accounts of the exception. 'Law itself', says Nancy, 'does not have a form for what would need to be its own sovereignty'.[27] In its responsiveness to the infinity of possible relation in our being together, law has to be ever changeful and, in some ultimate sense, a vacuity. As such, it cannot in itself, in any formed self, enduringly unite its determinate and receptive dimensions. That same vacuity, however, renders law intimately receptive to power. And it is in the formation of the 'modern' national polity that we find a power endowing law, a power concentrated in the persistence of a pre-modern conception of sovereignty.[28] Taking matters that far would help explain the subjection of law to the sovereign within Schmitt's and Agamben's exception. What would still need explaining would be the saturation of Schmitt's sovereign exception with legal matter and Agamben's unwitting extension of law beyond the sovereign power that somehow also encompassed it.

---

26 This is not to deny that the position apart may provide an opening typically more wide in some legal situations than in others. The situation most frequently instancing the exception, a declaration of emergency, is but an example at the wider end. Congeries of 'exceptional' laws can now serve the same function as that performed by the supposed exception to the law (see Hussain, op. cit., n. 2). Standard lamentations, such as Schmitt's, about the spread of discretion and our being moved 'further and further from the ground or juridical certainty' (as quoted in Agamben, op. cit., n. 14, p. 172), manage to ignore the intrinsic ability of law to become other to itself. Even the most seemingly stable law carries with it a power of being radically revised or reversed.

27 J.-L. Nancy, *Being Singular Plural* (2000) tr. R. Richardson and A. O'Byrne, 131.

28 This mode of sovereign appropriation is, of course, not the only way in which law's dimensions have been or are combined.

70

For sovereignty to endow law with determining force, for it to bring together effectively the determinate and receptive dimensions of law, it must share those dimensions with law. In modernity, and like law, sovereignty cannot seek resolution of disparate dimensions in some transcendent reference apart from itself. Hence its starkly dual characteristics delimited by Derrida. Sovereignty, says Derrida, 'is undivided, unshared, or it is not'; yet he would ask: 'What happens when . . . [sovereignty] divides? When it must, when it cannot not divide?'[29] There is some merging of these seeming opposites when Derrida talks about ipseity in terms of 'the sovereign and reappropriating gathering of self in the simultaneity of an assemblage or assembly, being together or "living together," as we say'.[30] Transposing this in terms borrowed from law's dimensions, the determinate dimension could be seen as calling for an experientially undivided cohering; the receptive dimension could be seen as matching the necessity for sovereignty, like any vital organization, to incorporate responsively and assemble the multitude of disparate forces that continually come to (re)constitute it. For this projected assembling, sovereignty must be intrinsically receptive to plurality. To be so receptive, sovereignty must always be incipiently vacuous, always capable of emptying any existent content. So, appropriating another arcanum, Nancy would find that 'sovereignty is nothing', 'bare', an 'empty place'.[31] So a 'modern' sovereignty, like its exhausted sacral predecessors, must marvellously fuse being determinate with a receptiveness prehensively subjected to that sovereignty's unconstrained efficacy. Such a sovereign power can enclose itself yet extend indefinitely, subsist finitely yet potentially encompass what is beyond its existent content.

To do all this, however, sovereign power cannot simply and purely in itself match the dimensions of law. It has also to be dependent on law. For the sovereign to sustain its being in an importunate futurity, no amount of the present assertion or exercise of power ('exceptional' or otherwise) would suffice. That being is of necessity oriented in a claim of right, a claim that projects sovereign power beyond its determinate dimension and attaches it receptively to what is beyond. Law, then, as the carrier of that right, provides this continuously projected, amenable, and generally enforceable means of combining the determinate and receptive dimensions of sovereignty. In all, as the mutual contamination of Schmitt's law and sovereign intimated, law and sovereignty subsist in a constituent mutuality. It is also possible now to reconcile Agamben's contradiction. In its vacuity law is indeed needful of sovereign assertion, yet law extends beyond such assertion in the cause not just to its own but also the sovereign's continuance 'in being'.

29 J. Derrida, *Without Alibi* (2002) tr. P. Kamuf, xix–xx.
30 J. Derrida, *Rogues: Two Essays on Reason* (2005) tr. P.-A. Brault and M. Naas, 11.
31 Nancy, op. cit., n. 27, pp. 36, 147.

Democracy, like law, finds its being in this position of exception – in an opening to what is beyond itself and in bringing what is beyond to itself. There is more here than a simple correspondence between democracy and law. Rather, there is an integral tie in which law creates, and continuously generates, democracy. The necessity for law specifically to do this can be derived from a seeming contradiction in democracy itself.

Democracy is rule by the people, but the people in itself cannot rule. This is the gist of Plato's complaint about democracy in *Republic*.[32] He, or his *dramatis personae*, concentrate on the quality of the democratic individual, but they do so in order to derive the quality of a 'corresponding ... democratic political system'.[33] Such an individual 'indulges in every passing desire that each day brings', submits to 'every passing pleasure as its turn comes to hold office, as it were'; and, in all, 'his lifestyle has no rhyme or reason'.[34] The corresponding political system is promiscuously 'open' and potentially 'adorned with every species of human trait'.[35] It is, in short, this illimitable openness that is the prime and impelling constituent of democracy. Putting this in terms relevant to modern democracy, for Lefort, democracy 'inaugurates the experience of an ungraspable, uncontrollable society in which the people will be said to be sovereign, of course, but whose identity will constantly be open to question, whose identity will remain latent'.[36] Hence Lefort's thesis that the place of power in democracy is an 'empty place'; and the empty throne becomes the 'normal' condition.[37] It is not, however, a condition that simply and somehow results from naturalistic traits that Plato, for example, would attribute to it a crucial point that will now be taken up.

The immediate problem is how the people, the demos of democracy, can assume any determinate existence at all, let alone a position of sovereignty. Democracy's pre-modern forms could resort to a defining force of the natural or of the supernatural to selectively constitute the people. With modernity, and as Lindahl incisively notes, 'the people' is incapable of coming together to constitute itself as a political unity and from there institute a political and legal order; rather, they come to be a people through the creation of that order.[38] So, this very people, in a feat of what Derrida

32 Plato, *Republic* (1998) tr. R. Waterfield, 293–302 (555a–560b).
33 id., p. 296 (557b).
34 id., p. 301 (561c–d).
35 id., p. 296 (557c–d).
36 C. Lefort, *The Political Forms of Modern Society: Bureaucracy, Democracy, Totalitarianism* (1984) tr. J. B. Thompson, 303–4.
37 id., p. 303; C. Lefort, *Democracy and Political Theory* (1988) tr. D. Macey, 86, 225–6; S. Žižek, *For they know not what they do: Enjoyment as a Political Factor* (1991) 267–8.
38 H. Lindahl, 'Constituent Power and Reflexive Identity: Towards an Ontology of Collective Selfhood' in *The Paradox of Constitutionalism*, eds. M. Loughlin and N. Walker (forthcoming).

would call 'fabulous retroactivity',[39] is a creation of what it is taken in standard perspectives as creating, a creature of the constitution and of laws made pursuant to it – electoral laws, laws to do with citizenship and immigration, laws to do with mental capacity, and so on. What is more, law produces the definitive processes of democratic, and of sovereign democratic, assertion. Such production extends to the vacuity, the empty place of democracy. In constituting democracy and its definitive processes, this production does so in a way that gives force and effect to this empty place. Law, that is, integrates into democracy's form and processes the ability to be other than what it may determinately be at any one time. With modern democracy, in short, power is purposively constituted or constructed as empty.[40] More specifically, this is achieved through law's sharing in and making operative:

> ... a discourse which reveals that power belongs to no one; that those who exercise power do not possess it; that they do not, indeed, embody it; that the exercise of power requires a periodic and repeated contest; that the authority of those vested with power is created and re-created as a result of the manifestation of the will of the people.[41]

This generative emptiness, then, is embedded in democracy's determinate composition – embedded as a template, no matter how varied its realization. The commensurate ability of democracy to be other than its determinate existence cannot extend to being other to this template securing its emptiness. Democracy then, and like law, imports an 'exceptional' position. It is oriented beyond and as other to its determinate existence but still relates and returns to that existence.

DEMOCRACY'S EMPIRE

Finally, then, to the question of whether this 'normal' exception accords with democracy's empire, relating this to the promised case of the empire of the United States. The issue can be condensed in Jefferson's conceiving of the United States as 'the imperial republic'. This republic was imperial in that the ability and even the duty of the United States was to expand hugely, but it was republican in that the 'territories' so acquired had eventually to be admitted to the union as new states.[42] Imperial expansion beyond the existent range of the republic was justified because of the eventual return to a

---

39 J. Derrida, 'Declarations of Independence' (tr. T. Keenan and T. Pepper) (1986) 15 *New Political Science* 7, 10.
40 Žižek, op. cit., n. 37, p. 276, fn. 52.
41 Lefort, op. cit., n. 37, p. 225.
42 J. Wilson, *The Imperial Republic: A Structural History of American Constitutionalism from the Colonial Era to the Beginning of the Twentieth Century* (2002) 63, 73.

73

republican and democratic fold. All of which may seem to accord with the exceptional quality of democracy. Indeed, democracy and its law could be seen in ways as attuned to the imperial. Their vacuity makes them receptive to imperial power, specifically to the assertions of the sovereign of the imperial nation. And their orientation beyond the determinate can serve the expansionary grasp of empire, law having long been part of the 'civilizing mission', even if democracy has joined that mission only recently. So, updating the Jeffersonian model to the current formation of American empire so-called, we find its expansionary 'influence' is justified by the mantric insistence that, in the result, others will be brought within the fold of democracy and the rule of law.[43]

The grand solipsism of empire radically qualifies this easy correspondence with democracy and law. Modern imperialism has been and remains based on national sovereignty, a sovereignty bound in terms that are elevated exemplarily. So, Jefferson's model, which was to be 'an empire of liberty', became racially qualified in its application leaving some indefinitely outside the range of achievable civilization.[44] Leaping over to the current scene, we find an imperium officially asserted in terms that are naturalist and divisive, yet transcendent. These are terms laying down 'a single sustainable model for national success'; a model in which the market and an economic orthodoxy are enshrined as natural; a model in which certain attendant values are affirmed as 'right and true for every person, in every society'; a model in which there has to be limited government and the 'unleashing [of] the power of the private sector'; and, more generally, a model in which, conveniently, markets and 'societies' have to be 'open', especially to foreign investment.[45] This imperative openness turns out to be not quite universal. It excludes the United States which must always, so it is officially ordained, be 'strong enough' to counter any 'surpassing, or equalling, [of its] power': it must, then, 'maintain a military without peer'; and it can use the 'global commons' ('space, international waters and airspace, and cyberspace') so as to 'project power anywhere in the world from secure bases of operation.'[46] If this nationally enclosed predomination were incompatible with the 'open' quality of democracy and its law, then we would expect it to find an antithesis when it encountered the rough democracy of the international and its law.

---

43 For example, G.W. Bush, *The National Security Strategy of the United States of America* (2002); G.W. Bush, *The National Security Strategy of the United States of America* (2006) introduction, 10–11.

44 Wilson, op. cit., n. 42, p. 107. For 'empire of liberty' see, for example, A. Stephanson, *Manifest Destiny: American Expansion and the Empire of Right* (1995) 22. The phrase was not quite so original in that the British had used it to describe their early empire by way of a contrast with the Spanish. The heavy historical irony is that the 'empire of liberty' of the United States was set against British imperialism, among others.

45 Bush, op. cit. (2002), n. 43, introduction; Bush, op. cit. (2006), n. 43, pp. 4, 27, 31–2.

46 id. (2002), Part IX; id. (2006), introduction; D. Rumsfeld, *The National Defence Strategy of the United States of America* (2005) 13.

74

Such proves to be the case. To take a stark example, in his 'address to the nation' prior to the invasion of Iraq, a putative President Bush declared: 'The United Nations Security Council has not lived up to its responsibilities, so we will rise to ours'.[47] This self-elevation of the United States and of its conveniently constituted 'responsibilities' did not simply involve the embroiled question of whether the invasion of Iraq was 'legal'. The breach of international law does not necessarily or usually entail the assertion that, as here, one is superior to it, and superior to the institutions of the international community that create it. The quality of a breach could, however, be quite telling in this respect. Violation of standards, of human rights for example, that are taken to be definitive of the international community, or violation that would seek to undermine the hold of law and its processes, could evidence a hostility or disregard that affirmed superiority at least implicitly. That much could also be extracted from not only the refusal to enter into treaties of a like quality but also from the assiduous undermining of them. And activities of these kinds have been plentiful in the recent history of American empire.[48] Any doubt that these activities are superordinate may diminish on a reading of the *National Defence Strategy of the United States of America* for 2005 where 'our strength as a nation state' is pitted against 'those who employ a strategy of the weak using international fora, judicial processes, and terrorism'.[49]

CONCLUSION

Agamben begins his *State of Exception* with this epigraph, as translated: 'Why are you jurists silent about that which concerns you?'[50] Perhaps the point of the question, and accusation, is that jurists should conspicuously

---

47 G.W. Bush, 'Address to the Nation on Iraq' (17 March 2003) 39 *Weekly Comp. Pres. Doc.* 338, at 339.

48 See, for example, P. Fitzpatrick, ' "Gods would be needed . . .": American Empire and the Rule of (International) Law' (2003) 16 *Leiden J. of International Law* 429, 457–66. Another indicative instance could be that the United States has not notified any derogation from the provisions of the International Covenant on Civil and Political Rights, as provided in Article 4, despite being in breach of several of its provisions. Or perhaps it could not justify a derogation because Article 4 relates to a 'time of public emergency which threatens the life of the nation and the existence of which is officially proclaimed'. Compare, however, Human Rights Committee, *Consideration of Reports Submitted by States Parties under Article 40 of the Covenant – Third periodic reports of States parties due in 2003: United States of America,* UN Doc. CCPR/C/USA/3, 28 November 2005, Annex I, 'Territorial Scope of Application of the Covenant'.

49 Rumsfeld, op. cit., n. 46, p. 5. The terminology could be a tribute to R. Kagan, *Paradise & Power: America and Europe in the New World Order* (2003), widely hailed for its eternal verities about this 'new world order', an order in which it is 'the weak' who place ultimate reliance on law, the United States having to be strong and act in ways untrammelled by law: at 38–39, 102.

50 Agamben, op. cit., n. 1, epigraph.

75

condemn the disregard and desecration of the law and legal values in the 'exceptional' use of sovereign power he would instance with Guantánamo. In finding that the exception is not *to* but within law, this paper would question a silence that is more 'normal', a silence walled in the determinative elevation of naturalist and imperial categories that would deny the responsibility freighted with law's illimitable responsiveness. A like silence diminishes democracy, as we saw. If being modern is to be in a 'world of movement, of transformation, of displacement, and of restlessness, this world that is in principle and structurally outside itself, this world where nature does not subsist but steps out of itself into work and into history',[51] then one can only conclude, borrowing that most resonant of titles, 'we have never been modern'.[52]

---

51 J.-L. Nancy, *Hegel; The Restlessness of the Negative* (2002) tr. J. Smith and S. Miller, 6.
52 B. Latour, *We Have Never Been Modern* (1993) tr. C. Porter.

JOURNAL OF LAW AND SOCIETY
VOLUME 34, NUMBER 1, MARCH 2007
ISSN: 0263-323X, pp. 77–98

Post-Apartheid Social Movements and the Quest for the Elusive 'New' South Africa

Tshepo Madlingozi*

The South African Constitution guarantees justiciable socio-economic rights such as the rights to access to housing; to sufficient food and water; to social security and health care services. This 'transformative constitution' is meant to help rid the country of legacies of apartheid such as huge economic inequalities and entrenched poverty. The government's embrace of neoliberalism has, however, meant that these legacies have not only remained largely untreated but have also become entrenched. Poor communities have started organizing themselves in order to challenge the government's neoliberal policies as well as marginalization from structures of governance. This paper evaluates the nature of these 'social movements' as well as their impact on democracy and development.

The leader ... asks the people to remember the colonial period and to look back on the long way they have come since then. Now it must be said that the masses show themselves totally incapable of appreciating the long way they have come. The peasant who goes on scratching out a living from the soil and the unemployed man who never finds employment do not manage, in spite of public holidays and flags, new and brightly colored though they may be, to convince themselves that anything has really changed in their lives.[1]

* *Faculty of Law, University of Pretoria, Pretoria 0002, South Africa*
tshepo.madlingozi@up.ac.za
Tshepo Madligozi is also advocacy coordinator for Khulumani Support Group, a membership-based organization comprising of over 44000 members, which fight for the rights of people who suffered gross violations of human rights under apartheid (visit www.khulumani.net). I owe a lot of gratitude to Stewart Motha for his generous encouragement, patience and inspiration during the course of writing this paper. I cannot thank him enough for providing me with invaluable written comments on earlier drafts. The usual disclaimers apply.

1 F. Fanon, *Wretched of the Earth* (1963) 136.

Mandela has been the real sell-out, the biggest betrayer of his people. When it came to the crunch, he used his status to camouflage the actual agreement that the ANC was forging with the [white] South African elite.[2]

INTRODUCTION

Just over a decade ago progressives all over the world looked admiringly as Nelson Mandela became the first democratically elected president of South Africa. For those who were involved in the international anti-apartheid movement, this was a sign that the mission had been accomplished. Given the legacy of centuries of racial oppression and conflict, many observers were confounded by the relative peace that accompanied the transition period and quickly declared South Africa a 'miracle nation'.

Twelve years down the line, and three successful elections later, democratic institutions are being consolidated. These include a robust and independent Constitutional Court as well as a very vibrant media. All of this takes place against the background of a Constitution that contains a supreme Bill of Rights which entrenches an impressive catalogue of first-, second-, and third-generation rights ranging from the right not to be discriminated against on the basis of sexual orientation, to justiciable rights to access to adequate housing, health care services, and sufficient food and water.[3] It is because of these advances that globally, the country is often hailed as a successful model of 'Third Wave' democratization. This, however, is only one side of the story.

Apartheid left a legacy of great economic inequality and abject poverty. The ruling African National Congress (ANC) election campaign tagline, 'a better life for all', is therefore recognition that the struggle for liberation was also a struggle to eradicate the effects of racial capitalism. Indeed, township struggles that were taking place in the 1980s were about 'transforming the racial status quo, the prevailing set of stultifying and subjugating conditions of existence for those deemed not white.'[4] However, twelve years down the line, not much has change for South Africans now grappling with unemployment that stands at around 40 per cent. Half the population is living below the poverty line and millions remain landless and ravaged by HIV and AIDS.

The ANC's decision to embrace a liberal macroeconomic paradigm was made official in 1996, when the Growth, Employment and Redistribution

---

2 Trevor Ngwane, former ANC councillor, now a leading member of the Anti Privatisation Forum, cited in A. Desai and R. Pithouse, ' "But We Were Thousands": Dispossession, Resistance, Repossession and Repression in Mandela Park' (2004) 39 *J. of Asian and African Studies* 239–69, at 239.
3 See Bill of Rights in the South African Constitution of 1996 ('the Constitution').
4 D. Goldberg, *The Death of Race* (2004) 9, cited in Desai and Pithouse, op. cit., n. 2, p. 246.

Programme (GEAR) was unveiled.[5] GEAR promised to 'increase annual growth by an average of 4.2 per cent, create 1.35 million jobs by the year 2000, boost exports by an average 8.4 per cent per annum through an array of supply-side measures, and drastically improve social infrastructure.'[6] In order to achieve these targets, the plan hinged on massive increases in private sector investment. This would be achieved by, amongst other things: cutting government spending; keeping inflation in single digits; encouraging 'wage restraint'; speeding up privatization of 'non-essential' government assets; provision of tax breaks for corporate capital; and creation of a flexible labour market.[7]

GEAR was drafted in very secretive conditions. As one participant in its drafting would later comment:

> close affinity with the 'Washington Consensus' characterised not only the substantive policy recommendations of GEAR, but also the process through which it was formulated and presented publicly ... This was 'reform from above' with a vengeance, taking to extreme the arguments in favour of insulation and autonomy of policymakers from popular pressures.[8]

GEAR was quickly declared 'non-negotiable' by the Minister of Finance, Mr. Manuel, and by Mandela. Members of the Tripartite Alliance (consisting of the ANC, South African Communist Party (SACP), and the Congress of South African Trade Unions) who expressed dissatisfaction with the new policy were ordered to toe the line, threatened with disciplinary measures, and regularly marginalized from the centres of decision-making and power.[9] This authoritarian imposition of neoliberal policies is to be expected because, as Marais points out:

> neoliberal policies require a powerful, centralized and effective state – not to manage national development projects, but to neutralize and/or co-opt those social formations that under normal circumstances mediate relations between individuals and the market. Key among them is trade unions and other social movements.[10]

In the case of South Africa, the embrace of neoliberalism has led to policy-making that Bassett aptly describes as 'relatively closed hierarchical and expert-driven ... [making] it difficult for popular movements to par-

---

5 Unveiling the new macroeconomic policy, Mbeki told journalists to 'call me a Thatcherite', *Business Day*, 13 May 1997, cited in S. Terreblanche, *A History of Inequality in South Africa 1652–2002* (2002) 145.

6 H. Marais, *South Africa Limits to Change: the Political Economy of Transition* (2001) 163.

7 id., p. 164.

8 S. Gelb, 'The Politics of Macroeconomic Policy Reform in South Africa' (History Workshop of the University of the Witwatersrand, Johannesburg, 18 September 1999) 16–17, cited in id., p. 162.

9 D. McKinley, 'Democracy, Power and Patronage: Debate and Opposition within the African National Congress and the Tripartite Alliance since 1994' in *Opposition and Democracy in South Africa*, ed. R. Southall (2001) 183–206, at 192.

10 Marais, op. cit., n. 6, p. 153.

ticipate.'[11] The centralized and closed manner in which important economic policies are being drafted run contrary to the ANC historic commitment to participatory democracy.

Given this background, not many would disagree with Andreasson's assessment that the ANC's neoliberal restructuring of the economy has become an instrument 'for empowering (ANC) elites' hold on state power and for, simultaneously, marginalizing and disempowering opposition to this neo-liberal turn from within the Alliance and from society in general.'[12] He further argues that this neoliberal restructuring of the economy fits in with the definition of 'predatory liberalism':

> a cocktail of market capitalism, the neoliberal restructuring manifested in the Growth, Employment and Redistribution (GEAR) macro-economic programme, state authority (government neo-liberal restructuring and black empowerment as instruments for disciplining and marginalizing opposition) and oligarch power (entrenched apartheid-era capitalists along with an ANC-affiliated emergent 'black bourgeoisie').[13]

Under GEAR, unemployment, wage disparities, landlessness, and poverty have worsened. At the same time, the privatization and commodification of municipal services has meant that basic services such as health care and the provision of water and electricity have become inaccessible to the majority of South Africans.[14]

The state's turn to neoliberalism has effectively negated the Constitution's promise to 'improve the quality of life of all citizens and to free the potential of each person'.[15] In line with the logic of neoliberalism, most of the socio-economic rights that are guaranteed in the Constitution in order to realize the Constitutional values of 'dignity, equality and freedom' are only realizable 'progressively' and not immediately and only when there are 'available resources.'[16] John Saul has thus accurately elucidated that South Africa has experienced a 'dual transition' in the early 1990s: on the one hand, a transition from a racially driven, authoritarian rule to a more democratic (institutional) system of governance; on the other, a reintegration in the global capitalist economy along neoliberal lines.[17]

---

11 C. Bassett, 'The Demise of the Social Contract in South Africa' (2004) 38 *Cnd. J. of African Studies* 544, cited in S. Andreasson, 'The African National Congress and its Critics: "Predatory Liberalism", Black Empowerment and Intra-Alliance Tensions in Post-Apartheid South Africa' (2006) 13 *Democratization* 303–22, at 310.

12 Andreasson, id., p. 304.

13 id.

14 For comprehensive and critical analyses of the effects of GEAR, see Terreblanche, op. cit., n. 5; Marais, op. cit., n. 6; P. Bond, *Elite Transition: From Apartheid to Neoliberalism in South Africa* (2005).

15 See the preamble to the Constitution.

16 See, especially, ss. 26 and 27 of the Constitution.

17 J. Saul, 'Cry the Beloved Country: The Post-Apartheid Denouement' *Monthly Rev.*, January 2001, as summarized in D. McKinley and A. Veriava, *Arresting Dissent: State Repression and Post-Apartheid Social Movements* (2005) 8.

Because of the horrors occasioned by neoliberalism, poor communities throughout the country have banded together to challenge the effects of the state's macroeconomic policy and also to demand to be included in governance, an arena which is increasingly the sole preserve of state officials, NGOs, and other experts and professionals. Community organizations that are mounting these struggles have been characterized as new social movements. The state's response to these poor communities has been at best to marginalize them and at worse to criminalize them.

McKinley has argued that the rise of these social movements is due to the need to 'push for more inclusive and meaningful forms of direct and participatory democracy, that have little to do with the institutional forms of representation within bourgeois democratic society', and that 'these movements have arisen out of the very failures and betrayals of the "main currents" and the institutional framework that gives them contemporary legitimacy.'[18] This article evaluates the counter-hegemonic prospects of these social movements. It is therefore a tentative evaluation of whether these movements will manage 'to dislodge their national and local government's commitment to neoliberalism and increasingly repressive governance'[19] and whether they have the ability to ultimately 'open up new spaces and prefigure forms where alternative ideas of post-apartheid South Africa can be organized and discussed.'[20]

Before engaging in any in-depth analysis of these movements, it is first necessary to place them in a historical context. The first section of this article therefore aims to show that South Africa has a long and proud history of highly politicized community organizations. It was these organizations, together with the trade unions, that mobilized oppressed communities around issues of social justice and active citizenship. These community organizations banded together to mount a formidable resistance against apartheid. It is therefore important to see what lessons post-apartheid social movements could obtain from the struggles of anti-apartheid social movements. An attempt to get to grips with post-apartheid social movements and to evaluate their prospects is made after that section. By most accounts, South Africa's democracy is a very limited one. McKinley has thus proposed that 'it is the ANC that has now become the standard-bearer of liberal democracy in South Africa ... This has happened despite the ANC's long history of association with more radical notions of mass participatory

---

18 D. McKinley, 'Democracy and Social Movements in SA' (2004) 28 *Labour Bull.* 39–42, at 40.

19 P. Bond, 'South Africa's Resurgent Urban Social Movements: The Case of Johannesburg, 1984, 1994, 2004' in *Challenging Hegemony: Social Movements and the Quest for a New Humanism in South Africa*, ed. N. Gibson (2006) 103–24, at 124.

20 N. Gibson, 'Calling Everything into Question: Broken Promises, Social Movements and Emergent Intellectual Currents in Post-Apartheid South Africa' in Gibson, id., 1–53, at 41.

and non-capitalist democracy ...'.[21] This article takes as its point of departure the claim that if democracy is to be meaningful to the millions and millions of South Africa's poor and unemployed, a more human-centred development trajectory is needed. This in turn requires the presence of effective social movements in South Africa.[22]

SOCIAL MOVEMENTS AND THE ANTI-APARTHEID STRUGGLE

Between the late 1960s and the early 1980s, when the two major anti-apartheid political parties, the ANC and the Pan Africanist Congress were banned, there was no effective national movement that mounted a challenge against the apartheid regime. Such a popular national movement only came to the fore in the 1980s with the formation of the United Democratic Front (UDF).

The UDF brought together under its umbrella a coalition of civic associations, student organizations and youth congresses, women's groups, trade unions, church societies, sports clubs, and a multitude of organizations. The formation of the UDF was made possible by the emergence and proliferation of community organizations which began in the 1970s and continued throughout the 1980s.[23] The first wave of township resistance after the 1976 uprising was caused by the decision by the state to introduce community councils in 1977.[24] The main cause of popular resentment against these community councils was the fact that because the state wanted to make these councils self-financing, the major source of revenue for the community councils was rent and service charges.[25] Community organizations mobilized communities in resistance, employing a wide variety of tactics including electoral boycotts, calls on councillors to resign, and physical attacks on some councillors or their property.[26]

Most of these organizations mobilized locally around single issues and in relative isolation from each other. The effect of this was that they were not

---

21 McKinley, op. cit., n. 9, pp. 183–4. Also, see K. Johnson, 'State and Civil Society in Contemporary South Africa: Redefining the Rules of the Game' in *Thabo Mbeki's World: The Politics and Ideology of the South African President*, eds. S. Jacobs and R. Calland (2002) 221–41, at 222.

22 See R. Ballard, A. Habib, and I. Valodia, 'Conclusion: Making Sense of Post-Apartheid South Africa's Voices of Protest' in *Voices of Protest: Social Movements in Post-Apartheid South Africa*, eds. R. Ballard, A. Habib, and I. Valodia (2006) 397–417, at 415.

23 For a detailed history of the emergence and proliferation of these organizations, see A. Marx, *Lessons of Struggle: South African Internal Opposition, 1960–1990* (1990) and M. Mayekiso, *Township Politics: Civic Struggles for a New South Africa* (1996). Also, see G. Houston, *The National Liberation Struggle in South Africa: A Case Study of the United Democratic Front, 1983–1987* (1999) 37–57.

24 Houston, id., p. 46.

25 id.

26 id.

able to keep their members actively engaged in collective action, let alone link up their struggles with other organizations in order to mount a decisive challenge against the entire system that oppressed and exploited them. It was only with the formation of the UDF that isolated struggles could be linked together and directed against the apartheid juggernaut. Popular struggles, which were both national and local, were soon extended to resist state reform initiatives, to fight against hikes in rent and service charges, bus-fare increases and food prices, forced removals, and incorporation into the homelands.[27]

The inaugural conference of the UDF in August 1983 brought together 565 organizations with a total membership of 1.65 million.[28] The creation of the UDF brought together a range of independent organizations of differing class origins and with differing political and ideological agendas. The main thing that brought these organizations together was that they had a common enemy: the apartheid system of exploitation and domination.[29] The opposition that emerged under the banner of the UDF was therefore shaped more by pragmatic efforts than by ideology.[30] Guidelines that were drawn up at a conference that called for the establishment of a 'united front' against the apartheid regime included dedication to the '"creation of a non-racial, unitary state, undiluted by racial or ethnic considerations as formulated in the bantustan policy", the adoption of a non-racial form of organization, and the need to consult with "all democratic people wherever they may be".'[31]

With the formation of the UDF, struggles over grassroots issues were combined with those that amounted to direct challenge against apartheid state power. The leaders of the UDF obtained momentum for action from below, where the people were themselves politicized and mobilized.[32]Although the prevailing view when it was formed was that the UDF would just coordinate

---

27 id., p. 48.
28 id., p. 56.
29 id., p. 5.
30 See Marx, op. cit., n. 23, pp. 106–46.
31 Houston, op. cit., n. 23, p. 63.
32 Murphy Morobe, then acting publicity secretary of the UDF, explained what the Freedom Charter catchphrase 'The People Shall Govern' meant for the UDF:
> When we say that the people shall govern, we mean at all levels and in all spheres, and we demand that there be a real, effective control on a daily basis ... The key to a democratic system lies in being able to say that the people in our country can not only vote for a representative of their choice, but also feel that they have some direct control over where and how they live, eat, sleep, work, how they get to work, how they and their children are educated, what the content of that education is; and that these things are not done for them by the government of the day, but [by] the people themselves.

See M. Morobe, 'Towards a People's Democracy: the UDF View' (1987) 40 *Rev. of African Political Economy* 81–7, quoted in M. Neocosmos, 'Intellectual Debates and Popular Struggles in Transitional South Africa: Political Discourse and the Origins of Statism' (1999) Seminar Paper, Centre for African Studies UCT.

opposition to government reform, by the mid-1980s, the role of the UDF included the coordination of resistance to apartheid and thus around 1987, the UDF is said to have claimed a prime role for itself in the struggle for liberation: 'that of organising the masses of people in an unstoppable tide towards liberation.'[33]

If we accept the definition that says that social movements could be seen as collective enterprises that have their inception in conditions of unrest and seek to create a new order of life, it is clear that the UDF was a social movement. Although the UDF was formed as a response to fake state reforms and thus engaged in 'reactive' politics, it later metamorphosed into a movement that focused on the total liberation of South Africans.

Houston has therefore argued that the UDF strategies conformed to three of Antonio Gramsci's central requirements for a revolutionary movement in its struggle for hegemony:

> These are the need to 'begin with the concrete particulars of people's everyday lives' (which was done by focusing on rent and education issues), the need to be 'prepared to seek durable alliances that transcend a class base' (which the UDF did by gathering organizations 'under the broad Charterist rubric of non-racial democracy') and the need to 'transform the particular, often economic, demands of interests groups into a universalistic political challenge of the dominant system' (which the UDF did in its popular campaigns which 'systematically sought to unite participants in the expression of national political demands').[34]

For the purposes of this article, it is important to note that although the UDF was the coordinating body for the liberation struggle in South Africa, its expanding political and ideological leadership was made possible by its affiliates such as the civic associations, student and youth organizations as well as women organizations. The key roles played by these organizations were in the form of mass mobilization and the spread of revolutionary consciousness.[35] However, during the last phase of the UDF, Houston argues that state repression on the structure and activities of the UDF 'resulted in the centralisation of decision making and the transformation of the UDF into a vanguard party.'[36]

At the time when mass mobilization was happening under the umbrella of the UDF, the ANC found itself at the 'leading' position of the liberation against apartheid. This leading position:

> had come about not as a result of being at the practical forefront of the student, worker and community struggles that had erupted across the country but rather as a result of the ANC's ability to politically absorb these struggles within their broad-church strategy of the 'national democratic revolution' (NDR).[37]

33 Houston, op. cit., n. 23, p. 85.
34 id., p. 2.
35 id., p. 5.
36 id., p. 7.
37 McKinley and Veriava, op. cit., n. 17, p. 5. For an extensive treatment of these developments, see D. McKinley, *The ANC and the Liberation Struggle: A Critical Political Biography* (1997) and M. Neocosmos, 'From Peoples' Politics to State

84

The ANC's 'capture' of the UDF was made 'official' in 1987 when the UDF leadership adopted the Freedom Charter, a move 'symbolizing the centralization of the movement under its leadership and the reduced concerned for accommodating alternative views.'[38] The language that was used during the adoption of the Freedom Charter as a 'comprehensive political program' shows the lack of tolerance for ideological plurality that had up until then been the mainstay of the UDF. The leadership of the UDF then declared the UDF to be the only viable political home for those in the legal opposition movement and who stand for genuine change.[39]

The hegemony of the ANC and its allies over the national liberation struggle had devastating consequences for ideological and organizational diversity represented by grassroots organizations affiliated to the UDF. According to McKinley and Veriava:

> [b]y the time the ANC was firmly in the seat of institutional (state) power, the vast majority of those community organisations that had been so central to the radicalisation of the anti-apartheid struggle and that had sustained the hope of millions for a more radical (and potentially anti-capitalist) transformation of South African society, had been swallowed by the ANC and, to a lesser extent by its Alliance partners.[40]

This section was not an attempt to give an exhaustive history of the UDF, let alone that of the liberation struggle in South Africa. Rather, my intention here was to demonstrate the rich history of popular struggles through social movement activism in South Africa. The UDF experience has been described as an 'attempt to develop genuinely popular forms of democracy in both ideology and practice'.[41] The tactics, repertoires and orientations of the 'new' or re-emerging post-apartheid social movements display some continuities and discontinuities with these social movements. It is important to record the history of demobilization of popular organizations as it might account for the lack of popular resistance in the face of the ANC's shift to the right. It is also important to have reference to these organizations as this might go a long way in explaining the character of most post-apartheid social movements as well as providing valuable historical lessons on how to organize, how to build up counter-hegemonic discourses and power, and the need to be cautious when building alliances.

Politics: Aspects of National Liberation in South Africa' in *Opposition in Contemporary Africa*, ed. A. Olukoshi (1998) 195–240.
38 Marx, op. cit., n. 23, p. 177.
39 id.
40 McKinley and Veriava, op. cit., n. 17, p. 7.
41 Neocosmos, op. cit., n. 37, p. 206.

POST-APARTHEID 'SOCIAL MOVEMENTS':
CAUGHT BETWEEN A ROCK (STATE REPRESSION)
AND A HARD PLACE (MIDDLE-CLASS LEFTISTS)

1. *Post-apartheid 'social movements'*

According to Desai and Pithouse:

> revolts have ebbed and flowed in poor communities all over the country since 1996 ... [when] the African National Congress [ANC] became the first African government to ever voluntarily seek the help of the World Bank to design and impose a structural adjustment programme on its people.[42]

While most of these revolts have often been the result of acts of mobilization by community organizations, some of them have been uncoordinated violent revolts by poor communities against poor service delivery, cost-recovery policies in respect of basic services as well as marginalization from structures of governance. Do these community protests amount to the emergence of 'social movements'?

In its 'social movements directory', the Centre for Civil Society (CCS) – a research institution based at the University of KwaZulu-Natal, and a leader in research projects that pertain to post-apartheid social movements – lists seventeen South African organizations as 'social movements'.[43] In the preface to this directory, the constituting elements of what makes an organization or collective a social movement are not listed. As a result, the directory contains diverse organizations including NGO-type organizations like Earth Life as well as political parties such as the South African Communist Party. So what makes a social movement a 'social movement'?

Definitions for what constitutes a 'social movement' abound. Snow et al. suggest that although most definitions of social movements differ in terms of what is emphasized or accented, most are based on three or more of the following axes: 'collective or joint action; change-oriented goals or claims; some extra- or non-institutional collective action; some degree of organization; and some degree of temporal continuity.'[44] In his seminal study entitled *Power in Movement: Social Movements, Collective Action and Politics*, Sidney Tarrow defines social movements as 'collective challenges by people with common purposes and solidarity in sustained interaction with elites, opponents and authorities.'[45] From this definition, Tarrow distils the following as constituting the 'basic properties of movement': collective

---

42 Desai and Pithouse, op. cit., n. 2, p. 241.
43 See <http://ukzn.ac.za/ccs/default.asp?6,20>.
44 D. Snow, S. Soule, and H. Kriesi, 'Mapping the Terrain' in *The Blackwell Companion to Social Movements*, eds. D. Snow, S. Soule, and H. Kriesi (2004) 3–6, at 6.
45 S. Tarrow, *Power in Movement: Social Movements, Collective Action and Politics* (1994) 3–4.

86

challenge, common purpose, solidarity, and sustained interaction.[46] From the above outline, it should be clear that social movements come in all shapes and sizes and with varying agendas.

In a conclusion to a collection entitled *Voices of Protest: Social Movements in Post-Apartheid South Africa*, Ballard et al. have proposed a typology to show the heterogeneity that is found in the social movements' landscape in South Africa.[47] This typology is based on what social movements in South Africa are opposing.[48] The first set of social movements are said to be those which direct much of their activism against government on distributional issues especially with regard to access to basic services by poor South Africans.[49] These organizations perceive privatization and cost recovery policies as the key elements debilitating delivery. Some of the most prominent social movements engaged in these campaigns include the following movements:

- The Soweto Electricity Crisis Committee (SECC). This organization campaigns for the provision of affordable, or where possible, free electricity to the poor residents of Soweto township. The most commonly used tactic by the SECC is the illegal reconnection of electricity supply that has been cut-off; [50] and

- The Anti-Privatisation Forum (APF): the APF is an umbrella body made up of organizations and activists who share an anti-privatization agenda. Some of the key issues that have been undertaken by the APF include electricity cut-offs, evictions, and support for workers' struggles against the privatization of Johannesburg and the University of Witwatersrand.[51]

The second set of organizations are said to be ones that 'oppose the state, banks and private landlords through opposition to evictions and attempts to secure land tenure'.[52] Some of the most prominent organizations in this regard include the following:

- The Landless People's Movement (LPM): the LPM is a national movement of landless people dissatisfied with the slow pace of the government land reform programme. Besides engaging in protest marches to highlight issues facing landless people, the LPM has also engaged in campaigns urging its members not to vote and have also threatened to occupy vacant land.[53]

---

46 id., pp. 4–6.
47 Ballard, Habib, and Valodia, op. cit., n. 22, p. 399.
48 id.
49 id., p. 399.
50 For a detailed study of the SECC, see A. Egan and A. Wafer, 'Dynamics of a "Mini-Mass Movement": Origins, Identity and Ideological Pluralism in the Soweto Electricity Crisis Committee', id., pp. 45–65.
51 See 'About the APF' at <http://www.apf.org.za/article.php3?id_article=2>. For more on the APF, see S. Buhlungu, 'Upstarts or Bearers of Tradition? The Anti-Privatisation Forum of Gauteng', in Ballard, Habib, and Valodia, id., pp. 67–87.
52 id., p. 399.
53 See S. Greenberg, 'The Landless People's Movement and the Failure of the Post-Apartheid Reform', id., pp. 133–53.

87

- The Western Cape Anti-Eviction Campaign (AEC): the AEC is an umbrella movement that consists of various community organizations from poor, marginalized areas in Cape Town. These community organizations are said to 'share threats and experiences of evictions and water disconnections, discontent with state policies of cost recovery on public services, and dissatisfaction with local political representation'.[54]

The third set of social movements that Ballard et al point out are unions that oppose government policy on employment conditions as well as the labour practices of business.[55] These would include most of the labour unions that are affiliated to the Congress of South African Trade Unions (COSATU) as well as COSATU itself which, although is part of the Tripartite Alliance led by the ANC, has nevertheless continued to engage in adversarial mass action and other protest actions.[56] The fourth set of social movements outlined by Ballard et al. consists of those who advocate around issues of pollution and degradation of the environment.[57] A very active umbrella organization here is the Environmental Justice Networking Forum (EJNF). This movement describes itself as a:

> democratic network, a shared resource, a forum which seeks to advance the interrelatedness of social, economic, environmental and political issues to reverse and prevent environmental injustices affecting the poor and the working class.[58]

Fourthly, Ballard et al. identifies those organizations that campaign for the right of vulnerable groups in society such as refugees and sexual minorities by seeking to influence government policy.[59] The last category is identified as those movements, notably Jubilee South Africa (JSA), that campaign against multinational corporations in relation to debt incurred during apartheid, or in terms of claiming reparations from multinational corporations that operated in South Africa during apartheid.[60] From the brief outline above it should be clear that post-apartheid South Africa is inhabited by a wide variety of 'social movements'.

The 'political opportunity structures'[61] that gave rise to post-apartheid social movements are first, the political openings made possible by

---

54 See S. Oldfield and K. Stokke, 'Building Unity in Diversity: Social Movement Activism in the Western Cape Anti-Eviction Campaign', id., pp. 111–32, at p. 111.
55 See id., p. 399.
56 id.
57 id.
58 See J. Cock, 'Connecting the Red, Brown and Green: The Environmental Justice Movement in South Africa', id., pp. 203–24, at p. 207.
59 id., p. 399.
60 id.
61 Tarrow defines 'political opportunity structure' as 'consistent – but not necessarily formal, permanent or national – dimensions of the political environment which either encourage or discourage people from using collective action', see Tarrow, op. cit., n. 45, p. 18.

democratization, and secondly, the adoption of GEAR which has led to social dislocation and hardships as well as the state's lack of responsiveness to the plight of the poor.[62] Put differently, the re-emergence of social movements is due to the fact 'the poor are progressively squeezed between state repression and the commodification of the basic means of life.'[63]

As can be expected in such a diverse setting, relations amongst various social movements are sometimes beset by a lot of tension. One reason that may account for this tension is the fact that unlike their anti-apartheid counterparts, post-apartheid social movements do not collectively share a common counter-hegemonic political project. From the above typology of social movements, Ballard et al. submit that the political projects of post-apartheid social movements can be taken in one of two directions: rights-based opposition and counter opposition. In the former position, 'rights-based opposition attempts to hold the government to constitutionally enshrined rights within the current liberal order',[64] whereby the problem is understood to be one of 'deficient policy or its compromised implementation'.[65] On the other hand, those social movements that see themselves as articulating a counter-hegemonic project suggest that they draw from 'class-based ideologies with notable self-descriptions such as: anti-neoliberal, anti-capital, anti-Gear, anti-globalisation, anti-market, socialist and Trotskyist.'[66] Movements represented in this school of thought include the ones that fall under the first set of social movements in the typology above. Although these movements campaign on the basis of single-issues, Ballard et al. point out that 'they can become vehicles for articulating broader challenges against the state's economic path and have, at times supported the need for a socialist alternative.'[67] These movements see themselves as constituting the '"real" social movements of the country in contrast to more collaborationist and reformist organizations'.[68]

The way in which an organization sees itself obviously influences the choice of tactics it uses. Tactics and strategies employed by post-apartheid social movements could be said to run along a continuum with one end being more 'in-system' tactics and, on the other extreme, more extra-institutional actions. However, as Ballard et al. point out the distinction between movements that practice in-system tactics and those that undertake extra-institutional action cannot be drawn simply because:

---

62 See M. Mbali, 'TAC in the History of Patient-Driven AIDS Activism: The case for Historizing South Africa's New Social Movements' in Gibson, op. cit., n. 19, pp. 129–55, at p. 131. For a contrary view see Mbali, id.
63 Desai and Pithouse, op. cit., n. 2, p. 21.
64 Ballard, Habib and Valodia, op. cit., n. 22, at p. 400.
65 id.
66 id.
67 id.
68 id., p. 401.

in their efforts to avoid collaboration, movements that frame their operations in explicitly counter-hegemonic terms would adopt a mix of strategies, but in-system strategies would often be used as a supplement to more extra-institutional action. Conversely, movements with an explicit rights-based agenda would be at the in-system pole of the continuum, practicing a mix of strategies with extra-institutional action often used to supplement in-system strategies. [69]

Examples here would be a movement like the Treatment Action Campaign (TAC) which has successfully used the courts to force the government to offer treatment to HIV-infected people. However, in instances where the government is perceived to be slow in implementing court orders, the TAC has engaged in civil disobedience campaigns. Conversely, Jubilee South Africa, an organization that mainly engages with the state and multi-national companies in very adversarial terms, also supports the international reparations lawsuit that has been instituted in New York by Khulumani Support Group. Of course, strategies of contention also depend on how other actors react to forms of innovation and mobilization undertaken by adversaries and allies. Koopmans has thus convincingly demonstrated that:

> selection of contentious innovations takes the form of strategic decision-making by individual contenders, either in the form of anticipation of other's reactions, or by way of a process of adaptation in which previously unsuccessful strategic models are abandoned, and successful ones are retained. [70]

Response by the state to agitation by social movements has varied. In most instances, various organs of state have responded by criminalizing[71]

---

69 id., p. 407.
70 R. Koopmans, 'Protest in Time and Space: The Evolution of Waves of Contention' in Snow, Soule, and Kriesi, op. cit., n. 44, pp. 19–46, at p. 41.
71 See, in general, McKinley and Veriava, op. cit., n. 17; Desai and Pithouse, op. cit., n. 2 as well as Mzi Memeza, *A Critical Review of the Implementation of the Regulation of Gatherings Act 205 of 1993: A Local Government and Civil Society Perspective*, at <http://www.fxi.org.za>. The view that the state is engaged in systematic harassment and repression of social movements, is quite pervasive among social movements organizations. In August 2002, a week before the World Summit on Sustainable Development, the Social Movements Indaba (SMI) organized a march dubbed a 'freedom of expression march' to highlight issues of harassment and imprisonment of social movement activists. This march was violently disrupted by members of the South African Police Services. The SMI reacted by releasing a press release that made the connection between the horrors of apartheid-era repression and repression allegedly carried out by the post-apartheid government. In part, the press release said the following:
The events of this evening are only further confirmation of the ever-narrowing space in the 'new' South Africa, for the exercise of constitutional and human rights to freedom of expression and assembly. If it was not before, it should now be crystal clear that the South African government is hell-bent on smashing legitimate dissent by whatever means they deem appropriate, including peaceful marchers and terrorising children. The ghosts of the South African past are returning with a vengeance.
Cited in McKinley and Veriava, id., pp. 43–4.

90

and marginalizing[72] the various movements and imposing harsh restrictions on them. In some cases the state has only made strategic and temporary concessions. These are usually granted just before elections. However, overwhelmingly, the state has been careful not to make concessions that could amount to it being perceived as moving away from its commitment to neoliberalism.

2. Post-apartheid 'social movements', democracy, and development

If we agree with McKinley's submission that:

> it is the ANC that has now become the standard-bearer of liberal democracy in South Africa [and that] [t]his has happened despite the ANC's long history of association with more radical notions of mass participatory and non-capitalist democracy ...[73]

what can social movements do to reverse this? In their study of the impact of community organizations that have risen to challenge government on lack of basic services, Desai and Pithouse proclaim that 'it is in organizations like these that our nation has come alive and it is here that the real fight to defend and deepen our democracy is being fought'.[74]

Neocosmos is however more circumspect and warns against an uncritical enthusiasm for social movements because:

> an organization cannot be said to be either democratic or progressive (despite the possible justice of its demands) just because it is opposed to the state. Its politics may simply be concerned with incorporation into the existing system, and/or with providing a simple mirror image of state politics, and not with transformation in a popular democratic direction.[75]

In the absence of a strong political party to the left of the ANC, social movements represent an avenue for channelling the interests of the poor and putting their agenda on the national psyche. Post-apartheid social movements thus add a welcomed political plurality to South Africa's political landscape. As Barchiesi so convincingly argues:

> [t]he growth and transformation of social movement politics in South Africa over the past few years have not only redefined the terrain of contestation over communities' solidarity, identity and loyalty. In a more far-reaching way, social movements have grown into a potent and decisive force in shaping the political agenda and strategies of the state, showing cracks, lines of fissure and

---

72 This mainly consists of acts of intimidation and vilification of movements as 'ultra-leftists', 'counter-revolutionary', and 'enemies of the people'. The general tone of an article by Michael Sachs, a key ANC strategist, exemplifies this approach. See M. Sachs '"We don't Want the Fucking Vote": Social Movements and Demagogues in South Africa's Young Democracy' (2003) 27 *Labour Bull.* 23–7.

73 McKinley, op. cit., n. 9, pp. 183–4.

74 Desai and Pithouse, op. cit., n. 2, p. 24.

75 M. Neocosmos, 'The State of the Post-apartheid State: The Poverty of Critique on the South African Left' (2004) 23 *Politeia* 137–57, at 151.

91

potential basis of anti-systemic support in what, on the surface, seems an almost monolithic political mandate for the ruling party.[76]

In an assessment of the impact of post-apartheid social movements, Oldfield and Stokke take as their point of departure that 'in simplified terms, the South African political field is marked by a competition over the right to be the legitimate representatives of poor people in struggle'.[77] They then argue that 'whereas the government alliance relies on extensive objectified political capital, the power of movements ... originates in their ability to mobilise communities for public acts of resistance';[78] and further that 'this symbolic capital holds the potential of being transformed into institutionalised political power through political negotiations or future electoral contestation.'[79] This 'symbolic capital' should not however be overestimated. The fact is that most of the members of these organizations still have some affinity to the ANC. Further, as Friedman and Mottiar warn, 'the legitimacy of the government and the popularity of the ruling party are also new realities which activists tackling the government policy forget at their own peril.'[80] In fact, in every instance when these social movements have fielded independent candidates in local elections, they have fared very badly.

From the section preceding this one, it is clear that struggles of poor communities that make up post-apartheid social movements respond largely to the impact of poverty and marginalization. Their struggles are often localized and issue-based. Desai and Pithouse bring this point to the fore by pointing out that:

> it must be remembered that people are fighting militant struggles to keep themselves in apartheid's satanic ghettoes ... The community movements respond to attempts to evict people from their homes or to exclude them from water, electricity and education with actions designed to prevent and reverse dispossession. Their actions are largely defensive and reactive. Generally, they are periodic mobilizations around single issues that do not develop into an ongoing mass-based confrontation with the ANC's neo-liberal juggernaut. The lack of resources and the ANC's ability to enforce repression and make strategic concessions all feed into the inability to sustain mobilization.[81]

As we have seen with the practices of the community organizations affiliated to the UDF in the mid-80s, fundamental change can only come

---

76 F. Barchiesi, 'Classes, Multitudes and the Politics of Community Movements in Post-apartheid South Africa' in Gibson, op. cit., n. 17, pp. 209–42, 214–15.
77 Oldfield and Stokke, op. cit., n. 54, p. 130.
78 id.
79 id.
80 S. Friedman and S. Mottiar, 'Rewarding Engagement?: The Treatment Action Campaign and the Politics of HIV/AIDS' at <http://www.nu.ac.za/ccs/files/FRIEDMAN%20MOTTIER%20A%20MORAL%20TO%20THE%20TALE%20LONG%20VERSION.PDF>.
81 Desai and Pithouse, op. cit., n. 2, p. 260. This is the unequivocal position of Zakie Achmat, chairperson of the TAC, who asserts that: 'We want to get medicine to people – we don't want to cause a revolution'. Cited in Friedman and Mottiar, id.

about when community organizations engage in sustained collective actions that focus the struggle on wider social change and not just single issues impacting on their communities. This might involve building strategic alliances with others, and forming a 'united front' which will ensure that particularistic struggles of different communities gets coordinated at a national level. In an empirical study of social movements worldwide, Rucht demonstrates that:

> most social movements would not come into existence, let alone survive, if there was no cooperation between groups and organization that consider themselves to be parts of a broader entity. Though these components may differ considerably in size, shape, concrete aims, and preferred activities, they tend to exhibit a readiness to participate in joint activities or structures, be it at a major protest event, a loosely coordinated but temporary campaign, or permanent umbrella organization or federation.[82]

In the same vein, in their analysis of whether the TAC is a model for other social movements, Friedman and Mottiar conclude that 'the TAC experience also suggests that social movements who do not "think alliances" are likely to remain isolated and weakened.'[83] While this is clearly true, the history of the UDF also shows that, taken too far, the idea of building alliances at all cost could be detrimental to community organization and the richness of their plurality. The unification of particularistic struggles, and eventual replacement thereof, by grandiose ideas of national struggle was a factor that led to the demise of many of the UDF affiliates. Yet, it seems that this historical lesson was never learned. A number of prominent leaders of various post-apartheid social movements have recently displayed a very centralist attitude. As Greenstein points out, 'in this process, the incoherent and untidy diversity and multiplicity of social movements are overcome and superseded'.[84] How can community organizations strike a balance between the need for sustained nationally coordinated actions that would pose a challenge against the neoliberal juggernaut, whilst at the same time retaining their autonomy?

On how this balance is to be struck, Barchiesi incisively deploys Paolo Virno's concept of 'multitude',[85] to define the way in which the plurality of social experience can be a condition for progressive social movement politics. He indicates that in the politics of multitude:

> the convergence of multiple social experiences around unitary forms of political representation (as in discourses of 'class,' 'people' and 'nation') is

82 D. Rucht, 'Movement Allies, Adversaries, and Third Parties' in Snow, Soule, and Kriesi, op. cit., n. 44, pp. 197–216, at p. 203.
83 Friedman and Mottiar, op. cit., n. 80.
84 R. Greestein, 'Civil Society, Social Movements and Power in South Africa' (2003) 17, unpublished RAU Sociology seminar paper, available at <http://general.rau.ac.za/sociology/Greenstein.pdf>.
85 P. Virno, A Grammar of the Multitude (2004).

seen as the contingent and often contested product of historical circumstances, rather than as the necessary outcome or the expression of a higher, truer form of collective consciousness.[86]

Barchiesi further argues that:

> the process of social change ushered in by the politics of the multitude is non-teleological, in the sense that it does not assume pre-constituted finality and direction for change as a source to validate practices of social conflict. Rather than building a cumulative path towards social transformation, the politics of the multitude 'inhabits' events and situations, shifting power relations by acting upon a multiplicity of sites of contestation.[87]

Similarly, Greenstein argues that:

> it is the emphasis on self-organization, internal diversity and resistance to forcible unification of social movements under a universal banner, which allows elements within civil society to develop its radical potential.[88]

Just like the community organizations of the 1980s, post-apartheid community organizations are providing new spaces for popular democracy by empowering its participants to *take their lives in their hands*[89] and organizing organically. If this popular democracy is to be preserved, these community organizations must see to it that they preserve their autonomy and that their particularistic interests are not sublated by universalistic claims. As to the question of how these issue-based and particularistic struggles could still be harnessed into a force that could contest the way state power is put, Greenstein submits that this could be achieved:

> not by trying to impose unity that will meet power with counter-power, but by allowing the untidy nature of the new social movements to flourish and spread to hitherto unaffected aspects of society ... [t]he kind of politics advocated here conforms to Unger's notion of 'transformative politics', which focuses on shaping the practical and discursive routines of social life. It works towards 'empowered democracy' precisely by adopting a piecemeal and cumulative approach and eschewing grandiose revolutionary rhetoric that sounds radical but ends up achieving very little because it is removed from people's daily concerns.[90]

Another obstacle faced by social movements is one posed by middle-class left activists and academics who have been accused of having:

> systematically tried to recruit social movements' politics for the pursuit of political agendas that developed entirely above their heads: national liberation, the party of the working class, sustained development, international workshops.[91]

---

86 Barchiesi, op. cit., n. 76, p. 215.
87 id., p. 216.
88 Greestein, op. cit., n. 84, p. 16.
89 Slogan displayed at the launch of the Social Movement Indaba.
90 Greestein, op. cit., n. 84, p. 17.
91 Indymedia South Africa as cited in id., p. 14.

94

These activists and academics are also the ones engaged in the framing processes *for* some community organizations. These framing processes are meant to 'assign meaning to and interpret relevant events and conditions in ways that are intended to mobilize potential adherents and constituents, to garner support, and to demobilize antagonists.'[92] In an evocative piece, Ashwin Desai, a very prominent academic-activist, has recently argued that middle class academics and activists – 'outsiders' – are the ones who take up:

> [the] task of fashioning political meanings that flow from struggles ... It is this 'outsider' grouping who most furiously contest what particular social movements mean ideologically, technically, even cynically, among themselves. These battles sometimes play themselves out on the bodies and campaigns of social movements as various academics try to position social movements to best achieve their vision.[93]

Consider the following remarks by McKinley who portrays post-apartheid social movements as arenas of free democratic debate and participation epitomised in a 'principled internationalism, a socialist vision, and independent mass-based mobilisation and struggle as an ideological and organizational alternative to the capitalist ANC!'[94]

In conclusion, it is clear that, although the plurality and horizontality in the practices of community organizations provide space for participants to engage in popular democracy, this autonomy is threatened by vanguardists, who have appropriated for themselves the collective framing processes for these organizations. Following, Barchiesi's usage of politics of the

---

92 D. Snow and R. Benford, 'Ideology, Frame Resonance, and Participant Mobilization' (1988) 1 *International Social Movement Research* 197–217, at 198, as cited by D. Snow, 'Framing Processes, Ideology, and Discursive Fields' in Snow, Soule, and Kriesi, op. cit., n. 44, pp. 380–412, at p. 384.

93 A. Desai, 'Vans, Autos, Kombis and the Drivers of Social Movements', Harold Wolpe Memorial Lecture 28 July 2006, available at <http://www.ukzn.ac.za/ccs>.

94 D. McKinley, 'The Rise of Social Movements in South Africa' (2004) *Debate: Voices from the South African Left* 17–21, at 20, cited in Ballard, Habib, and Valodia, op. cit., n. 22, p. 398. The role of these mainly white middle-class activists has recently come under fire from a number of black activists. Thus, Andile Mngxitama, a former activist with the Landless People's Movement has complained that:

> to date, what has often happened in these social movements in South Africa is that historically dominant voices – primarily white-left intellectuals – have been the main mediators of the identity and aspirations of the poor of the country. In a sense we are witnessing the re-inscription of racial domination in the service of a 'greater good' – to hold back the tide of neo-liberal attack on black bodies.

See A. Mngxitama, 'Let Black Voices Speak for the Voiceless' *Mail and Guardian Online* 22 January 2004, available at <http://www.mg.co.za/articledirect.aspx?articleid=131236&area=%2finsight%2finsight__comment_and_analysis%2f>. See, also, M. Ndlovu, 'Social Movements, Representation and the Role of Supporters of People's Struggle' 14 September 2006, electronic paper available at <http://www.ukzn.ac.za/ccs/default.asp?2,40,5,1126> and N. Mthembu, 'The Role of White Activists in the Liberation of the Black Race', 12 September 2006, electronic paper available at <http://www.ukzn.ac.za/ccs/default.asp?2,40,5,1125>.

'multitude', it is important that community organizations engage in alliance with others without being coerced into unity, but where they converge with others, this should be based on 'commonality'. One way of achieving such commonality, whilst eschewing 'unity', is to join forces with others around specific issues and on a temporary basis. It is not a bad idea for organizations coming into an alliance to draft and agree on a Memorandum of Understanding which will specify areas of cooperation, broad tactics to be used, and who shall speak for the alliance, as well as the period of cooperation. This might go a long way in ensuring that organizational autonomy is maintained and that there is mutual accountability amongst the alliance partners.

CONCLUSION

One clear characteristic of post-apartheid South Africa is the 'stabilization of capitalist relations'.[95] To be sure, Szeftel[96] has argued that the ANC had three options when it took over state power. The first option would have been to embark 'on what we might term a "revolutionary path" in which the commanding heights of the economy were expropriated by government and land and other resources redistributed by compulsion'.[97] The second option, which Szeftel terms the 'radical reforming path', entailed a scenario 'in which liberal democratic political institutions would have been combined with high taxes, high spending on public projects and social investment as well as some nationalization'.[98] A third option, the 'neo-liberal path,' 'would emphasise the expanding links with the global economy, improving human capital and making the economy more internationally competitive by emphasizing growth and monetarist orthodoxy in fiscal policy'.[99] Szeftel correctly concludes that 'in the years since the 1994 elections, the South African government moved progressively away from the second option towards the third'.[100]

The result of this choice is a transition which Bond has described as follows:

> it is abundantly clear that the [South African] society suffered the replacement of racial apartheid with what can be accurately considered to be class apartheid: systemic underdevelopment and segregation of the oppressed majority, through structured economic, political, environmental, legal,

95 Saul, op. cit., n. 17.
96 M. Szeftel 'Two Cheers? South African Democracy's First Decade' (2004) 31 *Rev. of African Political Economy* 193-202, at 194–5.
97 id., at p. 194.
98 id.
99 id., at p. 195.
100 id.

96

medical, and cultural practices largely organised or codified by Pretoria politicians and bureaucrats.[101]

In this article, I evaluated the prospects of post-apartheid 'social movements' in mounting a serious challenge against the South African state's embracing of neoliberalism. The ANC government's turn towards neoliberalism has not only left the legacy of massive inequalities and structural poverty inherited from apartheid, but has actually exacerbated them. The turn to neoliberalism has also been accompanied by intolerance of dissent on macroeconomic policies as well as the conception of development as a top-down process. A minimalist conception of democracy had meant that democracy has become meaningless for the millions of 'poor' and unemployed who have been marginalized and disempowered.

Largely due to the neoliberal assault visited on poor communities, these communities have started organizing themselves to demand affordable basic services and an inclusion in decision-making. Because they are often organized organically, these 'social movements' have ensured a degree of popular democracy for their members. In order to mount a powerful resistance against the macro-economic policies of the state and their exclusion from governance, there is a need for these 'social movements' to come together with others, to come up and fight for counterhegemonic discourses that would provide alternatives to liberal capitalism. In joining with others, they need to remember the lessons that were taught by community organizations that were affiliated to the UDF, whose particularistic interests were sublated into the universal – a move which eventually led to their demise. Building strategic alliances is encouraged but it should only take place under conditions that eschew vanguardism and unity for 'commonality' as described by Greenstein and Barchiesi above.

Although the contribution of middle-class activists can be very useful to poor communities as they bring with them resources, useful contacts, and solidarity, the terms of engagements with community organizations needs to be reassessed. Similarly, academics and others reporting on social movements need to be honest about the faults and limitations of community organizations with regard to the possibilities of expanding the democratic space and influencing the state to turn away from its neoliberal policies. In his latest reflection on the role of intellectuals in the struggles of social movements, Desai decries what he sees as a dangerous and patronizing trend amongst those who report on social movements but turn a blind eye to their faults. He explains:

> the most alarming feature of the current, general mode of reporting on social movements is that it is often overblown, romanticized and, in many cases, just plain made up ... the epitome of this mode of thinking is the facile axiom that the poor, somehow are an embodiment of the truth and, as long as they

---

101 P. Bond, 'Ten Years of Democracy: A Review' in *Articulations: A Harold Wolpe Memorial Lecture Collection*, ed. A. Alexander (2006) 37.

97

organise democratically, the line of march they take will advance the cause of freedom ... It is simply nonsense to talk them up as the next revolutionary subject ...[102]

It is only by dealing with these community organizations honestly and respectfully that we can help them obtain their immediate needs, whilst at the same time ensuring that they survive. Any hope for a more popular democracy as well as a move towards a more human-centred development depends on the survival and flourishing of these social movements.

102 Desai, op. cit., n. 93.

JOURNAL OF LAW AND SOCIETY
VOLUME 34, NUMBER 1, MARCH 2007
ISSN: 0263-323X, pp. 99–115

The Violence of Non-Violence: Law and War in Iraq

Samera Esmeir*

The article examines the relation between war making in Iraq and juridical reforms aimed at instituting democracy, or what the article coins juridico-democracy. It is argued that a certain aspiration for global peace, global security, and non-violence to be instituted by juridico-democracy accompanies the war against Iraq. Rather than leave this aspiration intact, the article examines the extent to which this aspiration itself is conducive to the war's violence. The associations between violence and non-violence, war and peace, conflict and security are examined not as oppositions, but as cycles, where non-violence, peace, and security are performative of more violence.

We enter the twenty-first century witnessing a renewed coupling of the violence of wars and projects of democracy-promotion. Afghanistan, Iraq, and Lebanon are our most recent wars. The violence of these wars has been mobilized to fight other violence, which war-makers argue constitutes 'terror', making theirs a 'war on terror'. Simultaneously, as the twenty-first century commences, and alongside the violence-ending wars, our world is announcing ever more loudly the promise of different juridical projects – rule of law, separation of powers, human rights, and constitutions – charting our delivery from the suffering generated by violence to the non-violence, peace, and security promised by democracy. This is a perplexing joint entry of two seemingly oppositional political formations: war and democracy. To be sure, this joint entry is diachronic, not necessarily synchronic, in that the agents of democracy do not necessarily proceed following the agents of war. And yet, unless one declares the hypocrisy of democracy and dismisses it as a justification for the war machine, the question remains as to the renewed encounter between war and democracy, between violent and non-violent political formations.

* *Department of Rhetoric, 7408 Dwinelle Hall, University of California, Berkeley, CA 94720-2670, United States of America*
samera.esmeir@berkeley.edu
I wish to thank Michael Allen, Robert Avila, Stewart Motha, Stefania Pandolfo, and the two anonymous reviewers for their comments and suggestions.

The joint entry of war and democracy manifests itself most clearly in contemporary Iraq. The war waged against Iraq by a coalition of states led by the United States of America and Great Britain in March 2003 was accompanied by juridical projects aimed at establishing the rule of law, the drafting of a constitution, and the protection of human rights. As the war was being fought, engendering its own forms of violence, preparations for a democratic transition were underway to rid Iraq of its previous murderous regime and to install, instead, a democratic one. Already in January 2003, the Office of Reconstruction and Humanitarian Assistance (ORHA) was established by the American Secretary of Defense to prepare 'for the coordinated, balanced progress of economic and security reconstruction in a post-conflict Iraq'.[1] Noah Feldman, an American law professor, would join the 'reconstruction efforts' in April 2003 to become the advisor on the Iraqi constitutional process.[2] An army of juridical actors consisting of lawyers, non-governmental organizations, international institutions, and national justice ministries was deployed to Iraq, in the midst of the war, to assist in the enterprise of substituting a regime of democracy, non-violence, peace, and security for Saddam Hussein's regime of despotism, violence, and death.

What does the joint entry of the violence of wars with the juridical track to democratic non-violence signal to us? Does the entry index a relation of opposition between the violence of wars and the instantiation of democratic government? How do we make sense of juridical democratic projects taking place in Iraq in the midst of a war? What do we make of the mounting violence coinciding with the rising aid to 'nation-building' and to 'democratization' projects in Iraq? Can we announce a contradiction between the violence of the war, on the one hand, and reforms aimed at establishing the rule of law and the protection of human rights, on the other? Could it be that the latter are only justifications for the former? Or might it be, as I suggest in what follows, that another relation between the two sides is operative, one revealed only once we consider war's non-violence, war's aspiration for peace, or war's democratic ends?

To answer these questions, the article focuses on the dynamics of war in Iraq in relation to the first phase of the occupation, a phase that ended with the drafting of the Iraqi constitution. Specifically, the article examines the period between 2003 and 2005 when the occupying power and other juridical actors carried out juridical projects aimed at preparing the ground for the transfer of a 'limited sovereignty' to a democratic Iraqi government. I investigate the violence of the war in light of what I define as *juridico-democracy*, that is, the specific form of democracy I find operative in reforming Iraq during this period.

---

1 See statement by Douglas J. Feith, Under Secretary of Defense for Policy to the Senate Committee on Foreign Relations: <http://www.dod.mil/policy/speech/feb_11_03.html>.
2 For Feldman's understanding of his work in Iraq, see, N. Feldman, *What we Owe Iraq: War and the Ethics of Nation-Building* (2004).

Juridico-democracy, in my analysis, names a recent enterprise of the post-Cold War era where sites of 'transitions to democracy' have become zones of interventions, wherein the juridical is the main agent of the 'transition' not only to democracy but also to global peace and security. Juridico-democracy, I suggest, is not concerned with the cultivation of democratic political subjects as citizens, nor is it interested in maintaining democratic conflict and tension. Juridico-democracy in the post-Cold War era is, rather, focused on building nation-state institutions, in particular, security institutions, that would contribute to 'global peace' while eradicating conflict, disobedience, and resistance to the dictates of global peace. Under juridico-democracy, juridical formations commonly associated with liberal democracy – such as the rule of law, human rights, and constitutions – are folded into the security apparatus of the state.

To be sure, juridico-democracy does not promise to be, itself, purely non-violent. It punishes, employs measures of pain, and wages outright wars when necessary. But juridico-democracy also declares the confinement of its violence to the sphere of means employed to the end of eradicating all other violence threatening security.[3] It promises an endpoint of non-violence alongside its own *instrumentalized* violence, and proposes itself as an alternative to other non-juridical formations of violence that themselves anticipate nothing but further violence.[4] Moreover, the violence of juridico-democracy not only maintains the law and protects it, but also at once grounds and reconstitutes it.[5] That is to say, instrumentalized violence is not deployed to a fixed end (juridico-democracy) existing prior to violence. Rather, this end is constantly reconstituted by violence's protective operations, leading instrumentalized violence to work towards an end that has no termination point. It is due to this absence of a fixed means/ends relation that I call this violence 'instrumentalized', rather than 'instrumental'.

The recognition that juridico-democracy evinces its own violence in its theories and practice makes the critical recovery of the violence intrinsic to juridico-democracy unremarkable.[6] Therefore, in examining the relation of the violence of the Iraq war to juridico-democratic projects, I do not aim to

3 I make this argument about juridico-democracy's violence while following Walter Benjamin's critique of legal coercion. See W. Benjamin, 'Critique of Violence' in *Reflections*, (1978) tr. E. Jephcott, 277–300.
4 Peter Fitzpatrick, in an essay on violence and the law, argues for the significance of accounting for law's non-violence. Law must encompass and yet be 'in between' the violent particularity of action and the nonviolent infinite responsiveness of interpretation. See P. Fitzpatrick, 'Why the Law is Also Nonviolent' in *Law, Violence, and the Possibility of Justice*, ed. A. Sarat (2001) 142–74.
5 J. Derrida, 'The Force of Law: The "Mystical Foundation of Authority"' in *Acts of Religion* (2002).
6 Marianne Constable makes a similar argument in her reading of Robert Cover's examination of law *as* violence. See M. Constable, 'The Silence of the Law: Justice in Cover's Field of Pain and Death' in Sarat, op. cit., n. 4, pp. 85–101.

101

show that the joint entry of wars and juridico-democracy reveals itself in the violence they both share. I am less interested in arguing that juridico-democracy always contains its own violence, whether in its moment of origin, in the exceptions it provides for, or in the wars of tolerance it wages.[7] In other words, what follows is not a Schmittian critique of liberal democracy that insists sovereignty, the site of possible violence not constrained by formal rules, is constitutive of the 'juridical order'.[8] Rather, and without necessarily contradicting this Schmittian line of inquiry, my interest is in the non-violent components of juridico-democracy, its promise of security and peace, and the promise's *association* with the violence of war. I suggest that perhaps, faced with the declared violence of juridico-democracy, we might want to interrogate its more celebrated and less criticized promise of non-violence in relation to the violence of war.

My argument throughout is the following: a certain aspiration for global peace, global security, and non-violence to be instituted by juridico-democracy *accompanies* the war against Iraq. Rather than leave this aspiration intact, or else declare its hypocrisy or fallaciousness, I propose to interrogate the extent to which this aspiration itself is conducive to the war's violence. I wonder about the amount of violence needed if one is to achieve a non-violent end, a world of peace and security on a so-called global scale, where all violence, tension, and conflict are eradicated. I propose to begin an initial interrogation, therefore, of the associations between violence and non-violence, war and peace, conflict and security not as oppositions, but as *cycles*, where non-violence, peace, and security are performative of more violence.

In advancing this argument, I suggest not only thinking beyond the violence/non-violence distinction, but thinking this 'beyond' in a *reversed order*. It is not sufficient to locate traces of violence in non-violence, exceptions in the juridical, wars in democracy. If we do only this, we risk overlooking the extent to which the operations of global non-violence, security, and peace are themselves productive of their own violence, needed in order to bring about the global state of non-violence. We also confine our critique to violence while imagining a sphere of non-violence always yet to be and, thus, forever beyond our criticism. I, therefore, inquire into the power operations of jurido-democracy's promise of non-violence and whether it is conducive to the violence of war.

How is it possible to prove this cycle? Before laying out the structure of this paper, I should note that no empirical causal relation can be found between juridico-democracy and its end of non-violence, global peace, and security, on the one hand, and the violence of the war, on the other. Moreover, many other factors contribute to the violence of war, including the

---

7 See, for example, A. Sarat and T. Kearns (eds.), *Law's Violence* (1995).
8 See C. Schmitt, *Political Theology: Four Chapters on the Concept of Sovereignty* (1985) tr. George Schwab.

structure of the Ba'ath regime and the sectarianism unleashed by the war. This paper does not look to collapse all the violence of the war in juridico-democracy and its promise of non-violence. Rather, the attempt is both more modest and more tentative: to implicate the non-violence of juridico-democracy in the project of war not as an explanatory cause, but as an operative ideal. Because it can never be attained, it inspires more violence, including the violence of war.

It should also be noted, finally, that juridico-democracy and its associated end of non-violence are not the operative aspirations of war-makers only. Even if one is to reject the democracy rhetoric of the US administration, it is necessary to investigate the entire juridico-democratic industry operating in Iraq, most of which is not directly linked to the US administration. The administration's rhetoric, its institutional reflection as well as the practices of other juridico-democratic agents are all productive of a certain aspiration of non-violence that feeds into the violence of the war itself in its paradoxical ambition to rid Iraq of all violence.

The first section below inquires into the distinctiveness of the violence of the war against Iraq, developing the argument that the war's aspiration for peace, which in Iraq's case means the imposition of a juridico-democratic regime, is partially constitutive of the war's violence. The second section helps ground this theoretical argument by focusing on the specific institutional dimensions of juridico-democracy. The third section argues against much of the literature on law and war explaining the former as either facilitating or constraining the latter. Instead, I suggest that the war against Iraq was carried out *for* the law, the specific law of juridico-democracy. This section also addresses other practices of juridico-democracy not directly initiated by the war-makers. The fourth section discusses some connections between rule of law and human rights, on the one hand, and the global security project on the other. I argue that these two are not opposites but part of the same juridico-democratic project with its aspiration to kill insecurity for security, to defeat violence for peace. In the same section, I also examine how the logic of fighting violence and aspiring to its eradication, is constitutive of the Iraqi constitution.

WAR'S VIOLENCE AND PEACE

The productive power of the Iraq war, its promise of peace and juridico-democracy, should guide our inquiry into the violence of the war. Because this promise does not fully determine the violence of the war or cause it but, rather, only contributes to it, we might want to ask in what ways the project of juridico-democracy has unleashed specific formations of violence. This examination of peace and democracy as partially constitutive of the violence of the 2003 war departs from other possible interrogations revealing the particularities of this war in terms of the suffering it inflicted, the deaths it

103

caused, or the destruction it wreaked. This departure is necessitated partly by the fact that other formations of violence in Iraq were similarly cruel and destructive. For example, the 1990 war against Iraq, led by the United States and mandated by the United Nations, entailed significant destruction. During the war, more than one thousand sorties were launched per day; the air campaign against Iraq included 'smart bombs', cluster bombs, 'Daisy Cutters', and cruise missiles. The targets in Iraq included military facilities as well as civil facilities considered to have a military use, so that by the end of the war in 1991 Iraq's civilian infrastructure was completely destroyed.[9]

The widespread destruction brought by economic sanctions was similarly cruel. Authorized by United Nations Security Council Resolution 661 in 1990, the sanctions were maintained after the war.[10] Whereas their original purpose was to drive the Iraqi army out of Kuwait, after the war the sanctions regime was used to force Iraq to destroy its stockpile of weapons of mass destruction, and its capacity to produce them. Resolution 661 placed a blanket ban on all imports and exports excluding 'supplies intended strictly for medical purposes and, in humanitarian circumstances, foodstuffs'.[11] But because over 90 per cent of Iraq's hard currency income was cut following the ban on oil sales and the freezing of foreign assets, the purchase of such supplies and foodstuffs from abroad remained at best a theoretical possibility.[12] Numerous studies by the United Nations and NGOs during the sanctions period documented dramatic increases in malnutrition and disease, leading to the deaths of hundreds of thousands of children under the age of five since 1991.[13] The Oil-for-Food Programme established in accordance with Security Council Resolution 986 of 1995 encouraged the same short-term responses that have characterized international programmes in Iraq since 1991. It proved incapable of addressing the long-term crisis of poverty, lowered health and education standards, and infrastructural collapse.[14]

Given the steady empirical rise of cruelty, destruction, violence and suffering in Iraq, what can be said to be different about the 2003 war? The 2003 war, I argue, was uniquely (in the recent history of Iraq) productive of pacifying violence. The violence of the Ba'th regime, the oppression it

9 For the estimate of the amount needed to rebuild Iraq in order to prevent the unfolding of a humanitarian crisis in the aftermath of the 1991 war, see: *Report to the Secretary-General on the Humanitarian Needs in Iraq by a Mission led by Sadruddin Aga Khan*, UN Doc. S/22799 (1991).

10 UN Security Council, Resolution 661 (6 August 1990). The Resolution was passed in response to Iraq's invasion of Kuwait.

11 id., para. 6c.

12 See R. Normand, 'Iraqi Sanctions, Human Rights and Humanitarian Law' in *Middle East Report: Power and Politics of Difference*, July–September 1996, no. 200, 40–3, 46.

13 Food and Agriculture Organization of the United Nations, *Technical Cooperation Programme: Evaluation of Food and Nutrition Situation in Iraq* (September 1995).

14 S. Graham-Brown, 'Sanctioning Iraq: A Failed Policy' *Middle East Report,* Summer 2000, no. 215, 8–13, 35.

104

practiced, and the structure of death it literally relied on, was to be killed and eradicated so as to carve out a space for a juridico-democracy as envisioned by the rule of law and human rights, and as the agent of global peace and security. And because the aspiration for non-violence was total, and because violence lurked in every corner, non-violence begat a cycle of more violence.

In this section I develop this argument theoretically while relying on the rhetoric of the war-makers. The following sections elaborate on institutional manifestations of the cycle of non-violence and violence engendered by juridico-democracy, as well as on the work of other agents of juridico-democracy not necessarily synchronically, but diachronically, associated with war-makers.

In developing this argument, I am guided by Carl von Clausewitz's *On War*.[15] Clausewitz offers a definition of 'the conception of war,' while emphasizing that its conceptual purity does not necessarily translate into reality every time a war is waged. For Clausewitz, war is 'nothing but a duel on an extensive scale'. It is 'an act of violence intended to compel our opponent to fulfill our will. Violence, in the framework of war is the *means*; the compulsory submission of the enemy is the ultimate *object*'. As to what constitutes the 'compulsory submission of the enemy', Clausewitz mentions three elements. First, the military power of the country must be destroyed. Second, the country must be conquered and out of the country a new military force must be formed. Third, the will of the enemy must be subdued. 'That is, its [the country's] government and its allies must be forced into signing a peace, or the people into submission'.[16] Clausewitz maintains that the third condition is of central significance, as whatever may take place after the war is over, 'we must always look upon the object as attained, and the business of war as ended, by peace'.[17]

Central to Clausewitz's analysis is the attainment of peace, however tentative, as the end of war. The enemy must not only be destroyed and subdued; the enemy must be made to live and to sign an imposed peace treaty. Most war literature repeats this concern with peace. With similar logic, Angelo Codevilla and Paul Seabury explain that the only significant question to ask about any war is 'what do we have to do to earn the peace we want'.[18] This peace, to be sure, is 'no picnic'. It is not a peace in which 'everyone lives happily ever after'. It is, rather, a peace 'under which a given people can live in a way that more or less satisfies their essential needs'.[19] And despite the fragile nature of the divide between war and peace evident in

---

15 C. von Clausewitz, *On War* (1976) tr. M. Howard and P. Paret.
16 id., pp. 25, 26.
17 id., p. 26.
18 A. Codevilla and P. Seabury, *Wars: Ends and Means* (2006, 2nd edn.) 5.
19 id., p. 15.

the many wars of the twentieth century, the distinction, the authors insist, remains central to Western politics.[20]

The end entailed by peace in both accounts is a vision of non-violence and non-war. But it is an end that feeds back into war, and becomes its new staging ground. Non-violence is turned perfomative of violence. Peace, in these accounts, is an end of a productive war, an end concerned with non-violence after violence, and with regulating this non-violence in the shadow, not in the midst, of violence. And it is this aspect of war, Clausewitz's war *par excellence*, that I argue is made visible in the 2003 war against Iraq, and with the forms of violence engendering it. If Clausewitz, however, spoke of a 'peace treaty' as an end to war, the Iraq war has its peace achieved by juridico-democracy.

The 2003 war against Iraq is said by some of those who waged it, and others who supported it, to have partly deployed violence to build a nation, to institute democracy, and to deliver Iraqis from their dehumanized past. These were the declared ends of the war that I argue became its new launching ground. To be sure, I follow the declared democracy rhetoric literally not because I do not recognize that the pursuit of economic gain is an important constitutive aspect of this war.[21] Rather, I follow the rhetoric of democracy because I argue that it needs to be interrogated on its own terms, and examine how it, itself, is productive of a certain security power field equal in its importance to the economic power field. Furthermore, these ends of democracy building need not be fully attainable, or even pursued on a daily basis, for them to chart the horizon for the war and to constitute a power field wherein the war takes place.

The theoretical formulation I am suggesting helps us understand the debates around the US government's 'failure' to draft an effective plan for what is coined 'Phase 4' of the war, that is, 'the period of conflict termination and the creation of an effective nation building office'.[22] The failure of the war's violence to fully plan for a new era, not only to destroy an old one, is thought to be the war's main shortcoming. This 'failure' is conceptualized as such precisely because the Iraq war was supposed to achieve something other than violence.

The National Security Council's 2005 report, 'National Strategy for Victory in Iraq', opens with a quote by President Bush: 'Rebuilding Iraq will require a sustained commitment from many nations, including our own: we will remain in Iraq as long as necessary, and not a day more'.[23] The report defines victory in Iraq in three stages. In the short term, 'Iraq is making

---

20 id., p. 17.
21 See, for example, R. Khalidi, *Resurrecting Empire: Western Footprints and America's Perilous Path in the Middle East* (2004).
22 Quoted in B. Hoffman, *Insurgency and Counter Insurgency* (2004) 2.
23 President George W. Bush, 26 February 2003, quoted in the National Security Council, *National Strategy for Victory in Iraq* (2005).

steady progress in fighting terrorists, meeting political milestones, building democratic institutions, and standing up security forces.' In the interim, 'Iraq is in the lead defeating terrorists and providing its own security, with a fully constitutional government in place, and on its way to achieving its economic potential.' And finally, in the long term, 'Iraq is peaceful, united, stable, and secure, well integrated into the international community, and a full partner in the global war on terrorism.'[24] This Iraq will be a democratic one, 'where Iraqis have the institutions and resources they need to govern themselves justly and provide security for their country.'[25]

The rhetoric of peace is central to the report of victory. This centrality is not a sign of logical contradictions, nor does the rhetoric of peace mask other non-peaceful ends. To follow the arguments of contradictions or rhetorical masking is to assume a priori, and against much historical evidence, that peace and war are simple oppositions. These arguments also have the effect of concealing that war and violence are the grounds from which life under peace is realized. And finally, these arguments make it impossible to interrogate, as in the case of Iraq, how the aspiration for non-violence is itself productive of a very specific kind of war that knows no end and in which definite victory can never be declared.

The argument I am developing can be also derived from Michel Foucault's arguments about war and peace. In *Society Must be Defended*, Foucault directs his critical investigations at the productive power of war.[26] Foucault argues that the confusion and noise of war, as well as its muddy battles, are the principles that explain order, institutions, and history – indeed, power relations. Foucault is careful to note this is not an ideal war, the one imagined by philosophers such as Hobbes, but real wars and actual battles. Wars continue 'to rage within the mechanisms of power at least to constitute the secret motor of institutions, laws, and order'. 'We have to rediscover the war', Foucault writes, as 'war is the cipher of peace'.[27]

In taking Foucault's argument a step further, while drawing on his insight into the productive power of war's violence, I suggest that because war has been productive of peace's power relations, then peace, too, needs to be thought of as belonging to the era before the war was waged. The productivity of war's violence articulated by Foucault compels us to incorporate the product in the process of production. This does not mean that we become theorists of order and prioritize peace over war. Rather, it means that we investigate the association between war and peace, not only in terms of the second being the product of the first, but also in the sense that the second might be the engine of the first.

---

24 id., p. 4.
25 id., p. 3.
26 M. Foucault, *Society Must be Defended: Lectures at the College de France, 1975–1976* (2003).
27 id., p. 269.

I have been suggesting that in order to understand the distinctiveness of the violence of the 2003 war, one needs to consider the aspiration for global security and non-violence that accompanied it, shaped its conditions, and made it brutal in a place where there was violence in every corner. The aspiration for global security necessitates the substituting of an entire social and political fabric – not the arrest of fifty ministers and high officials in the Ba'ath government, as the coalition forces declared when they occupied Iraq in 2003. Juridico-democracy constituted the substitute. What did the institutional configuration of juridico-democracy look like?

Citing UN Security Council Resolution 1483 (2003) and the laws of war, the Coalition Provisional Authority (CPA) vested itself with executive, legislative, and judicial authority from the period of the CPA's inception on 21 April 2003, until its dissolution on 28 June 2004. Similar to the OHRA mentioned above, one of the objectives of the CPA was to establish security:

> [S]ecuring, protecting, and preserving peace and justice for all Iraqi citizens, their property, and possessions will enable citizens to participate fully in political and economic life … In order for Iraq to make a smooth transition to sovereignty, the people of Iraq must be free from fear of terror and a return to power of Saddam Hussein loyalists. Advancing towards a secure and stable environment requires that Coalition and Iraqi partners work in close cooperation to defeat the terrorists and insurgents that seek to hijack the emerging future for Iraq …[28]

I recount this familiar history not only to point to the association characteristic of civilian/bureaucratic and military forces, but to the centrality of security to the 'sovereignty' envisioned by the CPA. Note that this security is rather particular. It is a security that means to eradicate fully the violence of the past. This security, with its totalizing aspirations, cannot be achieved without forcing Iraq to suffer endless insecurity.

Since its inception, the CPA operated in the space the war opened between the end of non-violence and the necessity of destruction. Future Iraqi governments would continue to operate in the same space. One of the first orders that Paul Bremer issued, as the second head of the CPA appointed in May 2003, was the dissolving of most state entities that were responsible for 'the repression of the Iraqi people'. The order states, among other things, that the 'prior Iraqi regime used certain government entities to oppress the Iraqi people and as instruments of torture, repression and corruption,' which were thereby declared dissolved.[29]

---

28 See Coalition Provisional Authority website: <http://www.iraqcoalition.org/security.html>.
29 Coalition Provisional Authority, Order No. 2, Dissolution of Entities (CPA/ORD/23 May 2003/02).

The attempt to exclude the 'violent agencies' of the past proved impossible. Crime raged out of control and violence only escalated. As of the fall of 2003, new Iraqi government institutions were being established to replace old brutal ones, resulting in further attacks by insurgent and criminal forces against these institutions.[30] The difficulties, indeed the impossibility of replacing an entire fabric of a society aside, the CPA maintained that all previous state entities were responsible for oppression, torture, and corruption. Dissolving them, that is to say destroying them, opened a space for the formation of new 'democratic entities' to endow Iraq with a future of non-violence distinct from its past of violence. The text that most explicitly articulates that killing of violence performed by juridico-democracy is the Law of Administration for the State of Iraq for the Transitional Period (TAL). Noah Feldman advised the drafters of TAL. Its preamble states:

> The people of Iraq, striving to reclaim their freedom, which was usurped by the previous tyrannical regime, rejecting the violence and coercion in all their forms, and particularly when used as instruments of governance, have determined that they shall hereafter remain a free people governed under the rule of law.

TAL dictates the rejection of the past, its violence, despotism, and tyranny, introducing instead a new regime of juridico-democracy guaranteeing freedom and security. A series of new juridico-democratic reforms followed thereafter. Such were the reforms in judicial and penal institutions.[31] By 2004, all Iraqi judges had been vetted,[32] and the CPA established the Central Criminal Court to try cases regarding attacks on coalition forces, organized crime, and governmental corruption.[33] In June 2004, the CPA passed the Charter for the Iraqi National Intelligence Service (INIS). It defined the threats to the security and democracy of Iraq: domestic insurgency, espionage, narcotics production and trafficking, weapons of mass destruction, serious organized crime.[34] Together these reforms worked out the juridico-democratic aspiration to eradicate all non-juridical violence. More importantly, together they stood for the promise of total peace, security, and stability that might have inspired more violence in the effort to fulfil this promise.

---

30 See S. G. Jones et al., *Establishing Law and Order After Conflict* (2005) 112–13.
31 See CPA, 'Management of Detention and Prison Facilities' (CPA/ORD/30 May 2003/ 09).
32 id., p. 137.
33 CPA, 'The Central Criminal Court of Iraq (Amended)', CPA Order 13, 22 April 2004g. Prior to that, and in September 2003, the CPA reestablished the Council of Judges abolished in 1979. The Council was given authority over courts, budgets, personnel, security and property: CPA, 'Re-Establishment of the Council of Judges', CPA Order 35, 15 September 2003e.
34 CPA, 'Charter for the Iraqi National Intelligence Service' at <www.cpa-iraq.org/ regulations/20040402_Annex.pdf>.

The discussion of the relation between the American-led war against Iraq and democracy promotion commonly focuses on the Bush administration, its neoconservative ideologues, and their project of promoting democracy in the world, though not necessarily strengthening it at home. The discussion typically revolves around a few radical conservatives, their ideas, and their struggle to decide America's future.[35] And yet, critics also suggest that the neoconservative democracy project is not genuine, but concerned with making profits, as democracy and human rights cannot be brought about by means of war.

As important as these criticisms are, I suggest they limit our understanding of the current juridico-democratic practice to what the neo-conservatives do or do not do. Consequently, we cease to see the many other actors, some of whom are well-intentioned liberals, carrying out the work of juridico-democratization in Iraq as elsewhere in post-conflict zones. These are actors publishing books on the rule of law, holding conferences on human rights, advising the judiciary on how to appoint judges, training the judiciary, drafting constitutional documents, carrying out field trips to (post)conflict zones, empowering women, publishing law review articles on effective legal reform, reforming law school curricula, purchasing books for the new law libraries, and innovating legal practice. In short, alongside the army of occupation is another army of lawyers, NGOs, human rights activists, jurists and judges. This army might not have necessarily supported the war against Iraq, but nevertheless seized the opportunity, made available during the period of chaos characteristic of post-conflict, to introduce a new juridico-democratic regime.

In conquering Iraq, contributing to a conflict, dismantling the old regime, and creating an era of post-conflict, the army of the occupation opened a space for the agents of juridco-democracy to intervene in yet another country, and to welcome the Iraqis into the ever-expanding universe of juridico-democracy. These agents constitute the nation-building industry. They advocate for, supervise, or monitor legal reform activity in Iraq. They constitute a human-rights international, a rule-of-law international, or a constitutional international.

Many institutions and groups constitute the juridico-democratic industry. They include governmental and nongovernmental organizations such as the

---

35 See, for example, on the question of Iraq, G. Packer, *The Assassins' Gate: America in Iraq* (2005). The book recounts how the United States set about changing the history of the Middle East. Packer brings to light the men and their ideas that created the Bush administration's war policy. Also, see G. Rosen (ed.), *The Right War: The Conservative Debate on Iraq* (2005). This volume brings together some of the most influential voices in the debate among conservatives over American's involvement in Iraq and includes a diverse collection of opinion pieces and journal articles written by people who belong to the political right.

110

RAND Corporation (a non-profit research organization that provides analysis to government and private sectors), the US Institute for Peace, as well as USAID. In a RAND monograph series, *Establishing Law and Order After Conflict*, the authors provide a study of 'the United States and allied efforts to provide security and rebuild internal security institutions in post-conflict environments'. The authors argue that 'establishing order during the "golden hour" should be the most immediate concern of policymakers to avert chaos and prevent criminal and insurgent groups from securing a foothold in society.' As to the definition of the 'golden hour', it is the 'critical hour following a life trauma when intervention – or lack thereof – determines the fate of the victim.'[36]

Post-conflict intervention practitioners realize that the period of post-conflict, if they can delineate it, is a golden opportunity for intervention, allowing them to reform a country before local elites emerge and begin to influence its future. Following the logic of post-conflict interventions, it is therefore imperative not to delay the intervention, so that the country does not enter a post-post-conflict stage in which elites have gained power and have begun to shape the future.

A number of juridico-democracy groups were involved in the drafting of Iraq's constitution. These included the United States Institute for Peace (USIP), USAID, The Carnegie Council, The International Human Rights Law Institute at De Paul University College of Law (IHRLI), and other non-affiliated individuals. USIP's Rule of Law Program provided in-country support for constitution-making to Iraqi political, governmental, and civil society actors. The IHRLI, with a contract from USAID, carried out a major publication project to support the process of writing the Iraqi constitution. This project involved the creation and publication of critical legal materials in Arabic, which were distributed to members of the Constitutional Drafting Commission, the Iraqi National Assembly, and others working in support of the new constitution. The IHRLI publications draw attention to international human rights law standards as they compare with Iraqi and Arab constitutions. They also set forth guiding principles regarding the basic rights protected by international human rights instruments. One of the books presents a collection of original essays and critical studies by twenty-two leading Iraqi and Arab constitutional experts, legal professionals, and academics regarding major constitutional issues.[37]

---

36 CPA, op. cit., n. 31.
37 See IHRLI, *Compilation of Arab Constitutions and a Comparative Study of International Human Rights Standards* (2005); *Compilation of Iraqi Constitutions and Comparative Studies of International Human Rights Standards* (2005); *Compilation of Legislative Laws and Regulations of Select Arab Legal Systems* (2005); *Gender Justice and Women's Rights in Iraq* (2005); *Iraqi Constitutional Studies: Basic Principles for the New Iraqi Constitution* (2005) (all in Arabic).

111

That the projects and the practices of these actors manifest the desire of the law to carve out a space for its operations remains underappreciated in legal literature. In many accounts of the war in Iraq, the law appears as either facilitating the work of the war, legitimizing it, constraining it, criticizing it, or carrying out the work of reform in its shadow. A considerable amount of the legal literature on law and the war in Iraq focuses on the legal options, or lack thereof, available to war-makers. Law in this literature is a matter of knowledge to be acquired in order to better wage a war or better criticize it. The themes covered in this literature are the following: whether law can assist in categorizing terrorism as war or as crime;[38] that the American soldiers deployed to the Middle East should receive education addressing how Muslims view the law of war and how to best use this knowledge;[39] the various bodies of law under which Iraqi insurgents could be prosecuted;[40] the legal options available for the prosecution of Saddam Hussein;[41] whether or not the war against Iraq spelled the death of international law; and whether the law can play a role in enhancing global security in the face of emerging threats.[42]

What unites this literature is its understanding of the law as a knowledge resource according to which the war is evaluated. Law in these accounts is not associated with the machine of death, but maintains its ground as knowledge independent of death and unshaken by it. Most crucially, by insisting on evaluating war through law, these accounts further separate non-violence from violence, juridico-democracy from war, thus allowing more violent wars to bring about juridico-democracy.

But if law's promise of peace is central to the operations of war, then the agents of juridico-democracy must also take responsibility for the deaths of the battlefield. This responsibility is avoided in most legal analyses because they rest on distinctions between non-violence and violence, law and wars; distinctions that allow the law to disassociate itself from the deaths of wars. But if one considers, as I have been suggesting, that the life of juridico-democracy is the engine of bloody wars, then death comes back to inhabit the legal arguments, demanding that we inquire into the responsibility of the agents of juridico-democracy for deaths in wars.

Unlike this legal scholarship, then, my analysis suggests that the law is not a resource for knowledge. In my analysis, the war against Iraq was

---

38 N. Feldman, 'Choices of Law, Choices of War' (2002) 25 *Harvard J. of Law and Public Policy* 457.

39 M. Supervielle, 'The Geneva Convention and the Rules of War in the Post 9/11 and Iraq World: Islam, the Law of War, and the U.S. Soldier' (2005) 21 *Am. University International Law Rev.* 191.

40 N. Canestaro, '"Small Wars" and the Law: Options for Prosecuting the Insurgents in Iraq' (2004) 43 *Columbia J. of Transnational Law* 73.

41 E. Chamblee, 'Post-War Iraq: Prosecuting Saddam Hussein' (2004) 7 *Californian Crim. Law Rev.* 1.

42 See J. Stromseth, 'Law and Force after Iraq: A Transitional Moment' (2003) 97 *Am. J. of International Law* 628–42.

waged *for* the law: a series of juridico-democratic reforms instituting the rule of law, constitutionalism, human rights, and separation of powers; in short, juridico-democracy.

KILLING VIOLENCE

It is possible to dismiss the rhetoric of democracy as empty and meaningless in the face of the horrors Iraq is witnessing. Critics of the United Sates administration have shown how it failed to protect the basic rights of individuals in Iraq as well as Iraq's cultural heritage.[43] What these critics share with juridico-democrats, however, is the belief that human rights is an avenue for security against the threat of terrorism. They hold against the United States administration its failure to fully pursue human rights as a measure of security. For them, as for juridico-democrats, the insecurity of the world is partly due to the absence of human rights.

In its report on law and order in post-conflict zones, RAND lists the justice system as an internal security apparatus, next to the police, military, and other security bodies. The justice system, in RAND's definition, includes the Ministry of Justice, federal and local courts, correction facilities, law schools, and the rule of law. The reconstruction of the justice system, as well as security sectors, is a constituent piece of so-called post-conflict operations. RAND's report belongs to a larger geopolitical context. Since the 1990s, human rights gained a prominent role in the conceptualization and realization of security.[44] Human rights law has furnished the dominant vocabulary in foreign affairs, despite being controversially linked to neo-liberal economies.[45] The United Nations and government aid agencies insisted upon human rights, the rule of law, and accountability as a central part of their reconstruction strategy in post-conflict zones. For governments, as well as for social movements, human rights grounded a range of activities and initiatives in fields such as economic development, reconstruction, and political reform.[46]

Similarly, the rule of law is promoted in a multitude of countries in Asia, the former Soviet Union, eastern Europe, Latin America, sub-Saharan Africa, and the Middle East. Rule of law initiatives include rewriting constitutions, laws, and regulations; training judges, lawyers, and bureaucrats; reconstructing court systems, police forces, and prisons; and educating

---

43 See, for example, T. Farer, 'The Interplay of Domestic Politics, Human Rights, and U.S. Foreign Policy' in *Wars on Terrorism and Iraq: Human Rights, Unilateralism, and U.S. Foreign Policy*, eds. T. Weiss et al. (2004) 29–60.
44 See T. Weiss et al., 'The Serendipity of War, Human Rights and Sovereignty' in id., pp. 3–26.
45 R. Falk, *The Great Terror War* (2003) 147–51.
46 R. Wilson, 'Human Rights in the "War on Terror"' in *Human Rights in the 'War on Terror'*, ed. R. Wilson (2005) 1–33, at 4.

113

citizens about certain conceptions of law and justice. Promoters of 'rule of law' include Western nations and private donors investing hundreds of millions of dollars.[47]

Both rule of law and human rights are classified by juridico-democrats, such as RAND, USAID, and USIP as security initiatives. They are meant not to replace the violence of the previous regime, but also to eradicate the violence of the present, especially that of the insurgency. Both initiatives celebrate themselves for their power to strengthen the security of Iraq against the threat of violence. They stand for the promise of security, of non-violence in the face of the heritage of violence. And it is this aspiration for peace, guaranteed by juridico-democracy, which is productive of a war that kills violence in order to bring about non-violence, of a war whose violence is, therefore, intensified.

One document that manifests these juridico-democratic sensibilities to violence is Iraq's constitution of October 2005. The text of the constitution is by no means remarkable or exceptional compared to other constitutions. And yet, the text is perhaps unique because it is drafted in era in which the aspirations for global peace and non-violence as the end of wars (that never end) have never been so central to the geopolitical order. I quote some passages from the constitution's preamble:

> Acknowledging God's right over us, and in fulfillment of the call of our homeland and citizens, and in response to the call of our religious and national leaderships and the determination of our great (religious) authorities and of our leaders and reformers, and in the midst of an international support from our friends and those who love us, marched for the first time in our history toward the ballot boxes by the millions, men and women, young and old, on the thirtieth of January two thousand and five, invoking the pains of sectarian oppression sufferings inflicted by the autocratic clique and inspired by the tragedies of Iraq's martyrs, Shiite and Sunni, Arabs and Kurds and Turkmen and from all the other components of the people and recollecting the darkness of the ravage of the holy cities and the South in the Sha'abaniyya uprising and burnt by the flames of grief of the mass graves, the marshes, Al-Dujail and others and articulating the sufferings of racial oppression in the massacres of Halabcha, Barzan, Anfal and the Fayli Kurds and inspired by the ordeals of the Turkmen in Basheer and as is the case in the remaining areas of Iraq where the people of the west suffered from the assassinations of their leaders, symbols and elderly and from the displacement of their skilled individuals and from the drying out of their cultural and intellectual wells, so we sought hand in hand and shoulder to shoulder to create our new Iraq, the Iraq of the future free from sectarianism, racism, locality complex, discrimination and exclusion.
>
> ... We the people of Iraq who have just risen from our stumble, and who are looking with confidence to the future through a republican, federal, democratic, pluralistic system, have resolved with the determination of our men, women, the elderly and youth, to respect the rules of law, to establish justice and equality, to cast aside the politics of aggression, and to tend to the

---

47 T. Carothers, 'The Rule-of-Law Revival' in *Promoting the Rule of Law Abroad: In Search of Knowledge,* ed. T. Carothers (2006) 3–14, at 4, 5.

114

concerns of women and their rights, and to the elderly and their concerns, and to children and their affairs and to spread a culture of diversity and defusing terrorism.

The preamble begins with the violence of the past, takes us to its massacres, reminds us of the tragedies of Iraq's martyrs – Shiite and Sunni, Arabs and Kurds and Turkmen – and recollects the pain of sectarian oppression. It does so in order to show Iraqis the path to non-violence, freedom, and the nation-state that the constitution, and thus juridico-democracy, guarantees. In its democratic rhetoric, the constitution makes the death of the past ever more legally transparent, ever more visible to the inspecting eye of the public, to the judgement of the citizens, in order to bring about a non-violent Iraq. But has this constitution delivered Iraq from the violence of the past to the path of freedom, or has it sparked more violence? Could it be that by articulating violence so clearly, by spelling out violence, by making death ever more comprehensible, the constitution risks underpinning violence? Might it be that in law's desire to survive violence, the constitution must confine violence to a series of events that then prevent us from seeing the degree to which our life is premised on violence? And finally, if the constitution is killing violence by promising a world beyond it, then what possibilities for life are there in a law giving birth to a world that constantly fights violence?

I conclude with these questions, because this article is only an initial inquiry into the violence that arises from juridico-democracy that wishes to institute a state of non-violence. But some additional tentative concluding remarks are in order. They concern a possible alternative to the cycle of non-violence and violence that kills violence and incites more violence. It seems to me that rather than aspire to global security that would rid us of all violence, rather than imagine an end of non-violence where violence is made to evaporate, and rather than have this aspiration and imagination perform more violence, we might think of ways to work through violence. These ways of 'working through' would look to regulate violence, live with the loss it generates, and mourn the lives it shatters. This article does not investigate this alternative, but I mention it in order to allude to what the article does not do and where more research can be conducted.

JOURNAL OF LAW AND SOCIETY
VOLUME 34, NUMBER 1, MARCH 2007
ISSN: 0263-323X, pp. 116–38

Performing Power: The Deal, Corporate Rule, and the Constitution of Global Legal Order

FLEUR JOHNS*

This article presents a stylized account of legal work involved in doing a corporate deal transnationally, drawing inspiration from the work of American legal realist, Robert Hale. In so doing, it seeks to show that legal institutions on which transnational corporate power depends are far more plastic, discordant, and irresolute than commonly recorded. By tethering global legal order to the decisive interiority of the transnational corporation, while taking that interior for granted, recent accounts (such as those of Michael Hardt and Antonio Negri or A. Claire Cutler) may do more to fortify than query the contemporary 'rule' of global capital.

> [T]he legal infrastructure of deals provides ... a window through which [one] can view, or imagine, the soul of the company.[1]

INTRODUCTION

The title of this special issue – Democracy's Empire – evokes a concern that has preoccupied legal scholars for centuries: how is it that the plasticity of democratic and market 'freedom' sustains distributional inequality and

* *Faculty of Law, University of Sydney, 173–175 Phillip Street, Sydney NSW 2000, Australia*

fleurj@law.usyd.edu.au

Numerous debts have been incurred in the writing of this article: to Stewart Motha for editing of extraordinary skill and patience; to Peter Fitzpatrick, for unfaltering generosity, including in commenting on earlier drafts; and to Dan Danielsen and two anonymous referees for invaluable comments and suggestions. Work on this article was supported by the Leverhulme Trust, the School of Law at Birkbeck College, University of London, and the Faculty of Law at the University of Sydney.

1 V. Fleischer, 'Brand New Deal: The Branding Effect of Corporate Deal Structures' (2006) 104 *Michigan Law Rev.* 1581, at 1585. See, also, V. Fleischer, 'Deals: Bringing Corporate Transactions into the Law School Classroom' (2002) *Columbia Business Law Rev.* 475.

116

political unfreedom of such apparent rigidity and durability? Moreover, what role might law play in this dynamic? Legal and political academics offer a range of studies responsive to this concern. Many of these report a global 'expansion of corporate power resulting from the juridification, pluraliza- tion, and privatization of commercial relations'.[2] Within such accounts, transnational corporations tend to feature prominently. In A. Claire Cutler's thoughtful study *Private Power and Global Authority*, for instance, trans- national corporations 'use their nationality to avoid or evade responsibility'; they exert 'overwhelming influence on the creation of international commercial arbitration law and institutions'; they 'manipulate ... rules' in pursuit of a 'disciplinary neoliberal agenda': in short, they are regarded as 'central players in this restructuring process'.[3]

While many of the insights put forward in Cutler's and other recent scholarship on transnational private power are compelling, there remains something curious about that scholarship's construction of corporate agency and influence. For all the critical vigour of these accounts, the transnational corporation seems to emerge from them critically unscathed. The legal formalist curtain is lifted and – lo and behold – we find fully formed entities 'in fact function[ing] as legal subjects' who seem to be pulling all the ropes.[4] When it comes to critical scholarly accounts of transnational corporate action, the model of law, lawyers, and legal institutions that tends to prevail is a pre-realist one.

Part I of this article works against the predestination with which many 'juridical' accounts of global corporate rule are invested, by presenting a stylized account of the legal work of cross-border investment. This re- description begins with an expression used by lawyers working in or on the global market: 'the deal'. Corporate lawyers use the language of the deal to name a multi-party transaction, often transnational in scope. However, deal- making implies much more than the striking of economic bargains through law. Deals have trajectories that digress wildly from the passage of a particular group from disagreement to agreement. Deals take on multi- dimensional lives that do not map neatly onto the 'corporate cultures' or plans of their participant-makers. The transnational deal is not simply a pooling of corporations' directive agency. Rather, it is a site for the enactment of identities and the production of values 'tenuously constituted in time, instituted in an exterior space, through a *stylized repetition of acts*'.[5]

The account of deal-making advanced here pays attention to those acts. It seeks to show that whatever version of corporate personality or global legal order one adopts, the gains and losses faced by bearers of global capital on a

---

2 A.C. Cutler, *Private Power and Global Authority: Transnational Merchant Law in the Global Political Economy* (2003) 242.
3 id., pp. 203–4, 234, 238.
4 id., p. 239.
5 J. Butler, *Gender Trouble* (1999) 191 (emphasis in original).

deal-by-deal basis cannot be deduced from those generic identities or principles. In so doing, it draws upon the early twentieth-century legal realist attack – in particular, Robert Hale's – upon laissez-faire constitutionalism.[6] As Hale sought to show that 'concepts that had conventionally been thought to establish categorical limits on the constitutional exercise of legislative powers ... did no such thing', so this article argues for a reading of legal institutions in transnational corporate settings as far more plastic and irresolute than commonly recorded.[7] Also, when seeking to explain the relatively predictable trajectories of transnational corporate work that nonetheless *do* ensue, Part I argues, as Hale did, for attention to a broader array of 'rules' than those of overtly 'constitutional' character. Amid the vagaries of a deal, it becomes clear that employment laws, partnership structures, service contracts, office leases, educational loan arrangements, billing and time-keeping standards, and the litany of norms that condition workplace interactions in and by large law firms have as much to do with the allocation of capital as the mere 'fact' of their clients' corporate form or balance sheet.[8]

Part II of this article then returns, by way of a more direct critique, to the representation of law and corporate action within recent commentaries on the global rise of private power, taking Michael Hardt and Antonio Negri's *Empire* and Cutler's *Private Power* as indicative texts. Robert Hale's scholarship equips us with a contrary and, I argue, more compelling understanding of the relationship between law and power: one that calls Hardt and Negri's and Cutler's influential studies of global legal order into question. In staging an encounter between Hale and these contemporary scholars, the concern of this article is with the politics of the tendency to frame the power (or pathology) of transnational corporations as determinative, and to regard law as a mere expression of that power. This configuration merits question because it anticipates – and, as it were, guarantees – the very global legal order with which it takes issue. By tethering global legal order to the decisive 'interiority' of the transnational corporation, while taking that interior for granted, recent accounts may do more to fortify the 'rule' of global capital than work towards its unravelling.

---

6 See, generally, G. Alexander, 'Comparing the Two Legal Realisms – American and Scandinavian' (2002) 50 *Am. J. of Comparative Law* 131; W. Fisher III et al. (eds.), *American Legal Realism* (1993).

7 B.H. Fried, *The Progressive Assault on Laissez Faire: Robert Hale and the First Law and Economics Movement* (1998) 20. See, generally, W. Samuels, 'The Economy as a System of Power and its Legal Bases: The Legal Economics of Robert Lee Hale' (1973) 27 *University of Miami Law Rev.* 261; N. Duxbury, 'Robert Hale and the Economy of Legal Force' (1990) 53 *Modern Law Rev.* 421.

8 Compare Miller and O'Leary's account of the impact of standard costing and budgeting, in conjunction with scientific management and industrial psychology, in constituting the firm as a space populated by 'governable persons': P. Miller and T. O'Leary, 'Accounting and the Construction of the Governable Person' (1987) 12 *Accounting, Organizations and Society* 235.

This critique begins with an account of some of the stylized acts through which corporate lawyers perform transnational corporate deals. This account mobilizes, obliquely, identities ranging from the transnational corporation and the corporate lawyer to those of 'global capital' and *lex mercatoria* (or transnational merchant law). Each term has been, in recent literature, invested with an interiority from which directive force is said to emanate. Yet, experiences of corporate transactional work yield no sullied corporate 'soul' amenable to saving or condemnation on a disciplinary, organizational or individual level.[9] Whereas Hardt and Negri insist, in *Empire*, that there is 'no more outside' to global capital or Empire,[10] this article proceeds in the opposite direction: towards a claim that there may be no *inside* to these phenomena that regulates their every performance, however unassailable their 'properties' appear. The following sketch of corporate dealing suggests that there may be more undecidedness to the legal dimensions of Empire or global mercatocratic rule than much recent critical scholarship would have us believe. Lived deal experiences register a sense of those legal decision(s) of which corporate 'rule' and 'identity' are forged as decisions 'overflowing with the performative'; one might even say, with madness.[11] This article seeks to evoke this familiar sense of decision-madness.

The particular decisional scenario at issue here is an apparent conflict between the necessity of the oft-drawn trajectory invoked above (the incessant piling up of capital in corporate hands) and the conviction that people can and do derail that trajectory in certain instances (in favour of capital erosion or capital redistribution). This article enacts the confrontation of a group of lawyers with this scenario, or with the 'laws' of global capital, in a particular deal.[12] It is, however, a starting point for this redescription that the

9 Contrary to Fleischer, op. cit., n. 1 and related text.
10 M. Hardt and A. Negri, *Empire* (2001) 186.
11 The description of the instant of decision as a 'madness' that is 'overflowing with the performative' is Derrida's (borrowing, in relation to the madness, from Kierkegaard): J. Derrida, 'Force of Law: "The Mystical Foundation of Authority"' in *Acts of Religion*, ed. G. Anidjar (2002) 228–98, at 255; S. Kierkegaard, *Concluding Unscientific Postscript* (1968) tr. D. Swenson and W. Kowrie, 173–5. Compare D. Kennedy, 'Freedom and Constraint in Adjudication: A Critical Phenomenology' (1986) 36 *J. of Legal Education* 518.
12 Marx's writings yield, among others, the following 'laws' of capital: (a) that capital 'preserves and perpetuates itself in and through circulation' (that is, the continual transfer of its ownership); (b) that capital accumulates in the course of this circulation in an upward 'spiral' motion, impelled by an in-built propensity to maximize the productivity of social labour (that is, its production of surplus value for the benefit of the capital-holder); and (c) that the growth of capital through the 'capitalist process of production' reproduces the capital-relation, that is, the relation of property-holders or capitalists on the one hand, and wage-workers on the other. See K. Marx, *Grundrisse: Foundations of the Critique of Political Economy (Rough Draft)* (1973 [1953]) German edn. tr. by M. Nicolaus, 262 and 250–370; K. Marx, *Capital: A Critique of*

119

re-enactment of transnational corporate power does not render that power up for grabs, any more than a deal is sure to yield return on capital in all cases. The deal is not, in this account, entirely pre-codified in either direction, even as it is patently not a domain of pure freedom. Rather, this article seeks to evoke an experience in which, first, law's significance to the accumulation of capital is brought into the foreground, and second, both the inflexibility and the pliability of legal decision-making surrounding that accumulation are experienced anew.

Importantly, the redescription that follows is not metaphoric. Here, the deal is not intended as a stand-in for anything but that which it presents: haphazardly recorded notes from days spent as a corporate lawyer. More-over, this record does not purport to erase transnational corporate subjec-tivity in favour of some 'improved' explanatory point(s) of reference: a now routine gesture that often enshrines, as an on/off phenomenon, the very subjectivity it claims to disaggregate or surpass. The notes that follow are concerned with 'how' rather than 'what' questions: in particular, how does the *necessity* of transnational corporations prevailing across the global legal order get produced through 'freely' negotiated transactions? The ensuing account implies that the idea of a corporate actor as a coherent, will-bearing subject is one medium for that necessity's production. However, this account will suggest that self-consciously contingent identities work rather well in that capacity too.[13]

In short, it is not contended here that, in the rabbit warren of a deal, one might (or should seek to) outrun normative coercion. Rather, this brief study of a deal is undertaken towards continued excavation of the innumerable background 'rules' by which legal choosers and choices are shaped and circumscribed. As discussed further in Part II, the work of legal realist scholars such as Robert Hale shows us much about how the inevitabilities of the global corporate domination are produced, day by day, decision by decision, deal by deal. It is in debt to Hale's study of the regulatory power borne by 'unofficial minorities', and Hale's attention to the endowments of intangible privilege as well as tangible property, that the daily life of a deal is sketched here.[14]

Political Economy, Volume 1 (1992) [1867] tr. B. Fowkes, 724, 780 and, more generally, 711–33, 794–802, 949–1065. The nature of capital, as well as the rigid categorization and opposition of 'wage-workers' and 'capitalists' has been the subject of extensive critique and re-thinking. See, for example, P. Bourdieu, 'The Forms of Capital' in *Handbook of Theory and Research for the Sociology of Education*, ed. J.G. Richardson (1986) 241–58; R. Marsden, *The Nature of Capital: Marx after Foucault* (2000) 123–42.

13 Contrary to M. Dan-Cohen, 'Responsibility and the Boundaries of the Self' (1992) 105 *Harvard Law Rev.* 959.

14 See, for example, R.L. Hale, 'Law Making by Unofficial Minorities' (1920) 20 *Columbia Law Rev.* 451.

1. *Doing deals: the vocabulary of the market*

When corporate lawyers engaged in the 'American mode of production of law' talk to each other about international transactional work in which they are engaged, they use the nomenclature of the deal.[15] 'We just won a mining deal in Chile.' 'I know [X] from that deal we did last year.' 'I can't do [Y] until this deal closes.' Among legal elites dedicated to transactional work in the international financial sector, these are the terms in which lives are punctuated. While scholarship concerning transnational corporate law has tended to prefer the vocabulary of agreements, regulations, firms, and institutions (with important exceptions),[16] industry rags announce 'deals of the year'. Under the banner of a deal, industry publications summarize an assemblage of legal and non-legal arrangements among participants public and private.[17]

Documenting all of the arrangements between the parties involved in a deal, and their authority to enter into those arrangements, is the responsibility of lawyers. For the lawyers concerned, 'getting the deal done' will mean, at a minimum, getting those documents prepared, negotiated and signed, so that money (debt and equity) may start to move. Included in that task will be the satisfaction of a litany of legal and non-legal conditions precedent to financing. The issues to be negotiated to that end are numerous and often fraught. In the project finance context, for example, they typically revolve around the entitlement of foreign lenders to oversee a project's day-to-day financial and technical management and, should problems arise, to step in and take over. This is the sort of scene that I wish to evoke in this section: a complex transaction, presenting an array of multi-jurisdictional, multi-disciplinary issues for negotiation, in which sizeable amounts of money and the provision of basic services (via energy infrastructure, for example) are at issue.

2. *Performing (corporate) power: pace, place, and projected returns*

Each occasion of a deal's performance is, in some sense, an abyss. Nevertheless, some stylistic markers recur. These are the focus of the following account. This account considers, initially, what might be thought of as

---

15 The notion of an 'American mode of production of law' is taken from D. Trubek, Y. Dezalay, R. Buchanan, and J.R. Davis, 'Global Restructuring and the Law: Studies of the Internationalization of Legal Fields and the Creation of Transnational Arenas' (1994) 44 *Case Western Reserve Law Rev.* 407, at 413, fn. 5 and 419–26.

16 Compare M.C. Suchman, 'The Contract as Social Artifact' (2003) 37 *Law & Society Rev.* 91, at 96; J.M. Lipshaw, 'Contingency and Contracts: A Philosophy of Complex Business Transactions' (2005) 54 *De Paul Law Rev.* 1077, at 1077–8.

17 See, for example, the deal summaries published under the heading 'Deals and Developments – Oil & Gas' in *Project Finance Magazine* (June 2006), at <http://www.projectfinancemagazine.com>.

mechanistic or menial elements of a deal: questions of scheduling and venue often left to junior or non-professional staff. To locate, at this level, arrangements colouring the making of 'substantive' legal decisions, is to stress that power is ubiquitous across the deal's formulation as such (a point made, in relation to economic relations generally, by Hale).[18]

Typically, the first step in embarking upon a complex cross-border deal is for the sponsors' (or equity investors') legal or financial advisors to convene an 'all hands' meeting. So begin the successive rounds of meetings and conference calls that comprise the daily life of the deal, each oriented around a draft document, pending issue list, or logistical concerns. These are interspersed with periods of feverish document preparation on the part of lawyers and occasional lulls in activity. The tempo of the deal tends towards this faltering rhythm. Time drags in the long, air conditioned hours of a multi-party meeting. Then, periodically, it gets compressed and caffeinated – pushed against the railing of a deadline. Each time that a lawyer gets called upon to make a decision, however significant, its making will be inflected in some way by this discontinuous temporality.[19] Engineering the reduction of transaction costs is supposedly the lawyers' broader mandate. That is how, it has been claimed, lawyers 'create value'.[20] Yet neither the 'cost' of time and action, nor the 'value-creating' processes of its calculation and apportionment, are independent of the cadence of their performance.[21]

Where these meetings occur will be a matter for negotiation between the parties. Typically, 'high-level' strategic meetings will be convened in the principal financing venue, where the preponderance of the deal's international personnel are likely based. More technical, project-specific matters, such as regulatory filings and due diligence, will usually be dealt with in the country of investment. These latter meetings will often involve more junior lawyers: frequently those with the strongest language skills within international firms. In the navigation of deal-making locales, the deal is given a significant scalar dimension. Through the type of meetings convened in each locale, the country of investment is typically cast as the particularized ground to/from which deracinated 'internationals' seek both a knowing

---

18 R.L. Hale, 'Bargaining, Duress, and Economic Liberty' (1943) 43 *Columbia Law Rev.* 603, at 626.

19 The temporality to which I am referring is too erratic and deal-specific to be amenable to modelling in terms of time-inconsistent preferences. Contrast M.A. Utset, 'Ethics in Corporate Representation: A Model of Time-Inconsistent Misconduct: The Case of Lawyer Misconduct' (2005) 74 *Fordham Law Rev.* 1319.

20 See R.J. Gilson, 'Value Creation by Business Lawyers: Legal Skills and Asset Pricing' (1984) 94 *Yale Law J.* 239. See, further, S.L. Schwarcz, 'Explaining the Value of Transactional Lawyering' (2006) *Duke Law School Legal Studies,* paper no. 108, at <http://ssrn.com/abstract=901439>.

21 '[T]empo', wrote Nietzsche, 'is as significant a power in the development of peoples as in music': F. Nietzsche, *The Gay Science:With a Prelude in German Rhymes and an Appendix of Songs* (2001) tr. B. Williams, 36.

proximity (in the sense of 'having one's ear close to the ground') and the safety of distance (so as to be able to project a generalized business sense, attuned to the 'needs' of the global market).[22]

This scalar dimension, in turn, feeds into the range of legal possibility experienced within the deal. Consider, for instance, the issue of venue for arbitration arising under a material contract for an emerging market financing.[23] International counsel would commonly advise that the market norm is to convene such arbitration in a major international capital home to none of the potential disputants, in which some or all parties are presumed capable of feeling at home, or attracting sympathy, while insulated from unseemly, parochial influences.[24] In the interests of national pride, or for other practical or strategic reasons, local sponsors and their counsel might argue for arbitration to be seated at a local or regional centre for international commercial arbitration.[25] The former argument most frequently prevails, in part because of the interests of all persons concerned in presenting as fluent in the dispassionate language of global commercial norms.[26] However, where a local party has been able to secure the attendance of senior 'internationals' at meetings in the project's home country (in the protective bubble of a suitably generic corporate office), it might seem more plausible to the lenders to accept, say, ICC arbitration in the project region, in the event of dispute under a key agreement.[27] Aside from the implications of this for any dispute that eventuates, such a concession tends to take deal negotiation in a rather different direction. Struggles over schedule and venue function as struggles over authority within and over the deal and, obliquely, over its material outcomes. Of such quotidian stuff is 'global corporate rule' made and remade.

At this discontinuous tempo and at these various sites, participant-makers perform deal identities. How one does so, as a lawyer, will invariably shift:

---

22 See A. Riles, 'The View from the International Plane: Perspective and Scale in the Architecture of Colonial International Law' (1995) 6 *Law and Critique* 39.

23 See F. De Ly, 'The Place of Arbitration in the Conflict of Laws of International Commercial Arbitration' (1991) 12 *Northwestern J. of International Law and Business* 48.

24 See, for example, S.E. Cirielli, 'Arbitration, Financial Markets and Banking Disputes' (2003) 14 *Am. Rev. of International Arbitration* 243, at 249.

25 On the establishment of centres for international commercial arbitration in Asia, Africa and the Islamic world in the late 1970s, see C.N. Brower and J.K. Sharpe, 'International Arbitration and the Islamic World: The Third Phase' (2003) 97 *Am. J. of International Law* 643, at 653–4.

26 Judge Keba Mbaye (then of the International Court of Justice) observed that developing countries are rarely the venue of international arbitration: quoted in F.S. Nariman, 'Courts and Arbitrators: Paradigms of Arbitral Autonomy' (1997) 15 *Boston University International Law J.* 185, at 189–90.

27 The Arbitration Rules of the International Chamber of Commerce (the ICC) provide that the place of arbitration shall be chosen by the parties or, in the absence of parties' choice, fixed by the Paris-based Court of the ICC. See *Rules of the Court of Arbitration of the International Chamber of Commerce* (1998) Art. 14.

123

now one is speaking or writing as representative of another ('my client has instructed me to ...'); now as a principal (drafting an opinion of one's firm, for instance); now as employee or employer (when, for instance, lawyers within a firm speak to one another about the deal, partner-to-associate). Here one speaks as the most senior lawyer in the room; there one is the most junior lawyer; at another time, one talks as a lawyer to a non-lawyer (imparting advice to a non-lawyer client, instructing an administrative staff-person, or receiving information from an expert in another field). Learning by observation and imitation, lawyers acquire facility in these various roles. The lawyer-role that one is performing, at any given moment, sets a bearing for the legal decisions at which one arrives.

Other identities are also enacted that may wreak havoc with assigned roles and formal hierarchies. On a certain deal, a particular lawyer might be the quiet one, the belligerent one, the old hand, the work-horse, or the 'rain-maker' (that is, the one whose particular gift is bringing new clients through the door). A lawyer may also circulate through these roles over the life of the deal. She who seemed compliant on one occasion might later become 'the tough one'. How one does a deal, in a particular instance, will be informed by an implicit loyalty to the role that one assumes within the socio-political life of the deal. If I am the young one on this deal, I may defer to my older counterparty on a particular negotiating point or fight it to the death. If I am the funny one, I may be ill-inclined to rock one or other negotiating boat, for fear of losing my likeability. Conventionally, atomism and anomie are supposed to result from sustained engagement in the work of capital.[28] At close range, however, one finds that it is often through the cultivation and repetitive performance of 'personal' idiosyncrasies – and the momentum and loyalties generated thereby – that a deal gets done.[29]

Certainly, particular characters tend to recur, albeit in modes that vary significantly among corporate professionals. Ready-made scripts are received and sent on and these are often framed in terms of economic or strategic goals. Those in the role of investors will often understand themselves to be seeking a return on their respective investments: lenders, through the payment of interest; equity investors, through the sale of goods or services at a profit, after debt repayment. The parties may also have other objectives in engaging in a deal. One investor might be seeking particular tax or accounting treatment for an investment, to improve its balance sheet. Another might be pursuing vertical integration by, for example, extending a portfolio of downstream energy investments upstream. Among lenders, the project might complement an existing investment portfolio (spreading risk in terms of industry or geography), or may be responsive to client demand for access to

---

28 The classic account is H. Marcuse, *One-dimensional Man* (1964).

29 Consider, for example, the vivid portraits colouring the deal memoires of a United States corporate lawyer in L. Lederman, *Tombstones: A Lawyer's Tales from the Takeover Decades* (1992) 77 and 189.

124

certain types of investment opportunity. Legal counsel commonly understand themselves to be charged with ensuring that these various goals are met, and/ or with reconciling them, to the extent of conflict. Yet these roles too have an inherent volatility. One cannot be sure whether one's goal-oriented performance will arrive at its destination. Yesterday's visionary is often today's cowboy.[30] Moreover, the promise of projected returns depends upon an embrace of the risk that those returns might not eventuate.

In pursuing this or that goal, deal participants tend to understand themselves to be assuming a particular posture towards risk. This often folds into the performance of a corporate identity. Fleischer maintains that '[c]ontract design helps form the identity of the firm'.[31] One firm may be known to 'push the envelope' more than another. Whatever the institutional identity they are performing, lawyers engaged in cross-border transactional investment typically envisage themselves engaged in site-specific navigation of a matrix of risks.[32]

'Risk allocation' is engineered in the detail of deal agreements. One party may obtain certain representations or covenants from another party, for instance, the latter then assuming the financial burden of their proving untrue or being unsatisfied. Risk allocation is also effected in the design of relational structures. One might ensure, for example, that a host government stands to gain financially from a project, in order to mitigate the risk for private investors of project expropriation. Yet, for all the labours of risk calibration across a deal, this analysis is continually perceived as incomplete. Risk proliferates. Risk cannot be contained. One discerns at once an anxiety about risk and a belief in its centrality to legal work.[33] Among transactional lawyers, contingency is perceived as a life-giving and bountiful force.[34] With risk comes the promise of return for the client, and the invigorating sense that one is acting beyond the realm of precedent.[35]

It is, perhaps, this sense of proximity to risk that evokes such efforts of choreography among transactional lawyers. It is a dedication to the choreographic endeavour that one discerns, above all, in the daily work of trans-

---

30 The contrast between pre-bankruptcy and post-bankruptcy portrayals of Enron's top management is illustrative: C.S. Lerner, 'Calling a Truce in the Culture Wars: From Enron to the CIA' (2006) 17 *Stanford Law & Policy Rev.* 277, at 291–2.

31 Fleischer, op. cit. (2006), n. 1, p. 1588.

32 See, for example, Fleischer, op. cit. (2002), n. 1, p. 478; M. Kaplan and K. de Bartolomé, 'Risk Allocation' (1996) 2 *J. of Project Finance* 19; J. Flood, 'Doing Business: The Management of Uncertainty in Lawyers' Work' (1991) 25 *Law and Society Rev.* 41.

33 See, further, R. Kreitner 'Speculations on Contract' (2000) *Columbia Law Rev.* 1132; Lipshaw, op. cit., n. 16, pp. 1082–1100.

34 Lipshaw, id., observes that 'deal makers live with contingency, but they do not necessarily invoke the law to control it' (p. 1092).

35 See, for example, J.C. Freund, *Lawyering: A Realistic Approach to Legal Practice* (1979) at 3: 'For want of a better term, I consider myself an activist lawyer – I believe that … the practitioner must at all times … reach out and *accomplish*.'

actional lawyering: a persistent effort to ensure everyone involved in the deal a designated role, and have them perform it more or less to script. This commitment to orchestration extends well beyond the production of legal documents. Transactional lawyers tend to agonize as much over menus as they do over covenants. Logistical planning, project management, and hospitality may occupy lawyers' time almost as much as technical legal work. While academic commentators such as Hardt, Negri, and Cutler tend to cast transnational corporate power as supreme, those engaged in the doing of a deal seem scrupulously attentive to its fragility.

This hazard-riddled deal landscape will be terraced, in part, in terms of 'what the law requires' in the various jurisdictions concerned. Lawyers will delineate the range of permissible action under relevant national and international laws and tinker with the deal accordingly. Withholding tax might, for instance, be imposed on fund transfers out of the country of investment. In light of lawyers' advice as to those tax requirements, this would be built into the deal's financial model. If a state-owned company is involved in the deal, lawyers would focus on the range of activity in which that entity is permitted to engage, under applicable national laws and prior contractual commitments. And so on and so forth, the legal analyses continue. The implication of any such analysis is that capital must bend to the 'will' of the law.

The deal will also be demarcated, from time to time, in terms of 'what the market requires'. On the withholding tax issue mentioned above, for example, it may be understood (depending upon the tax rate and deal economics) that the 'market requires' that tax not attach to debt repayments to foreign lenders or dividends paid to foreign equity holders. Counsel would then dedicate themselves to devising a funds-flow structure to achieve that result. Each legal issue open for negotiation within a deal will be discussed (at least in part) in terms of market norms. The implication of any such discussion is that the law must bend to the 'will' of capital and its drive to accumulate.

Yet the promise of capital accumulation is, as already noted, one only ever expressed in forecast terms. Likewise, the assurance of lawfulness will become increasingly tentative the more that a deal is seen as breaking new ground (an alluring prospect for participant-makers vested in affirming their own creativity). Among the risks with which participant-makers will understand themselves to be intimate is the risk that their deal-specific approximation of either 'what the law requires' or 'what the market requires' might be controverted from somewhere beyond the deal. It might turn out that the lawyers' reading of pertinent bankruptcy law authorities does not conform to an appellate court's subsequent pronouncement on the same. The market's appetite for the product being produced by the borrower might wane. Thus, the deal hovers between deal-specific projections of two horizons – 'what the law requires' and 'what the market requires' – each one as unsettled, often, as the other.

126

3. *The model as master: deal as commodity*

If the undecidedness of a deal acquires an objective existence for its participant-makers, it is more or less encapsulated by the financial model that in-house and external financial advisors produce in the course of its planning. Literally, the model is a set of interlocking spread-sheets in which economic relationships are established between simulated variables in an attempt to calibrate the economic consequences of particular future scenarios.[36] The model represents an attempt to cultivate a master-narrative of uncertainty for the deal: both to entrain risk and to give the deal over to risk. Lawyers rarely engage with the details of the financial model, but nonetheless tend to regard it, if only obliquely, as an expression of the deal's animus and purpose. Its very impenetrability (for all but the few financial types who work on it) seems to augment the model's talismanic force.

The model also expresses another sense in which the deal tends to be experienced by participant-makers: as a work of art or industry operating independently of any would-be authors.[37] In the automated unity of the model, one gains an impression of the deal as belonging to no-one, yet the work of many. Transactional lawyers tend, accordingly, to experience the deal as a collaborative, creative work, at one remove from the grubby brawls in which their litigation colleagues engage.[38] This sense of the deal often exerts a pacifying effect on employer-employee relations. The law firm associate handed yet another urgent, late-night assignment tends to understand *the deal* to be doing this to her, not the partner communicating the demand. Through the deal's circulation as collective work, friction is assuaged and points of possible resistance smoothed away.

After closing, the autonomy with which the deal is invested subsists in the commodified mode of a precedent. A particular deal-structure gets invested with a brand value independent of the institutional or jurisdictional sites of its making.[39] Lawyers embarking on a new deal will often begin by collecting publicly available accounts of past deals bearing some connection to their yet-to-be-created work, from which a new deal is assembled like some Dada collage. In so doing, they insert their new deal into a deal-lineage associated with 'success': associative value is purloined, reputation bolstered, and anxiety about uncertainty of outcome further allayed.

Hence, the deal-commodity's circulation fosters reproduction of the very *'stylized repetition of acts'* by which it was produced. The deal evokes a

---

36 The Monte Carlo class of computation algorithms is often used for this purpose, the name of which signals their incorporation of randomness and repetition. See S. Savvides, 'Risk Analysis in Investment Appraisal' (1994) 9 *Project Appraisal J.* 3.

37 Fleischer casts deal structure as a product or advertising medium, the effects of which remain 'ethereal': Fleischer, op. cit. (2006), n. 1, p. 1586.

38 See, for example, Freund, op. cit., n. 35.

39 See, generally, Fleischer, op. cit. (2006), n. 1.

collective allegiance among participant-makers that sets it apart from relations among them, however fraught. Accordingly, the instability arising from the deal's performativity gets cast outwards (as market uncertainty or generalized systemic demands) rather than inwards (as, say, employer-employee or investor-state conflict). The standard scholarly rejoinder has been to redouble that movement away from the deal's performative terrain: to plumb the global market's 'interior', ascribing determinative force to a latent bias or culture within this entity or that. The foregoing account suggests the potential fruitfulness of a different engagement – moving *through* the substance of the market, the law, or the corporation, and into the mêlée of performances that their properties and powers are.

4. Hailing Hale

Tracking the deal-specific capillaries along which power erratically flows is, I suggested earlier, a task for which legal realist scholarship provides both inspiration and instruction. In the 1920s and 1930s, legal realists, working primarily in the United States and Scandinavia, took issue with both classical liberal and orthodox Marxist accounts of the market. Against the former, they rejected a bald opposition between capitalist freedom (the free market, freedom of contract, freedom of speech, and so on) and socialist coercion (the planned economy), drawing attention to the coercive dimensions of liberal 'freedom'. Against the latter, they refused to accept the inherent freedom of capital in opposition to the absolute subordination of the working class. Rather, they highlighted the extent to which capital and capitalists are both constrained and enabled by legal rules and policy decisions made by lawyers.[40]

The insights of legal realist scholar Robert Hale about the operation of law in the market retain particular purchase today, not least as rejoinders to recent scholarship in which transnational corporate power is analysed. 'Law', in Hale's work, did not operate only in the sense of 'norms, standards, principles and rules' that attract varying degrees of support from those recognized as 'global actors', 'function[ing] to secure [their] objectives and goals', as in John Braithwaite's and Peter Drahos's influential account.[41] It operated, also, to vest certain entities with greater or lesser agency and attribute certain phenomena with systematicity. Hale's work demonstrated

---

40 See D. Kennedy, 'The Stakes of Law, or Hale and Foucault!' (1991) XV *Legal Studies Forum* 327, at 328–9.

41 J. Braithwaite and P. Drahos, *Global Business Regulation* (2000) 19. Although it prefers Hale's account to Braithwaite and Drahos's, this article nevertheless shares the latter's sense of the 'basic "messiness" about the globalization of regulation', their intuition that management philosophy may have (potentially) subversive dimensions, and their conviction that 'no single player . . . and no single mechanism ever brings about global regulatory change alone' (pp. 23 and 612).

128

that 'decisions made [by corporations, for instance] are a function of the decision-making structure, [such that] that structure becomes the critical, if not always conspicuous policy issue'.[42]

Recalling Hale's work encourages one to see incremental power latent in the deal scenarios described above: in, for instance, the capacity of participant-makers to withhold delivery on a performative expectation (to *fail* to remain loyal to their assumed deal role) and thereby affect value (the exchange value of the 'successful' deal-commodity, for example).[43] Hale's work also highlights the extent to which capacity so to withhold – and the intangible value embodied therein – is differentially allocated by law. So, through a Halean lens, as law shapes the interaction between a mid-level associate and a senior partner over negotiation strategy, or between a 'local' equity holder and 'foreign' lender over the location of a meeting (both interactions from which material consequences may flow, as noted above), regulatory power is delegated to these parties, and to the corporations and partnerships for which they work, as 'unofficial minorities'.[44] Moreover, the variable allocation of value among them is both an *outcome* of those minorities' exercise of legal power and a factor *circumscribing* that exercise. Wealth allocations so often cast as the dictates of the 'free' global market, or (per Hale) the outcome of 'individual efforts under a system of government neutrality' can, Hale demonstrated, be recast as the work of social actors among whom the law distributes power unevenly.[45] Hale showed us that lop-sided resource distributions thought to be the outcome of unfettered economic choice are maintained as a matter (at least partially) of legal decision.

Yet the implications of Hale's studies of private market power (as both an exercise and product of legal force) extend well beyond the range of his work. This is what the foregoing notes have sought to indicate. Legal decisions account not only for the distribution of power *as wealth* within and as a consequence of the deal. Legal institutions account also (in part) for distributions of power in reputational, symbolic, geographic, temporal, gendered, and stylistic terms. If the allocation of gains and losses from deal to deal tends to be rather predictable, then that very predictability is part of the pattern for which daily 'life choices' of lawyers are partially responsible. Far from being the prerogative of legislatures (as Hale suggested), incremental alteration of these patterns takes place at the menial level of corporate scheduling, for instance, as well as at the level of regulatory enactment.[46] As

---

42 Samuels, op. cit., n. 7, p. 351.
43 Compare R.L. Hale, 'Coercion and Distribution in a Supposedly Non-Coercive State' (1923) 38 *Political Science Q.* 470.
44 Hale, op. cit., n. 14.
45 Fried, op. cit., n. 7, p. 89.
46 id., p. 107. ('Given the essentially legislative nature of the choice that had to be made between the existing scheme and an infinite number of alternative schemes ... Hale ... argued, the choice was properly left to the legislatures ...'.) Compare n. 54 below and related text.

129

in Hale's writing, the central point is not to bemoan coercion or to arrive at a single, sweeping reformist solution, but rather to highlight that, in legal work at every level, power is both omnipresent and (variably) amenable to reallocation.[47] In contrast, recent accounts of global corporate rule have yielded a version of corporate power that seems both too generic and too thin.

II. CORPORATE POWER AND JURIDICAL ORDER

The messiness and madness of legal work described in the preceding section are rarely discernible in contemporary accounts of global corporate rule. One reason for this may be the unwillingness of those accounts to mobilize critical resources available within the academic legal canon. Just as contemporary critical theorizing is inattentive to law's day-to-day deal enactment, so it frequently overlooks the critical riches of legal scholarship: those to be garnered from Hale's work, for instance.

Like contemporary scholars such as Cutler, Hale observed that 'private "usurpation" ... of governmental functions is more frequent than is conventionally recognized'; 'governing power is invisible save when exerted by public officials wearing the authentic trappings of the political state'.[48] In terms not unlike those of Hardt and Negri in *Empire*, Hale noted that 'there was more coercion, and government and law played a more significant part [in the so-called "free economy"], than is generally realized'.[49]

Yet Hale's account of law – specifically, the role of law and lawyers in actions attributed to the market – went beyond that offered by either Cutler or Hardt and Negri. It did so in two respects. First, Hale drew greater attention to the significance of law in private economic activity. In so doing, Hale refused to cast law as constraining or enabling in itself, nor did he read law as the direct outcome of a 'contest of principles' among social or economic groups.[50] Rather, law's significance in private economic activity arose in part from the fact that it was *not* the focus of an explicit 'contest'. Law, in Hale's account, was so constitutively embedded in 'the market' and

---

47 Hale, op. cit., n. 14, p. 456.:
   [Given] our whole scheme for distributing income [may be seen as] one vast structure of 'minority dictation', ... the remedy is no such simple matter as getting out an injunction against the 'usurpers'. It consists, if indeed there is any remedy, in the construction of new organs of law-making and in the creation of new law for these new organs to apply when they deal, as deal they must, with questions concerning the proper distribution of income.

48 id., p. 453; Robert Hale Papers, folder 80–4, quoted by Samuels, op. cit., n. 7, p. 299. Compare Cutler, op. cit., n. 2, pp. 1–2.

49 Hale, op. cit., n. 18, p. 603. Compare Hardt and Negri, op. cit., n. 10, p. 3.

50 This phrase is drawn from Braithwaite and Drahos, op. cit., n. 41, pp. 18–20.

130

'society' as to render law an unseen beneficiary of faith in economic or social determinism.[51]

Second, the legal 'background' to which Hale drew attention, although ordered and ordering, was not as rigid as many recent characterizations suggest. It had the status of a 'pattern' both pliable *and* predictable.[52] Its maintenance as such depended upon endless iterations of decision.[53] However, for Hale, the role of decision was not encapsulated by conventional readings of contractual freedom, any more than by an exclusive orientation towards government policy reform.[54] The interpenetration of the choices of many, and the extent to which the echoing effects of choice may not therefore be anticipated in advance, rendered legal decision 'blind' and both its voluntariness and its decisiveness somewhat hypothetical, in Hale's account:

> The power [of various individuals and groups] ... is derived in part from the law's *more or less blind and haphazard* distribution of favors and burdens in the shape of powers over others and obligations to others.[55]

In contrast, Michael Hardt and Antonio Negri's *Empire* has laid claim to a relatively omnipotent, clear-eyed vision of the global distribution of power and law's role therein. It is to that vision that I will now turn.

51 Samuels, op. cit., n. 7, p. 299:
> Hale argued that the economy, fundamentally, is at least partially a function of what the law makes it to be, that, notwithstanding the obtrusiveness of increasingly deliberate political guidance of the market economy, there has been and is a vast and neglected realm of hitherto generally unobtrusive legal participation, and that much of its lies behind what is nominally seen (and studied by economists and extolled by ideologists) as simple private economic activity.

52 Quoted in id., p. 343:
> While the same legal and constitutional arrangements will produce varying economic patterns if people's tastes and abilities vary, the fact remains that the powers of compulsion which the law grants or permit to each individual have a determining effect likewise on the pattern, which would be different if the legal arrangements were different, even though the tastes and abilities of the people were the same.

53 Samuels (id., p. 350) observes of Hale's work that '[t]he ubiquity of choice, or policy, is correlative to the ubiquity of coercion'.

54 R.L. Hale, 'Labor Legislation as an Enlargement of Individual Liberty' (1925) 15 *Am. Labor Legislation Rev.* 155, at 160:
> As there is no one set of inequalities that must necessarily flow from property and contract, it cannot be asserted dogmatically that a statutory rearrangement of the existing inequalities will necessarily involve more restriction on liberty and more impairment of property rights than the reverse.

On Hale's notions of 'coercion', 'voluntary freedom', 'volitional freedom', and 'liberty', see, generally, Samuels, op. cit., n. 7, pp. 280–95 and Freid, op. cit., n. 7, pp. 29–70.

55 Hale, op. cit., n. 14, p. 455 [emphasis added].

131

'Empire is materializing before our very eyes', Michael Hardt and Antonio Negri informed their (many) readers in *Empire*.[56] Famously, Empire is the name that Hardt and Negri gave to a 'new form of sovereignty' governing the world, a 'new paradigm' of 'both system and hierarchy ... spread out over world space'; a 'new supranational juridical order' comprising 'the center that supports the globalization of productive networks' engaged in biopolitical production.[57] In *Empire*, the 'juridical' construction of global authority is, it seems, brought to the fore for direct negotiation.

Law, in *Empire*, expresses both the totality of the sovereign power that Hardt and Negri describe (Empire being a 'juridical' model) and particular, 'constituted' features of it. To the extent that constituent power is described as 'alien to the law' and that which the law seeks to organize,[58] Hardt and Negri associate law, in large part, with constituted power: that is, with the impulse to rule, restrain, centralize, punish, and formalize and with the 'philistinism of traditional juridical theory'.[59] 'Normativity, sanction, and repression' are understood as primary outcomes of domestic and international ('supranational') law.[60]

Moreover, the juridical order of Empire, in Hardt and Negri's account, has a 'fundamental connective fabric'. That fabric is woven 'in certain important respects' by 'huge transnational corporations':

> Capital has indeed always been organized with a view toward the entire global sphere, but only in the second half of the twentieth century did multinational and transnational industrial and financial corporations really begin to structure global territories biopolitically ... The activities of corporations are no longer defined by the imposition of abstract command and the organization of simple theft and unequal exchange. Rather, they directly structure and articulate territories and populations. They tend to make nation states merely instruments to record the flows of the commodities, monies, and populations they set in motion. The transnational corporations directly distribute labor power over various markets, functionally allocate resources, and organize hierarchically the various sectors of world production.[61]

---

56 Hardt and Negri, op. cit., n. 10, p. xi.
57 id., pp. 13, 16, 20. For their mobilization of Foucault's notion of 'biopolitical power', see pp. 22-41.
58 A. Negri, *Insurgencies: Constituent Power and the Modern State* (1999) tr. M. Boscagli, at 1 and 9 (quoting Georges Burdeau).
59 id., p. 20. Although, note the ambivalence of law in Hart and Negri's account, highlighted by Peter Fitzpatrick: P. Fitzpatrick, 'Laws of *Empire*' (2002) 15 *International J. for the Semiotics of Law* 253. See, further, P. Fitzpatrick, 'The Immanence of *Empire*' in *Empire's New Clothes: Reading Hardt and Negri*, eds. J. Dean and P.A. Passavant (2004) 31–55, at 43–5.
60 Hardt and Negri, op. cit., n. 10, p. 16.
61 id., pp. 31–2.

For all the disavowals of any centre or univocality within *Empire*, transnational corporations rise within the book to assume the stature of juridical '[g]iants [that] rule' through and in spite of a 'rhizomatic' network of 'global constitutional elements'.[62] And as is wont to happen in stories of giants, more than one would-be David rises with them.

2. *Private power and global authority*

Despite the relative minimalism of their analysis of transnational corporate power, Hardt and Negri's version seems both influential in, and indicative of, a tendency within recent left theorizing about the operations of global capital to read the 'juridical rule' of transnational corporations in a particular fashion. That reading entails casting the constituted power of law, manifest in the subjectivity of transnational corporations, as resolved, ripe, and packaged for re-taking by political activists or legal reformers. Permit me to venture one further example of this tendency.

A. Claire Cutler's study of 'the historical and contemporary influence of private power in the global political economy' is, it must be acknowledged, deeply attentive to the sorts of concerns raised in this article. Nevertheless, in *Private Power*, Cutler contends that the disciplines of international relations and international law are facing 'theoretical obstacles' and experiencing 'crisis'. This she attributes to these disciplines' inability to account for the historical rise of:

> [a] global mercatocracy or an elite association of transnational merchants, private lawyers, government officials, and representatives of international organizations engaged in the unification and globalization of transnational merchant law.[63]

In particular, she argues, scholarship in law and international relations remains wedded to a view of private international law and/or transnational merchant law as 'technical, functional, and apolitical bod[ies] of law, operating neutrally amongst market participants which are deemed generally to be of equal bargaining power'.[64]

Thus, *Private Power* is, in part, a story of law's progressive historical capture by a 'global mercatocracy', indicated in 'formidable accretions of corporate power and authority', and the insulation of that capture from question through objectification and a detachment of 'theory' from 'practice'.[65] The

---

62 id., pp. 305, 319, 307. To be fair, Hardt and Negri have not, in *Empire*, advanced a detailed account of the role of transnational corporations in propagating the global sovereign order to which they give the name Empire. Transnational corporations are, nevertheless, named as vital productive agents in 'a new economic-industrial-communicative machine'. See pp. 40, 150–3, 316–19.

63 Cutler, op. cit., n. 2, p. 12.

64 id., p. 6.

65 id., pp. 180, 196, 204, 233.

cure that Cutler would prescribe is one of reunification around a new line-up of legal subjects, transnational corporations among them.[66] Cutler's work thus shares with Hardt and Negri's two tendencies outlined above. Her work takes as a given the supposedly ossified matter of law and the calcified status of legal scholarship (a favourite theme, of course, for legal scholars themselves). Her work also 'unveils' transnational corporations as de facto subjects of remarkable coherence and determinative power, waiting in the wings to be harnessed, redressed, and brought to centre stage.

3. Staging redemption

In relation to these influential accounts, the concern that I wish to raise is not merely a discipline-defensive gripe about inattention to the historical richness of legal scholarship (specifically, Hale's). Rather, the worries that I have are twofold. First, when read against Hale's careful, detailed account of the work of legal decision in a 'free market', and against working lawyers' experience of the performative volatility of the deal, Hardt and Negri's tendency to collapse law into 'constituted power' and Cutler's reading of law as the unalloyed vehicle of 'disciplinary neoliberalism' seem misrepresentative and strategically misguided. Second, the emancipatory promise carried by these recent books seems to render them more part of the problem that they seek to foreground, than assurance of its imminent (or immanent) redress.

In their shared affirmation of historical progression (read as decline) and political predestination, both *Empire* and *Private Power* seem to fold too easily into the very 'transcendental apparatus' with which *Empire*, at least, takes issue.[67] Hardt and Negri rail against the 'imposition of transcendent rule and order' that 'limit[s] a priori' the 'realm of potentiality, which had been opened by the humanist principle of subjectivity'.[68] Yet the 'being against' Empire from within cast as 'the essential key to every active political position in the world' does not seem to extend to being against the all-consuming embrace of their account.[69] What does '[d]isobedience to authority' imply when Hardt and Negri insist that '[t]he telos of the multitude must live and organize its political space against Empire ... within ... the ontological conditions that Empire presents'?[70] In *Private Power*, the exalted seat reserved for Empire and its architects is occupied by the 'mercatocratic' elite and, on occasion, by the transnational corporation. It is their 'subjective identity' and authority that, Cutler contends, law has 'suppressed or sublimated' and that Cutler promises to reinscribe so that law

66 id., pp. 239–40.
67 Hardt and Negri, op. cit., n. 10, pp. 78–85. See Fitzpatrick, op. cit., n. 59, pp. 260–1.
68 id., p. 80.
69 id., pp. 210–11.
70 id., p. 407.

134

might once again 'constitute, mirror, and, in some cases ... discipline ...: emerging social forces'.[71]

With *Empire*'s and *Private Power*'s folding into transcendence comes another nestling: in a smooth, tradable sameness that announces itself as a could-be-different. The collective overturning of transnational corporate power anticipated in *Empire* and *Private Power* is, to this reader at least, strangely pacifying. That may be so because that overturning is framed in terms that articulate so well *to* a crucial dimension of corporate power: the fetishized appeal of the commodity.[72] That is, it is expressed in terms that are at once generic and insistent of their amenability to being personalized.

Although commodities have a 'life of their own',[73] the commodity's appeal rests, in large part, with its invitation to agency: its call to make the commodity one's own or part of oneself.[74] It is through that call that the commodity sustains its fungibility and impels itself towards subsequent exchange. To make a commodity one's own is to integrate it into one's 'lifestyle', and to make it, or the value it embodies, integral to one's 'identity': most importantly, that of a self-authoring being.[75] That integration relies on the commodity's ability to stand generically for something other than itself. Such integration also involves a compulsion towards endless self-revision (self-authorship not being appreciable in a single act), necessitating the acquisition of additional commodities. In this way, commodities' appeal to personalization links to their incessant circulation, that circulation being axiomatic to the accumulation of capital.

The promise with which *Empire* and *Private Power* are loaded operates in a comparable way.[76] By promising readers that, following the authors' lead, they might make Empire or 'global authority' their own by, for instance, recapturing power from transnational corporations, these books impel their readers into an upward-spiralling fantasy of authorship, substitution, and exchange. The power of Empire, mercatocratic rule, and/or transnational corporate rule is to be exchanged for the power of the multitude or, according to Cutler, 'alternate institutions, laws and practices',[77] under the direction of a generalized self-emancipating agency. This evocation of a collective giant-slaying David in the image of the commodity-holder tends to immunize global capital from its own ambivalences by reproducing them as an essential ingredient of progressive social transformation.

71 Cutler, op. cit., n. 2, pp. 248–9.
72 See Marx, op. cit. (1867), n. 12, pp. 163–77.
73 id., p. 165.
74 id., p. 343: 'What seems to throb there [in the commodity exchange] is my own heartbeat'.
75 See F. Tönnies, *Community and Society: Gemeinschaft and Gesellschaft* (2002 [1887]) tr. C.P. Loomis, 94: '[T]he commodity is taken possession of as an object of one's own will and a supplement to one's own forces.'
76 Compare B. Maurer, 'On Divine Markets and the Problem of Justice: *Empire* as Theodicy' in Dean and Passavant, op. cit., n. 59, pp. 57–72, at p. 63.
77 Cutler, op. cit. n. 2, p. 258.

4. Hailing Hale, again

Whereas Hardt, Negri, and Cutler cast law as a captor of constituent power –
the arcane lion-tamer, and some-time cage, to the irrepressible humanist lion
– for Robert Hale, law was part of the pattern that held the very configuration
of lion, tamer, and cage in place. Consider Hale's brief exegesis on
bargaining in a 'free economy':

> The employer's power to induce people to work for him depends largely on
> the fact that the law previously restricts the ability of these people to consume
> [by barring access to goods produced absent the consent of those to whom the
> law assigns ownership], while [the employer] has the power, through the
> payment of wages, to release [employees] to some extent from these
> restrictions [although, Hale goes on to show that wage-paying power is itself
> endowed by and subject to property law] ...[78]

While Cutler would likely focus, in reading this paragraph, on the
subjectivity of the employer, Hale directed our attention elsewhere, towards
'government': 'Whenever we find some men compelling other men to obey
them', Hale wrote, 'there we find government'.[79] Moreover, 'government'
was not, according to Hale, a force conveniently located in, or equivalent to,
the institutions of the state, or indeed any singular agent. 'This invisible
government', he wrote, 'is not a single coherent unit. It is a cluster of
different groups and persons who hold sway in different fields'.[80]

Duncan Kennedy helps us to see how far this account of law and power
strays from Cutler's narrative of mercatocratic rule and Hardt and Negri's
story of Empire:

> To see the modern power of Hale's insight, we have to follow him in
> abandoning the on/off all-or-nothing understanding of capitalism and private
> property. What we have in fact is a 'mixed' capitalist system in which (a)
> nothing like the whole economy is organized in terms of wage labor and the
> confrontation between worker and capitalist, and (b) property rights are neither
> 'absolute' nor self-defining ... [T]he mere choice of a [capitalist] regime
> doesn't settle the thousands of questions that will arise about the ground rules
> in particular situations.[81]

In its attention to the 'thousands of [unsettled] questions ... about the ground
rules in particular situations', Hale's work set rich, perplexing and dynamic
legal scenes, closer than Hardt and Negri's or Cutler's to the lived experience of a transnational corporate deal. Such scenes, moreover, presented
myriad options for critical manoeuvre. The critically inclined could work on
any one of these unsettled questions, rather than confronting a paralysing,
phantasmal choice between revolutionary triumph and ignoble servitude.

78 Hale, op. cit., n. 18, pp. 627–8.
79 Quoted by Samuels, op. cit., n. 7, p. 296.
80 id.
81 Kennedy, op. cit., n. 40, pp. 339–40.

A second significant dimension of Hale's work is evident in the conundrum outlined above – the sense in which 'volitional freedom' cannot be assured any 'counter-coercive' effect. In contrast to *Empire* and *Private Power*, Hale's work did not feed conviction that an awakening to power might permit its being brought to heel. In this respect, Hale may be read as a Foucauldian *avant la lettre*.[82] Immersing himself in the twists and turns of case law, Hale cautioned:

> [i]t is no simple matter to reform this situation . . . power permeates the entire economic system, and attempts to alter it may have repercussions that require more comprehensive treatment than a court is capable of giving.[83]

In a similar vein, he wrote:

> There is no a priori reason for regarding planned governmental intervention in the economic sphere as inimical to economic liberty, or even to that special form of it known as free enterprise.[84]

Accordingly, in Hale's account, one cannot *know* that any reversal of whatever is taken to be the legal 'status quo' would yield greater equality or emancipation for 'the weak', because of the complex ways in which constraint and liberty operate within the law.[85] Hale was certainly committed to the cause of law reform: he advanced a legislative programme dedicated to equalizing, to the greatest extent possible, the coercive power to which private parties were subject.[86] Nevertheless, Hale's liberal reformist impulses did not surmount his attention to the 'thousands of questions that will arise about the ground rules in particular situations'. His energies were not expended in the pursuit of consummate liberation, but in persistent, laborious experimentation, unconcerned with the assurance of rectitude or redemption.[87]

Hale's account of law thus runs against the overall shape and direction of *Empire* and *Private Power* in so far as both books are animated by a

---

82 id.
83 R.L. Hale, 'Force and the State: A Comparison of "Political" and "Economic" Compulsion' (1935) 35 *Columbia Law Rev.* 149, at 199.
84 Hale, op. cit., n. 18, p. 628.
85 This complex interaction is captured in Hale's close studies of the impact of doctrinal reform. See, for example, R.L. Hale, *Freedom Through Law* (1952) 132 (highlighting that measures designed to bolster the position of the economically 'weak' may be read as a governmental deprivation of liberty and accordingly impugned under constitutional guarantees, while the 'weak' may not subject their original deprivation of property and liberty – that was the rationale for the legislative 'intervention' – to similar legal challenge).
86 See, for example, R.H. Hale, 'Rate-Making and the Revision of the Property Concept' (1922) 22 *Columbia Law Rev.* 209. As Fried observes, the affirmative agenda coursing through Hale's writings was 'internal to the liberal tradition that Hale was critiquing': Fried, op. cit., n. 7, p. 22.
87 Freedom, in Hale's account, was not something one enjoyed completely or not at all. See R.L. Hale, Review of M.J. Adler, *The Idea of Freedom* (1959) 59 *Columbia Law Rev.* 821, at 826.

137

powerful sense of historical linearity and predestination. Tracing 'fundamental reconfigurations of global power and authority' through 'three phases
in [the law merchant's] evolution' since medieval times, Cutler announces:
'The pressing problem is to reconceive the story.'[88] With similar
breathlessness, Hardt and Negri observe that '[t]he virtual powers of the
multitude in postmodernity signal the end of [the modern] rule [of capital
and its institutions of sovereignty]'.[89] Against these sweeping accounts,
much might yet be learned from Hale's painstaking work about locating
legal and political footholds on the surfaces of a corporate transaction. As
Part I of this article sought to show, in the familiar, mundane chaos of a deal,
clefts open in the triumphant face of global capital and these are neither
empty of power nor filled to the brim with necessity.

CONCLUSION

This volume of essays marks a sceptical revisitation of recent announce-
ments of the rise of an *imperium* without borders, as a global end unto itself.
This article has focused on two oft-cited vehicles for that *imperium*: the
global corporation and the law. Drawing upon the work of Robert Hale, it
has argued against the reading of legal decision as congealed power and the
tracing of that power to the transnational corporation. Inverting Hardt and
Negri's insistence that there is 'no more outside' to global capital or Empire,
there may be *no inside* to Empire or global authority in so far as the
interiority of those forces has been borne by the attribution of the law and the
corporation with certain defining properties. In the arena of the deal, this
article has depicted the performative enactment of those properties, seeking
to establish as political the very terms through which they get articulated and
to recapture some sense of the madness or undecidedness of that articulation.
In the layered artifice of the deal, one discerns the contingency of any
continuous law-capital lock-step, and senses both the possibility and the
difficulty of dancing to a different tempo, or indeed, to no tune at all.

88 Cutler, op. cit., n. 2, pp. 108, 241, 257.
89 Hardt and Negri, op. cit., n. 10, p. 367–8.

JOURNAL OF LAW AND SOCIETY
VOLUME 34, NUMBER 1, MARCH 2007
ISSN: 0263-323X, pp. 139–62

Veiled Women and the *Affect* of Religion in Democracy

Stewart Motha*

The veiled woman troubles feminism and secularism in much the same way. Both feminism and secularism face a problem of finding a position that respects individual autonomy, and simultaneously sustains a conception of politics freed from heteronomous determination. This article gives an account of what is being resisted and by whom in modes of politics which seek to produce an autonomous subject emancipated from 'other laws' (heteronomy). It also draws on Jean-Luc Nancy in order to consider what has been termed the problem of Islam in Europe as a wider juridical and political problem centred on the significance of affect as heteronomy. It thus explores the tension between piety and polity.

INTRODUCTION

Ministers of state and the Prime Minister of Britain have found a problem worthy of themselves.[1] Not just the emancipation of women but social

* Kent Law School, University of Kent, Canterbury, Kent CT2 7NS, England
s.motha@kent.ac.uk

I would like to thank Brenna Bhandar and Colin Perrin for the countless enriching conversations, and for continuing to be the most challenging interlocutors. Suhraiya Jivraj read a previous draft and offered incisive suggestions for which I am very grateful. The AHRC Centre for Law, Gender and Sexuality at the University of Kent provided the vibrant setting for exploring the concerns examined in this article. Any errors are mine.

1 For a similar account in relation to France, see A. Badiou's excellent reflection in 'The Law of the Islamic Headscarf' in his *Polemics* (2006) at 98–114. A sample of the statements by ministers and the Prime Minister about veiled Muslim women can be found in an excellent review of events and press coverage by Wendy Kristianasen, 'Britain's Multiculturalism Falters' in *Le Monde diplomatique*, November 2006. Ishah Azmi, a school teacher in Dewsbury, Yorkshire, who wore a *nikab* in the classroom ceased to be a worker whose rights should have been determined by an employment tribunal without politicians expressing their judgement before all legal processes were expended. The minister for race and faith, Phil Woolas, told the *Sunday Mirror* on 15 October that 'she should be sacked. She has put herself in a position where she can't do her job'. Her own MP, Shahid Malik, urged her not to pursue an appeal. Harriet

cohesion, even democracy itself, depends on their success. In France the *hijab* and other religious symbols have been outlawed in educational institutions. Muslim girls and women are to be saved from their fathers and brothers. These girls and women must show their hair and faces, for surely to think that the decision to 'veil' is a matter of autonomous choice, an exercise of freedom of conscience or religion long guaranteed by liberal juridical orders is nothing but 'false consciousness'. What is the reason for this rage against a few girls and women who wear headscarves or other forms of Islamic dress? What is behind this insistence that the woman, and especially the girl, must disrobe, must show herself?[2]

The current obsession of the state and media with woman in the United Kingdom wearing a *hijab, jilbab* or *nikab* has also led to calls to abandon the state-sponsored policy of multiculturalism. In France the debate has been centred on the secular character of the Republic, the principle of *laïcité*, the separation of religion and the state. In both cases the prevailing concerns are the absorption or integration of 'minority cultures' in order to produce some elusive notion of social cohesion, and to disrupt apparently oppressive practices. The claim that multiculturalism and feminism are inconsistent is not new.[3] 'Culture' is now the cipher for speaking about people and practices that were racialized in earlier times. To question 'culture' and thus multi-culturalism is the new way to speak about the 'difference' of Europe's others – especially at a time when Islam and 'terror' have been given a spurious equivalence. 'Multiculturalism' was itself a liberal attempt to pluralize the concept of equality – to 'respect difference', 'tolerate' heterogeneity of social and cultural practices, and value a diversity of life worlds.[4] But the 'culture' and religion of the occident's archetypical other is being re-branded – Islam is once again a threat to the democratic value of equal liberty for all, despite the suicide of liberality contained in such discursive and govern-mental strategies to limit religious practices.

The veiled woman troubles feminism and secularism in much the same way. Both feminism and secularism face a problem of finding a consistent position that respects individual autonomy, and simultaneously sustains a

Harman, minister in the Department of Constitutional Affairs, called for an end to the *nikab* 'because I want women to be fully included. If you want equality, you have to be in society, not hidden away from it'. Creating a timely distraction from the disasters in Iraq, Jack Straw initiated the furore when he asked a constituent (not a term to be taken literally any longer) that she should remove her *nikab* as he 'felt uncomfortable'. Prime Minister Blair intervened later stating that the *nikab* was a 'mark of separation' that makes others 'from outside of the community feel uncomfortable'. See Kristianasen's detailed contextualization of how the veil became a weighty matter of state.

2 Badiou, id.

3 See S.M. Okin, *Is Multiculturalism Bad for Women?* (1999).

4 There have, of course, been powerful and persuasive critiques of multiculturalism, see, especially, H. Bannerji, *Thinking Through: Essays on Feminism, Marxism and Anti-Racism* (1995); and *The Dark Side of the Nation: Essays on Multiculturalism, Nationalism and Gender* (2000).

140

conception of politics freed from heteronomous determination. In making this argument, this article takes much of its conceptual inspiration from the essay by Jean-Luc Nancy contained in this volume. As Nancy characterizes the problem:

> So everything happens as if the great alternative of modernity had been: either definitively emancipate politics so that it is entirely separate from religion, or expel them both, outside the effectivity and seriousness of the autoproduction of humanity. So either politics is conceived as the effectivity of autonomy (personal as well as collective), or politics and religion together are represented as heteronomous, and autonomy consists in freeing oneself from them. Resistance of the political to the religious or resistance to the politico-religious (and in this case, resistance of what, of whom? Let us leave this question in suspense).[5]

Inspired by this line of questioning, this article will seek to do two things: first, attempt to give an answer to what is being resisted and by whom in modes of politics which seek to produce an autonomous subject emancipated from 'other laws' (heteronomy). Second, it will consider what has been termed the problem of Islam in Europe as a wider juridical and political problem centred on the significance of *affect* as heteronomy. That is, it will explore the important tension between piety and the polity. But let us first consider some examples of how the problem of autonomy and heteronomy are presented in juridical and political discourse.

There is by now high judicial authority, in Europe and the United Kingdom, for governmental limits on religious dress. The Grand Chamber of the European Court of Human Rights in *Leyla Şahin* v. *Turkey*[6] endorsed a version of secularism that saw the ban on the 'Islamic headscarf' (the *hijab*) as a condition for maintaining the 'revolutionary values' that underpin the Republic of Turkey, and thus for guaranteeing equality, liberty, and democracy.[7] The prohibition on wearing the *hijab* by Leyla Şahin, a medical student at Istanbul University, was found to be a justifiable and proportionate means of dealing with a threat to 'public order' and for protecting the rights and freedoms of others. The Grand Chamber endorsed the following statement from the Chamber judgment of June 2004:

> The Court does not lose sight of the fact that there are extremist political movements in Turkey which seek to impose on society as a whole their religious symbols and conception of a society founded on religious precepts ... It has previously said that each Contracting State may, in accordance with the Convention provisions, take a stance against such political movements, based on its historical experience ... The regulations concerned have to be viewed in that context and constitute a measure intended to achieve the

---

5 J.-L. Nancy, 'Church, State, Resistance' in this Special Issue, (2007) 34 *Journal of Law and Society* 3–13, at 7.

6 *Leyla Şahin* v. *Turkey* (Grand Chamber, European Court of Human Rights, Strasbourg, 10 November 2005); see, also, *Dahlab* v. *Switzerland* (Application no. 42393/98, 15 February 2001).

7 See *Şahin*, id., para. 39.

141

legitimate aims referred to above and thereby to preserve pluralism in the university.[8]

This assessment equates the *hijab* and other forms of Islamic dress with 'extremism', and with political movements that threaten the secular character of the Republic of Turkey. With the vulnerability of the secular state in mind, the following account of secularism was endorsed by the Grand Chamber:

> Secularism is the civil organiser of political, social and cultural life, based on national sovereignty, democracy, freedom and science. Secularism is the principle which offers the individual the possibility to affirm his or her own personality through freedom of thought and which, by the distinction it makes between politics and religious beliefs, renders freedom of conscience and religion effective. In societies based on religion, which function with religious thought and religious rules, political organisation is religious in character. In a secular regime, religion is shielded from a political role. It is not a tool of the authorities and remains in its respectable place, to be determined by the conscience of each and everyone.[9]

The defence of the principle of secularism as distinct from state authority based on religious values is central to the judgment of the Grand Chamber, and to the wider disavowal of Islamic dress in the United Kingdom, France, the Netherlands, and Germany.[10] We see in this formulation of secularism a direct opposition asserted between a politics of individual autonomy and theocratic political organization. It is precisely this distinction between secular and religious order that I will challenge in this article.

Secularism has not been the key ground for limiting Islamic dress in the United Kingdom. The United Kingdom cannot lay claim to being a secular state – and the fact that liberty, equality, and pluralism have nonetheless flourished in this non-secular state was not a matter that interrupted the reasoning of the Grand Chamber in *Şahin* when it elevated secularism with such confidence. But the United Kingdom courts have also ruled on the (in)appropriateness of religious dress, most recently in *R (Begum)* v. *Headteacher and Governors of Denbigh High School*.[11]

---

8 id., para. 115, the Grand Chamber citing the decision of the European Court of Human Rights in *Şahin* with approval.

9 id., para. 39, decision of the Constitutional Court of Turkey, published in the *Official Gazette*, 5 July 1989, endorsed by the Grand Chamber at para. 115.

10 For an overview of the variety of reactions to Islamic dress in Europe, see T. Modood et al. (eds.), *Multiculturalism, Muslims, and Citizenship: A European Approach* (2006).

11 *R (Begum)* v. *Headteacher and Governors of Denbigh High School* [2006] UKHL 15. The dispute was between Shabina Begum, a minor of nearly 14 years when the dispute began, and Denbigh High School in Luton. The School prevented Shabina Begum from wearing the *jilbab* when she attended school, but denied that it had excluded her from the School. She was, according to the School, asked to conform to a 'uniform policy' (wear the shalwar kameeze and/or other forms of dress including a *hijab*) which had been drawn up, the School claimed, in a manner sensitive to Muslim

142

The grand revolutionary ideals of a secular state are absent from the character of the tension between autonomy and heteronomy in the United Kingdom. Instead, women's equality, freedom of religious practice, social harmony, and unity and public order have featured in the reasoning of the courts. In *Begum* it was a school uniform policy which permitted the *hijab* but prohibited the *jilbab* that was in issue. The majority of judges in the House of Lords concluded that Miss Begum's right to manifest her religion (guaranteed by Article 9 of the European Convention of Human Rights (ECHR)) was not infringed as she and her family had chosen that she attend this school knowing full well that there were limits on school uniform. The majority also concluded that if her Article 9 right was infringed, there was a justifiable and proportionate limitation of her right authorized by Article 9(2) of the ECHR. The limits on school uniform were also judged to have been arrived at with extensive and adequate consultation in a plural society – the Imams had been consulted![12] At stake, then, was the limitation of religious freedom and the extent to which this is consistent with a plural democratic polity.

The decision of Baroness Hale in *Begum* is of particular significance for the objectives of this article. That is because it so palpably struggles with the tension between autonomy and heteronomy. Thus individual autonomy is pitted against democracy (as multicultural social cohesion), and feminist arguments that both support girls who veil and eschew the practice are considered. The reasons given by Baroness Hale for approving the school's uniform policy include consideration of the individual choice of women,[13] women's equality,[14] the complex agency of Muslim girls in Europe,[15] the

girls and their religious beliefs, and after wide consultation. Shabina Begum argued that she had been excluded, and had thus been denied her Art. 9 right and freedom under the European Convention on Human Rights to manifest her religious belief. She also contended that she has been denied her right to education, but this was not pursued later on appeal. Once Art. 9 is engaged, and not all Lord Justices agreed that it was, the question was whether the interference was justified and necessary in a democratic society. The majority of the House of Lords concluded that there had been no interference with the right in Art. 9 to manifest the practices and observances of Shabina Begum's religious beliefs. Lord Bingham sets out the most comprehensive account of this position. Lord Nicholls and Baroness Hale stated that there was an interference with Begum's Art. 9 rights, but argued that the interference was justified.

12 See the judgment of Lord Bingham, id., at para. 34; and Lord Foscote, id., paras. 75–7.

13 id., para. 96: 'If a woman freely chooses to adopt a way of life for herself, it is not for others, including other women who have chosen differently, to criticise or prevent her'.

14 id., para. 95: 'A dress code which requires women to conceal all but their face and hands, while leaving men much freer to decide what they will wear, does not treat them equally'.

15 id., para. 94: citing Bhikhu Parekh's rebuttal of Susan Moller Okin in 'A Varied Moral World, A Response to Susan Okin's "Is Multiculturalism Bad for Women"' *Boston Review*, October/November 1997. Parekh wrote:

In France and the Netherlands several Muslim girls freely wore the hijab (headscarf), partly to reassure their conservative parents that they would not be

143

limited cognitive capacities of a child,[16] and then beyond the individual, the social cohesion that a school might foster.[17] Drawing on the dissenting judgment of Judge Tulkens in *Şahin*, Baroness Hale agreed that there should not be limits placed on an adult's individual autonomy to choose how religious belief would be manifested. But in the case of a child, such limits were said to be justified, particularly when a school was successfully implementing a policy that was aimed at creating the conditions for social cohesion.

At the heart of Baroness Hale's reasoning is an extremely limited notion of what it means for an individual to have autonomous agency ('formal operational thought') – and this despite the fact that she acknowledges the complexity of agentive decisions on veiling by girls and women.[18] Moreover, it features the elevation of the unity of the community – the commonality and cohesion produced by the school – over the complex concerns that inform the decisions of young women to 'veil'. It thus exposes how the exigencies of sustaining a particular formation of the political – the cohesive multicultural state – are dressed up as a defence of individual autonomy, or the protection of vulnerable girls. The production of a cohesive nation has to negotiate tensions between autonomy, democracy, secularism, and religion. It is precisely the relation between these phenomena that I explore here.

What, then, is the relation between autonomy, democracy, secularism, and religion? As we have seen, the equal liberty of the individual to practice her

corrupted by the public culture of the school, and partly to reshape the latter by indicating to white boys how they wished to be treated. The hijab in their case was a highly complex autonomous act intended to use the resources of the tradition both to change and to preserve it.

16 id., para. 93:
Important physical, cognitive and psychological developments take place during adolescence. Adolescence begins with the onset of puberty; from puberty to adulthood, the 'capacity to acquire and utilise knowledge reaches its peak efficiency'; and the capacity for formal operational thought is the forerunner to developing the capacity to make autonomous moral judgments. Obviously, these developments happen at different times and at different rates for different people. But it is not at all surprising to find adolescents making different moral judgments from those of their parents. It is part of growing up. The fact that they are not yet fully adult may help to justify interference with the choices they have made. It cannot be assumed, as it can with adults, that these choices are the product of a fully developed individual autonomy.

17 id., para. 98:
Social cohesion is promoted by the uniform elements of shirt, tie and jumper, and the requirement that all outer garments be in the school colour. But cultural and religious diversity is respected by allowing girls to wear either a skirt, trousers, or the shalwar kameez, and by allowing those who wished to do so to wear the hijab. This was indeed a thoughtful and proportionate response to reconciling the complexities of the situation. This is demonstrated by the fact that girls have subsequently expressed their concern that if the jilbab were to be allowed they would face pressure to adopt it even though they do not wish to do so.

18 See Parekh, op. cit., n. 15.

religion, or to engage in social or cultural practices (though the practice of 'veiling' cannot be reduced to that), has been opposed to civility, the emancipation of women, the defeat of Islamic fundamentalism, and the physical and psychological health of children. While the obvious conclusion to draw from all this would be that the 'sacred' is being unequivocally expelled in order to sustain some other basis of commonality, in this paper I argue that much more is at stake. The controversy in relation to Islamic dress, and more widely, the place of Islam in Europe, is an apt context in which to explore how formations of the 'sacred' mediate what is 'common' in secular political community. The contemporary crisis of liberal democracy stems, I wish to argue, from the inability to sustain a political formation either by monistic authority (of God, monarch, or its modern variation as 'people'), or by the various hetero-nomic formations of political community determined by history (class and labour), religion, culture, or ethno-nationality. Even the cosmopolitan polity buckles under the weight of the exigencies of 'necessity' which regulate the application of human rights. Nearly all human rights enunciated in post-Second World War charters and conventions (following the model of the French Declaration of the Rights of Man and Citizen 1789) subject such rights to limitations 'prescribed by law' and 'necessary in a democratic society'. That is to say, the violence that might legitimately be deployed in the name of sovereignty and community has multiplied in the age of human rights, and in a manner that specifically destroys the very liberties and autonomies purportedly founded and protected by such extreme measures. 'Democracy' is now invoked in order to legitimate violations of individual freedom and liberty, and to disregard fundamental legal protections such as habeas corpus. We must understand this undermining of freedom, equality, and liberty in the name of democracy by way of a complex relation between *autonomy* and *heteronomy* contained in the concept of politics itself.[19]

It is worth tracing some of the key modes of politics that have led to the oppositions we have just observed between autonomy/heteronomy, sacred/profane, liberty/democracy. Much of the rhetoric about women who veil has centred on questions of individual autonomy, agency, social cohesion, and political transformation. It is therefore useful to provide a map of the influential discourses on political subjectivity, agency, and social transformation. This is followed by an examination of piety and political community in the second part of this article. Islamic piety has posed particular challenges in democratic political orders. The objective here is to explore the contours of how piety is a problem of 'polity'. How does the opposition between religion and democracy arise in European modernity? Is the distinction between sacred and secular viable? How does the relation between autonomy and heteronomy undo the simplistic opposition between Islam and democracy?

19 I take this opposition of autonomy/heteronomy from Nancy, op. cit., n. 5.

145

1. *Autonomy*

Although the enlightenment and its bourgeois revolutions are not the only source of a 'proclamation of autonomy', their inspired formulation of 'no equality without liberty, no liberty without equality' is worth examining more closely.[21] As Balibar argues, 'equal liberty' stated in revolutionary terms has a logic that contains a 'self-refutation of its negation'.[22] It is logically impossible to base civil liberty on discrimination, privilege, and inequality just as it is not possible to institute equality by despotism, even 'enlightened' despotism.[23] This is a lesson that those who have intervened to save young Muslim women will do well to learn. But here the first *aporia* of autonomy also emerges to unsettle the 'purity' of the formulation set out above. Autonomy is only possible through the unfolding of a universalization of the claim to autonomy. For instance, in the Marxist tradition, the demand for emancipation was articulated through the universalization 'the people of the people', the 'universal class'.[24] The politics of autonomy which is first a negation of oppressive conditions, must then present as a 'negation of the negation', thus becoming an absolute.[25] As Balibar puts it, this 'idealisation expresses itself in namings, creations of keywords, whose power to seize the imagination is all the greater for the fact that they initially expressed a radical negativity'.[26] 'People' and 'proletariat' are such terms, and Balibar claims that 'woman' and 'foreigner' might be others.[27] The unfolding of the emancipatory politics of the claim to autonomy of women, in its universalization as an absolute, becomes an unconditional demand that sweeps away any claim that does not fit with the ideal. What content will be given to this ideal? What conditions of women's emancipation will be made absolute?

In the language of left progressive politics, autonomy as the unconditional base for an emancipatory politics turns against itself at the moment when it is invoked as a universal practice. The universalization of a particular political subjectivity appears to be, in various modern instantiations, a necessary condition of emancipatory politics. But the autonomy of the subject falls down at the frontier where it confronts the (other's) law from another place.

---

20 E. Balibar, *Politics and the Other Scene* (2002) 1–39. I draw the three concepts of politics discussed in this section from Balibar's account.
21 id., p. 2
22 id., p. 3.
23 id.
24 id., p. 6.
25 id., p. 7.
26 id.
27 id.

For instance, consider the claim made by some feminists in relation to multiculturalism – particularly in the controversial debate around Susan Moller Okin's essay, 'Is Multiculturalism Bad for Women?'[28] Here the claim is that respect for a plurality of cultural practices and normative frameworks can lead to normative paralysis in the face of practices that are harmful to women, such as polygamy, forced marriage, or genital cutting. But in an attempt to universalize the emancipated feminine subject, this feminist intervention undoes the very important negation of the abstract, autonomous liberal subject, exposed by an earlier feminist critique. More recently, Anne Phillips has presented an advance on Okin's concern, by suggesting that multiculturalism be emptied of 'culture'. It is a gesture that holds on to the possibility of universally applicable norms that can regulate practices in particular life-worlds:

> We need ... a multiculturalism without 'culture': a multiculturalism that dispenses with the reified notions of culture that feed those stereotypes to which so many feminists have objected, yet retains enough robustness to address inequalities between cultural groups; a multiculturalism in which the language of cultural difference no longer gives hostages to fortune or sustenance to racists, but also no longer paralyses normative judgment. Those writing on multiculturalism (supporters as well as critics) have exaggerated not only the unity and solidity of cultures but also the intractability of value conflict, and often misrecognised highly contextual political dilemmas as if these reflected deep value disagreement. Though there are important areas of cultural disagreement, most do not involve a deep diversity in respect of ethical principles and norms, and many are more comparable to the disputes that take place *within* cultural groups.[29]

What, in particular, is being negated here in the name of a feminist politics? There is of course a disavowal of cultural relativism and an affirmation of woman's agency 'within' particular cultural formations. There is also recognition of cultural difference, but a refusal to accept deep incommensurability with regard to ethical and normative principles. Most palpable, however, is the sense that one is either *inside* or *outside* a cultural and political group, and on the dominant side of such a binary opposition is a hegemonic capacity (of the feminists of the majority culture) to engineer a political consensus about what is beneficial to oppressed women.[30] On what basis can this political consensus be produced? This is a question that troubles all politics, and significantly, it leaves one wondering what is left of the demand for (the other's) 'autonomy' at the end of this process.

---

28 Okin, op. cit., n. 3.
29 A. Phillips, 'Multiculturalism without Culture' 4 (original emphasis), paper presented at conference on 'Beyond Feminism v. Multiculturalism', London School of Economics, 17 November 2006, to be published in A. Phillips, *Multiculturalism without Culture* (2007).
30 Later I will consider another feminist approach, by Rosi Braidotti, that eschews this inside/outside conception of politics and human subjectivity – but one that I argue has its own shortcomings.

We have just observed the tension between universalizing autonomy and producing political consensus at the same time. This is a particular problem when the cultural and political field is understood to be 'multicultural' or plural – by implication containing a multiplicity of normative frameworks. Let's consider this problem of politics in another register, this time, one that places emphasis on individual agency, and transformation of the conditions under which individuals make their own history.

2. Heteronomy

Famously, Marx gave an account of subjects' agency as 'politics under conditions not of their choosing'. For Marx: 'human beings make there own history, but they do not make it arbitrarily in conditions chosen by themselves, but in conditions always already given and inherited from the past'.[31] Balibar offers a persuasive account of the agency of the individual subject that can be derived from the 'conditions of history' as the *heteronomous* condition of politics.[32] Moreover, he combines this, following Foucault, with social and cultural structures, in order to avoid privileging structures of production and exchange.[33] For Marx, universalizing the economic base of history, 'man is first and foremost a labouring being'.[34] Revolutionary politics is developed by exploiting the contradictions that might ultimately rupture the economic base.

New social movements, including feminism, have followed a similar logic in arguing against patriarchy, or cultural modes of domination. The general pattern is to examine the material conditions of politics, exploit contradictions, and thus bring about *transformation* (there is no 'outside' to these conditions under which human agency is practiced).[35] It is a mode of politics which does not rely on a law from 'outside' to call forth emancipation, as we observed with the liberal politics of autonomy above. Politics is immanent to the conditions in which it arises. This concept of politics envisages a movement from material conditions, their contradiction, and finally the arrival of emancipatory transformation at some future point.

This distant horizon of politics-as-transformation is compressed by Foucault.[36] Rather than treating the conditions of politics as temporally or structurally distant from 'transformation', Foucault set out how the 'conditions of existence which are to be transformed are woven from the same cloth as the practices of transformation themselves'.[37] Here again we see the

---

31 K. Marx, *The Eighteenth Brumaire of Louis Bonaparte*, cited in Balibar, op. cit., n. 20, p. 8.
32 Balibar, id., pp. 8–21.
33 id., p. 9.
34 id., p. 10.
35 See discussion, id., pp. 10–12.
36 id., p. 16.
37 id., p. 15.

148

immanence of a politics of resistance. So for instance in his essay, 'The Subject and Power', Foucault explained how institutions should be analysed from the standpoint of power relations, rather than from the perspective of institutions.[38] The 'proper relation of power' is then 'an action upon an action', that is to say, 'deeply rooted in the social nexus' rather than in social relations constituted and determined above society in some structure whose effacement lies in some revolutionary future.[39] The 'distance between conditions and transformation is reduced to a minimum'.[40] The *body* becomes the ultimate referent/agent of politics, and with it, attention is drawn to techniques of normalization. Where for Marx liberty was the horizon of revolutionary politics, for Foucault politics is contingent on power relations which entail 'resistance'.[41] This is why Foucault urged that political actions should be thought of as 'strategies' which are ultimately directed within the self – that is, as technologies of the self which train bodies. What we have here, then, are two modes of conceiving a politics of transformation: the Marxist notion of *emancipation* as 'world historical change brought about by a universal class' or an analysis of power relations with respect to the singular being whose resistances in the mode of an 'action upon an action' brings about *transformations* in the conditions of individual existence.

Returning to the question of politics in the context of veiling in European liberal democracies, we should be cautious about making trite equations between resistant practices and the complex reasons attached to why girls and women may decide to 'veil'. Nonetheless, there is no shortage of evidence that veiling may well be seen as a form of resistance, 'an action upon an action', and not merely the crude absorption of a docile subject in a theocratic and patriarchal order.[42] This should cause concern for those who wish to produce social consensus from above as a means of liberating the oppressed woman. Moreover, the ease with which the judiciary has internalized threats by 'fundamentalists' and 'extremists' should give no comfort when feminist concerns are appropriated for the production of social cohesion, such as in the *Begum* case. In Şahin and *Begum*, the individual subject whose freedom was apparently at issue is left to confront yet another governmental and biopolitical action against her body. Autonomy and

---

38 M. Foucault, 'The Subject and Power' in *Michel Foucault: Beyond Structuralism and Hermeneutics*, eds. H.L. Dreyfus and P. Rabinow (1982), cited in Balibar, id., pp. 14–15.

39 Balibar, id., p. 14.

40 id., p. 15.

41 id., p. 17.

42 In particular, see my discussion of S. Mahmood's study of women's Mosque movements at pp. 153–5 below. See, also, Kristianasen, op. cit., n. 1; T. Asad, 'Trying to Understand French Secularism' in *Political Theologies*, ed. H. de Vries (2006); D. Lyon and D. Spini, 'Unveiling the Headscarf Debate' (2004) 12 *Feminist Legal Studies* 333–45, at 339–44; and Baroness Hale in *Begum*, op. cit., n. 15.

149

heteronomy cannot simply be opposed to each other. The desire and agency of the subject is conditioned by heteronomy, but not overdetermined by it.

To the modes of politics and related conceptions of the individual subject we have been considering, a third must be added. This is inspired by Spinoza, and developed by Deleuze and Guattari, and feminist philosophers influenced by their thought.[43]

3. *Becoming minority*

For Deleuze and Guattari, following Spinoza, elements do not have a particular form or function.[44] An element is distinguished by movement and rest, slowness and speed:

> Thus each individual is an infinite multiplicity, and the whole of Nature is a multiplicity of perfectly individuated multiplicities. The plane of consistency of Nature is like an immense Abstract Machine ... [I]ts pieces are the various assemblages each of which groups together an infinity of particles entering into an infinity of more or less interconnected relations.[45]

Individuation, which is only distinguished by movement, rest, slowness, and speed, takes place on a 'plane of immanence'.[46] In this plane of immanence, the individual is never fixed, that is to say, it is always in a process of becoming:

> To the relations composing, decomposing, or modifying an individual there correspond intensities that affect it, augmenting or diminishing its power to act; these intensities come from external parts or from the individual's own parts. Affects are becomings. Spinoza asks: What can a body do?[47]

The body is capable of affects within a given degree of power. Rather than defining the body through species or genus, Deleuze and Guattari state that we should try to count its affects.[48] Through affects, bodies can jointly compose a more powerful body, or destroy each other.

From this conceptualization of individuation – that is, bodies as multiplicitous desiring assemblages, Deleuze and Guattari proposed a notion of identity as 'territoriality'. This notion of identity as territoriality is especially pertinent to a discussion of veiling where women's bodies are *territorialized* as the site at which a political dispute about autonomy/heteronomy,

---

43 B. Spinoza, *Ethics* (2000); G. Deleuze and F. Guattari, *A Thousand Plateaus: Capitalism and Schizophrenia* (1987); and see M. Gatens, *Imaginary Bodies: Ethics, Power and Corporeality* (1996); M. Gatens and G. Lloyd, *Collective Imaginings: Spinoza, Past and Present* (1999); G. Lloyd, *Spinoza and the Ethics* (1996); A. Negri, *The Savage Anomaly: The Power of Spinoza's Metaphysics and Politics* (1991); and R. Braidotti, *Transpositions: On Nomadic Ethics* (2006).
44 Deleuze and Guattari, id., p. 253.
45 id., p. 254.
46 id.
47 id., p. 256.
48 id., p. 257.

secularism and *laïcité* take place. These territorialities/identities are either 'majoritarian' or 'minoritarian' – both expressing different modes of 'desire for otherness'.[49] 'Desire for otherness' involves two modes of being the 'fascinated self' – either desiring that the other remain other, or expressing a fascination for becoming other.[50] These modes of desire (and territorialities) are means of constituting collectivities that arise in a universal schema of majoritarian identity: 'a punctual system comprising five points: Man (central point), male (dominant point), adult (dominant point), woman, child'.[51] This notion of the 'majority' in Deleuze and Guattari's formulation is universal and without geopolitical or historical specificity.[52] As Goulimari explains, from the point of view of feminism, this majoritarian schema of identity provides 'a ready-made referent or political constituency, "woman" – in spite of her diversity and multiplicity'.[53] To the extent that feminism relies on this referent as the subjectivity in relation to which its claims are based, it corroborates the majoritarian schema of identity. What many feminists including Goulimari call for is a *minoritarian feminism* – a mode of *becoming minority* – that emphasizes the 'desire of becoming other' which builds 'lines of flight' or 'lines of escape' from the majoritarian schema.[54] I should emphasize that this is not about majority/minority as it is used in discussions about 'multiculturalism'.[55] It is rather about the concept 'woman' as a *territoriality*, and requires further explanation.

For feminists like Luce Irigaray who use the concept 'woman' as a 'strategic essentialism', woman is a referent for 'female sexed being', a being capable of building alliances across 'boundaries' of age, race, class, and sexual orientation.[56] In relation to political subjectivity, the Deleuzian and Guattarian schema poses an immediate dilemma for feminists who wish to hold on to the category 'woman' as a 'strategic essentialism' which grounds a politics of difference upon which they base a reformist agenda. Luce Irigaray advocates such an essentialism ('woman'), as does Rosi Braidotti: '"being-a-woman" is always already there as the ontological

---

49 P. Goulimari, 'A Minoritarian Feminism? Things to do with Deleuze and Guattari' (1999) 14(2) *Hypatia* 97–120, at 102.
50 id.
51 id.
52 id.
53 id.
54 id.
55 Feminist theory has attempted to take seriously the conundrum of imposing a feminist normativity on so called 'minority women' who are thus by definition 'outside' what is set out as a feminist emancipatory trajectory. A good summary of how feminism grapples with the rather problematic category of the 'minority woman' can be found in M. Malik, '"The Branch on which we sit": Multiculturalism, Minority Women and Family Law' in *Feminist Perspectives on Family Law*, eds. A. Diduck and K. O'Donovan (2007, forthcoming).
56 See discussion of Irigaray and Braidotti in Goulimari, op. cit., n. 49, p. 106.

151

precondition'.[57] As Goulimari argues, the problem in Deleuze and Guattari's terms is that:

> Strategic essentialism turns 'being a woman' into an artificial territoriality for feminism, thereby simultaneously turning race, age, and sexual preference into subdivisions, into subterritorialities of 'being-a-woman', with the result that it purports to be necessary for alliances across boundaries and between subterritorialities that it has constructed in the first place.[58]

The artificial territory, such as 'woman', involves processes of 'segregation' that are 'majoritarian'. For Deleuze and Guattari, the processes of artificial territorialization are omnipresent, and there is no point in trying to label them as bad or good.[59] The objective, rather, is to constitute a mode of 'becoming minoritarian' – that is, to create a 'nomadic' identity/territoriality.[60]

Rosi Braidotti, Moira Gatens, Genevieve Lloyd, and Antonio Negri have all drawn on Deleuze and Guattari to build a conception of human subjects as individuated 'bodies', differentiated parts of nature, but without essence.[61] For these bodies, freedom is tied to reason, but also shaped by environment and social organization. These 'nomadic subjectivities are defined in terms of processes of becoming'.[62] The desire of the individuated subject is capable of *affective force* and 'being together' – but a 'being together' which is radically 'post-human', that is to say, non-anthropocentric. Rosi Braidotti has put it like this:

> 'we' are in *this* together. What *this* refers to is the cartography as a cluster of interconnected problems that touches the structure of subjectivity and the very possibility of the future as a sustainable option. 'We' are in *this* together, in fact, enlarges the sense of collectively bound subjectivity to nonhuman agents, from our genetic neighbours the animals, to the earth as a bio-sphere as a whole ... How to do justice to this relatively simple yet highly problematic reality requires a shift of perspective. As Haraway suggests, we need to work towards 'a new techno-scientific democracy'.[63]

This 'post-human' mode of nomadic politics raises and addresses many important contemporary concerns, although its generality and abstraction conveniently elides some more conventionally territorialized bodies. Given the affinity of Deleuze and Guattari with Marx and Foucault, one is left to ponder the many connections between the politics of the nomad and the earlier concerns of politics as autonomy and heteronomy.

57 R. Braidotti, *Nomadic Subjects: Embodiment and Sexual Difference in Contemporary Feminist Theory* (1994) 187, cited in Goulimari, id., p. 106.
58 Goulimari, id.
59 id., p. 110.
60 id.
61 Braidotti, op. cit., Gatens, op. cit., Lloyd, op. cit., Negri, op. cit., all in n. 43.
62 Braidotti, id., p. 148.
63 R. Braidotti, 'Affirming the Affirmative: on Nomadic Affectivity' (2006) 11 *Rhizomes* para. 28, at <http://www.rhizomes.net/issue11/braidotti.html> – access verified 22 November 2006.

More specifically, what would it mean for a woman to speak in her own name, and be a desiring body that is a mere assemblage of affective forces oriented towards a minoritarian line of flight? Is autonomy obsolete when being-a-nomad is a condition of infinite multiplicity? Is the agentive subject redundant when the body is an affective assemblage? This is not the place to develop the responses that are available to these important questions. What we can take away from this discussion of modes of politics is that it is by no means adequate to pursue questions of equality and freedom, or religious and political life, as they have been dealt with by some liberal feminists or theorists of multiculturalism. Nor is it adequate to separate the child from the adult, the believer from the extremist, the democrat from the fundamentalist – simplistic oppositions that judges of the United Kingdom and European Courts have found to be expedient.

The Western popular media regularly assert that 'Muslim women are incomparably bound by the unbreakable chains of religious and patriarchal oppression'.[64] However, more informed research would suggest that conduct that follows strict adherence to some Islamic teachings cannot simply be rendered as a rejection of liberal pluralism, secularization, and modernization. As Mahmood has argued, feminist scholarship on the subjectivity of Muslim women has paralleled the New Left rejection of the classical Marxist formulation that the peasantry has no agency and thus no place in the making of modern history (the Subaltern Studies Project).[65] The Muslim woman has thus been reunited with her agency, but this important intervention by feminists is also attended by some problems. Most significantly, a feminist consciousness about gendered subjectivity, as we have seen, has tended to focus on the agency of an 'autonomous subject' whose actions can be universally mapped onto a terrain of repression and resistance.[66] Feminists have of course sought to depart from a liberal notion of individual autonomy by providing an account of woman's agency as embodied, relational, and socially embedded. Post-structural feminists have described how subjects performatively transgress norms by resignifying or subverting them. And as we have just seen, feminists inspired by Deleuze and Guattari, call into question the very existence of a unitary subject condemned to oppressive stasis. For these latter theorists, nomadic-being is a multiplicity of affective relations in constant movement. Hence, there are by now many familiar accounts of understanding 'resistance' to modes of normalization. But Mahmood asks whether this attention to norms as either consolidated or subverted by subjects does not ignore the fact that (religious) norms are also inhabited and experienced in a variety of ways.[67]

---

64 S. Mahmood, *Politics of Piety: The Islamic Revival and the Feminist Subject* (2005) 6–7.
65 id.
66 id., pp. 7, 14. Mahmood discusses the celebrated work of Lila Abu-Lughod, and the latter's own reflections on the need to depart from the binary of repression/resistance.
67 id., pp. 9, 22.

Importantly, Mahmood questions whether:

> it is even possible to identify a universal category of acts – such as those of resistance – outside of the ethical and political conditions within which such acts acquire their particular meaning. Equally important is the question that follows: does the category of resistance impose a teleology of progressive politics on the analytics of power – a teleology that makes it hard for us to see and understand forms of being and action that are not necessarily encapsulated by the narrative of subversion and reinscription of norms?[68]

Mahmood's answer to the need to avoid such a teleology of politics through analytics of power is to focus on the agency of the subject, for instance, in women's mosque movements. To cut a rather long and interesting story short, what Mahmood finds in the Egyptian women's mosque movements is a turn to religion precisely in order to resist the wider secularization of society that is regarded as dissolving the family, and other sources of social and cultural practices. The mosque movement is thus about new structures of learning that will generate an ethos that was previously sustained by family and society. In what follows I want to focus on the *affect* of community that is at the heart of the tension between religion and democracy. This is one way to juxtapose practices of religious piety with modes of subjection in political community.

PIETY AND POLITY

Wearing the *hijab* and other forms of Islamic dress has been infused with the power to undermine multiculturalism, liberal notions of equality, individual autonomy, and the secular state.[69] For most liberals, particularly of the muscular kind, the *hijab* is a sign of women's oppressive absorption in 'culture', and an intrusion of religion into the public sphere. This is apparently anathema to the modern conception of political life. In Turkey, as we observed above, the *hijab* has been associated with Islamic extremism and fundamentalism, and in the United Kingdom we observed how the *jilbab* and *nikab* have been associated with stifling the 'proper' development of a child, or being a symbol of separation and unacceptable difference. Saba Mahmood has pointed out how the question of women's 'piety' discussed in such disputes is always already a question of 'polity'.[70] In her book, *Politics of Piety*, she sets out the debates among Islamic scholars and activists in Egypt regarding whether religious piety should principally be about worship, ritual, and an entire mode of being (the version from the pious adherents of Islam), or a platform for a wider social and political project which has as its horizons 'truth, justice and freedom' (this is the view of people who eschew

68 id., p. 9.
69 See n. 1.
70 Mahmood, op. cit., n. 64, p. 53.

154

'religiosity', and want a wider dialogue about Islam and social change).[71] The cultivation of the living body as virtuous through its capacities to be constrained, limited, endure fasting and pain, punishment and even martyrdom, are common features of many religions, not least Christianity. In modernity these practices present a tension between individual *autonomy* (in the form of individual choice of religious practice) and *heteronomy* (being subject to a different, external law).

1. *Autonomy and heteronomy*

The tension between autonomy and heteronomy is especially troubling for democratic orders – and in two senses. First there is the obvious tension between the secular and the religious. Liberal democratic orders elevate the autonomous individual above the constraints of communitarian determinations, including the external (transcendent) law of religion. On this account Islamic dress is negated to protect a system of individual autonomies, including that of the apparently 'vulnerable' woman. But there is a second tension – this time between heteronomy and democracy itself. The individual right to freedom of religious practice contradicts the 'civil religion' of the secular state. In light of this, the seemingly obvious oppositions between sacred and profane, secular and religious, come unstuck.[72] *Heteronomy* is thus not only the transcendent, deific authority of conventional religion, but also the 'civil religion' of 'stable nations' and the patriotic fervour that is modernity's answer to what holds together our 'being-with' each other.[73] The problem of Islam in Europe is in that sense not just a clash between the enlightenment's self-legislating, autonomous individual and the religion to which she belongs, but is in fact a clash between which external law, of God or nation-state, will determine individual and collective practice.

The problem of Islam in Europe (as with Christianity in the United States) is that it has given rise to a *civil war of heteronomies*. The war of heteronomies is a struggle over which law (of nation/republic or theocracy) will prevail. Jean-Luc Nancy has elegantly encapsulated this conundrum of heteronomy and the nation-state:

> The sovereign State is the State that must derive its legitimation from itself. Without even emphasizing how essential the right to decide the state of exception from law (according to which Schmitt defines sovereignty) is in this context, we have to acknowledge that *autonomy*, as the principle of the political, here makes its major demand: it must or it should in one way or another found, authorize, and guarantee its own law by its own means. Is this possible in any other way than by invoking the necessities of security born of the weakness and the hostility of men? But can such necessities found more than an expedient – or even, in some cases, more than a usurped authority for

71 id., pp. 52–3.
72 The opposition between sacred and profane is interrogated below.
73 I will elaborate this point below with reference to J.-L. Nancy.

the sole good of some? Thus we see delineated the general scheme of the political problematic from the classical age onwards.[74]

How will the secular democratic state guarantee its own law by its own means? Have we not seen how questions of security (extremism and fundamentalism) operate as the expedient which mediates authority for the good of some? The *Şahin* case, for instance, highlights how liberal democracies contain what Jacques Derrida has called an *auto-immune* process, a capacity to self-destruct in the name of self-preservation.[75]

Demo-cracy, literally the rule of the *demos*, harbours several 'suicidal' possibilities. By giving over to the rule of the many, to rule by 'number', by a process of counting, a majority can come to power that can destroy all that democracy appears to stand for: the equal worth of each person (which of course is another form of counting, of being included or excluded), and the many freedoms of speech, association, or political organization with which democracy is associated.[76] In Turkey, an Islamic revival 'threatened' the secular Republic (and more specifically the reliability of a NATO ally crucially poised with a Euro-American geo-political orientation in the Middle East), and so the state responded by delimiting one of the very freedoms for which democracy stands by prohibiting the *hijab* in public institutions. This is one example of the auto-immunity or suicidal tendency in democracy.

There is a more direct 'suicide' which is a double appellation when the result of the counting for which demo-cracy stands yields a governing authority that is hostile to what has been called democracy.[77] Derrida gives the example of the Algerian election of 1992, when the state interrupted the electoral process in order to prevent an Islamic or Islamist group gaining power by democratic means – that is, by obtaining the support of the majority of eligible voters. The interruption of the electoral process was in the name of democracy, but also against the coming to power of Islamic groups that would introduce another *law* for the political community. The interruption of the election was decided in a sovereign fashion by the state because it held the view that a democratically elected Islamist organization would alter the constitution, and thus by democratic means, 'de-democratize' the political and juridical order. The interruption of the election was the suicidal immunization of democracy. It was a destruction of democracy in the name of its preservation. An obvious question, then, is whether what is called 'democracy' is much more than a process of counting – more than the rule (*cracy*) of the *demos*? The auto-immunity of democracy exposes the

---

74 Nancy, op. cit., n. 5, p. 9 (original emphasis).
75 J. Derrida, *Rogues: Two Essays on Reason* (2005) 35; but for a fuller account of the politics of friendship and fraternity that harbours this destruction, see J. Derrida, *Politics of Friendship* (1997); and for an excellent commentary see A.J.P. Thomson, *Deconstruction and Democracy* (2005).
76 Derrida, id. (2005), p. 30.
77 id., p. 33.

deep conundrum of 'guaranteeing your own law by your own means' highlighted by Nancy above. In this process, democracy turns in on itself, turns against itself.

These observations about the auto-immune processes of democracy are also pertinent to the election of Hamas in the Palestinian Authority elections in January 2006. This was a democratic electoral victory decried by western powers. Though the formation of a government by Hamas could not be prevented precisely because of their democratic mandate, Europe, the United States, and several other countries suspended financial aid and continue to insist that specific policies be adopted by the Hamas-led government before further 'recognition' of that power (*kratos*) of the people (*demos*) is given its due – the status of legitimate rule.[78] The unique feature in the Turkish, Algerian, and Palestinian examples is that Islam, in its many variations, has come to be regarded as 'resisting' what is being called the democratic principle – even though, in actual fact, the 'necessities born of expedience' (Nancy) are usurping democratic legitimacy. These examples yield an urgent and pressing conjunction of the 'demographic' (piety) and the 'democratic' (polity).[79]

We can now distil a general problematic that will be taken up in more detail here. The question is whether the 'political', the polity, can be conceived in a manner that resists both heteronomy (which clings to a transcendent source of law), and auto-nomy (a source of law which collapses under the weight of the many critiques of the atomistic liberal subject)? What is the permissible relation between the cohering *affect* of a certain demographic (such as a Muslim community) and democracy (the counting of each individual-as-one)?[80] This is a problem that has been posed in so-called 'multicultural societies' where the minority's attachment to the *affect* of community (usually centred around religion or culture) is opposed to the majority's apparently secularized citizenship. Again what is at stake (as with the Turkish example), I will argue, is one heteronomous determination verses another – the *civil war of heteronomies*. What we must consider is what these questions about *affect* reveal about the limits of secular formations of the political as they have hitherto been conceived.

Let me begin to approach these questions by elaborating how the principle of autonomy in liberal democracy surrenders to the heteronomous exigencies of the secular state. This will permit a refinement of how autonomy and heteronomy mutually undermine the expulsion of the 'sacred' from the political order. It will also set up an interrogation of the unsustainable opposition between democracy and theocracy which is so central to the interrogation of secular modernity and for considering the affect of religion in democratic political community.

---

78 See 'U.S. to Cancel $240m in aid over Hamas government' *Times*, 8 April 2006.
79 See discussion at pp. 154–5 above.
80 This is a problematic developed by Nancy in 'Church, State, Resistance' (op. cit, n. 5), and I will provide an account of his insights below.

2. Secular theology and the institution of democracy

The perception of 'Islam' is that it presents sharp contrasts and acute tensions with liberal values and respect for human rights. The 'Rushdie affair' or the controversy surrounding the recent publication of cartoons depicting the Prophet Muhammad are yet more examples of what is depicted as a challenge to 'Europe's modernity' from religious extremists, usually Europe's others, caught in their regular stasis of culture and tradition. Moreover, the struggle between theocracy and democracy is being posed through a discourse of human rights. The question of Islam in Europe, and especially in the United Kingdom, is a telling site for considering the problem of the sacred in modern political and juridical formations.

In what sense is the 'sacred' opposed to democracy in conventional rhetoric? To address this question we must have at least a working definition of the 'sacred'. The 'sacred' is more usually than not opposed to the 'profane', but that opposition is itself a product of the modes of classification particular to developments in anthropology and sociology in the nineteenth century.[81] An essential feature of the sacred is that it pertains to what is 'set apart' from the profane. The opposition between sacred and profane is determined by the essential character of this *setting apart*. This is a distinctly modern phenomenon according to Talal Asad, and can be contrasted with the opposition in medieval theology of divine/satanic (both transcendent powers) or spiritual/temporal (both worldly institutions).[82] Durkheim's *Elementary Forms of Religious Life*, for instance, presented 'all known religious beliefs' through a classification that could be reduced to two opposed groups or terms, the 'sacred' and 'profane'.[83] The sacred in modernity, then, is an external transcendent power or authority which is supposedly universally opposed to the worldly or profane.

Closer scrutiny reveals that the distinction between the sacred and profane is a conceptual mess compiled on contradictions. The 'sacred' has a very different inflection in the Christianity of early modernity where not all that is sacred is set apart. An object, person, institution, vessel, or the body and office of the King (who famously has two bodies), is not set apart and yet is called sacred.[84] The French Declaration of the Rights of Man and Citizen speaks of various rights, such as property, as sacred. Defying the opposition of religious and secular, it is no less than the 'sacralization' of the individual and people that marks the emergence of the *secular* state. This is something of a contradiction given the regular logic of the secular state has it that it is the re-presentation of individual or 'people'. Individual and people must be

---

81 See the excellent discussion in T. Asad, *Formations of the Secular: Christianity, Islam, Modernity* (2003) 30–7.
82 id., pp. 31–2.
83 id., p. 31.
84 id., p. 32.

158

anything but 'sacred' – they must be a source of authority that mark the opening of an *immanent* rather than a transcendent source of power.[85] Some of the confusion which attends the opposition between sacred/profane can be explained through the conceptual separation of 'nature', 'religion', and 'reason' that arises out of the European encounters with the colonized world.

For Asad, Europe's encounter with the non-European world helps to explain how the 'sacred' comes to be essentialized as that which is universally set apart from the profane.[86] It was through the designation of practices as fetish and taboo, and the allocation of these to 'Nature Folk' in the non-European world, that an essential separation was wrought between the sacred and the profane. The 'sacred' became universally associated with religion. The cultures and traditions of the 'backward peoples' of the world were understood as frozen in religion or myth. Europe came to be regarded as holding the prerogative of 'profanation', the capacity to reorder society through 'forcible emancipation from error and despotism'.[87] Liberal democracy as it is known today is informed by these movements in the eighteenth and nineteenth centuries. But let's be more specific about how the sacred continues to inhabit what is called the profane sphere of modern law, politics, and society.

Modern law and society is structured through what can be termed *onto-theology*. Modern sovereignty, for instance, secularizes a theological concept of power. As Derrida has put it, sovereignty is:

> the concentration, into a single point of indivisible singularity (God, the monarch, the people, the state, or the nation-state), of absolute force and the absolute exception. We did not have to wait for Schmitt to learn that the sovereign is the one who decides exceptionally and performatively about the exception, the one who keeps or grants himself the right to suspend rights or law; nor did we need him to know that this politico-juridical concept, like all the others, secularises a theological heritage.[88]

The retention of a theological heritage can be seen in numerous definitive texts of western modernity.[89] The persistence of the sacred (or what is set apart) in the historico-political formation of European modernity suggests that this secular theology deserves more attention when considering formations of the sacred in modern law and democracy. The secular theology of modernity is one explanation of why the sacred receives ambivalent treatment in liberal juridical orders. The sacred is at once guarded as

---

85 This move towards immanence is also a move towards transcendence, see, generally, F. Dallmayr, 'Postmetaphysics and Democracy' (1993) 21 *Political Theory* 101.
86 Asad, op. cit, n. 81, p. 35.
87 id.
88 Derrida, op. cit. (2005), n. 75, pp. 153–4.
89 For a compendious setting out of these, see P. Fitzpatrick, ' "What Are the Gods to Us Now?": Secular Theology and the Modernity of Law' (2006) 8 *Theoretical Inquiries in Law* 285.

'freedom of conscience', right to religion, or the event of *sacrifice*[90] on which the political is founded and sustained, and also expelled as not proper to the 'City', particularly in the case of what has been termed 'political Islam'.

What we must now decipher is how this problem of secular theology manifests the constitutive limits of liberal democracy. In brief, this is a question of how modern rationality is presented as the property of the inhabitants, all equal, who dwell in the *City* (as *polis*, Europe, western civilization, with their values of freedom and autonomy apparently hated by religious fundamentalists, and so on). To be free is to be charged with the freedom that is the property of equal, rational beings (all the social contract theories flow from this assumption). But since Charles Taylor and others imported a certain Hegelianism into liberal philosophy (where the community or collective is the source of normative life-worlds), there have been ongoing ripples of a dispute about the source of authority. What is at stake here is whether the autonomous individual or the community to which she belongs is to be the source of authority and value. Will the self-authorizing autonomous individual be the sole guide of her actions, or will the individual's life-world be determined from another place (heteronomy)? The problem of secular theology in modern formations of law and society can thus be addressed through the tension between the autonomous individual of liberal demo-*cracy*, and the stricture of another *'cracy'*, that of *theocracy*. As we have seen, Jean-Luc Nancy has recently condensed this problematic of secular theology into the tension between *autonomy* and *heteronomy*.[91]

To recap for a moment, I have set the stage for an undoing of the autonomous, self-legislating individual of western modernity by showing the extent to which this political formation contained a constitutive tension with heteronomy. Now I want to explain why this is the case. Why is there a persistent call on transcendent deities or their substitutes (such as nation, people, ethnicity)?

3. *The affect of religion in democracy*

'Autonomy' is a central principle of the political in modernity. The autonomy of the individual survives among competing heteronomies of theology and civil religion – what was termed secular theology above. Autonomy cannot deliver what J.-L. Nancy has termed the 'force of affect' – the 'fervour, desire, and sentiment' that is so central to our being-with. This autonomy must in 'one way or another found, authorize, and guarantee its

---

90 For instance, consider J. van der Walt, *Law and Sacrifice: Towards a Post-Apartheid Theory of Law* (2005). See his account of the inevitability of sacrifice in political community, in ch. 5.

91 Nancy, op. cit, n. 5.

own law by its own means'.[92] The modern invention of sovereignty is the dominant mode of answering this problem of autonomy. The State comes to embody the principle of 'atheistic' self-sufficiency with no legitimation from beyond itself. The intrinsic flaw in this formulation is the need for recourse to 'civil religion'. As Nancy points out, the separation of Church and State comes to rest on a principle of secularism and 'fraternity'. Through fraternity, and other denotations including 'friendship', solidarity, responsibility, and even 'justice' (think for instance of the various postcolonial struggles for independence), the 'affect' of the political as an autonomous phenomenon is 'perceptible to the hearts of citizens' (a phrase taken from Rousseau).[93] As an order of autonomy, something in the 'affect' of the political resists. It is this resistance in the autonomy of the political that comes to be in conflict with heteronomy.

'Affect' is also 'everyone's adhesion to community', and despite the secular imperative to separate this adhesion from all forms of 'worship', it takes the form of practices of observance which celebrate values, symbols or signs (think of flags, Independence Day celebrations, monuments to the war-dead, and so on).[94] The allure of the many forms of fascism, and even 'actually existing socialism', so-called, or the current 'force' of democracy carries the lure of this 'affect', and is central to the autonomy of the political.

Now, although 'autonomy' has resisted heteronomy (through notions of fraternity and secularism), what is crucial for understanding the significance of the 'sacred', and indeed piety, as a challenge to the present empire of democracy, is that 'heteronomy resists autonomy with the force of affect'.[95] For Nancy, 'affect is essentially heteronomous, and perhaps we should even say that affect *is* heteronomy'.[96] Because of the 'force of affect' exacted through Church or State, we are now facing the impossibility of a political institution constructed by autonomy. Autonomy fails because of the resistance of heteronomy. And heteronomy leads us to the disasters of patriotism, ethnicity, and religion. Hence the task now is to think the affect by which 'we' co-exist, but not through a politics that collapses under the force of affect generated by heteronomy. How do we separate Church and State and be-with each other in a way that does not fall into the civil religion of the Republic that demands sacrifice? What law, or indeed as Nancy suggest, what 'anomic' formation, will mutually resist autonomy and heteronomy?[97] This is the problem that remains to be thought through. The problem of *affect* in the political will have to be the site for this labour.

92 id., p. 8.
93 id., p. 9.
94 id., p. 10.
95 id., p. 11.
96 id. (original emphasis).
97 id., p. 13.

161

CONCLUSION

The juridification of politics has turned the veiled woman into a rights-bearing subject whose agency is subject to what is expedient in a democratic society. That is the banal reality of all human rights, and we should not be surprised that the state will clamp down on all heteronomous formations that resist the civil religions of the state. The feminist veneer of juridical and political pronouncements about the veiled woman must not distract us from the real political crisis – the apparent impossibility of recovering a political subject that might resist the proliferation of the exception as the norm, of consumption as freedom, of social cohesion through ignorant vilification of Europe's archetypical other. The suppression of religious expression and piety only exposes democracy's own lack – it cannot guarantee its own law by its own means unless the autonomy of the political is always already heteronomous. For the time being we are left with 'convert or perish' as democracy's oxymoronic cry.

The subject of politics who makes her own history under conditions not of her choosing then appears to be left with a stark choice. Either convert to political formations that absorb her as a 'citizen', or rely on the other heteronomous forms that inspire the desire and fervour of all affected beings. If being is singular-plural and always affected by the force of heteronomy, then her de-territorialization, the fact that she is a relational assemblage, is already part of her 'becoming minority'. What will be a line of escape, a line of flight, from heteronomy? That is what remains to be thought.

Printed and bound by CPI Group (UK) Ltd, Croydon, CR0 4YY

09/06/2025

14685980-0002